Making Sense of Astrology

Making Sense of Astrology

Ronny Martens and Tim Trachet

Prometheus Books
59 John Glenn Drive
Amherst, New York 14228-2197

English language edition licensed by permission of Uitgeverij Hadewijch,
Vrijheidstraat 33, B–2000 Antwerp, Belgium.

Published 1998 by Prometheus Books

Making Sense of Astrology. Copyright © 1998 by Ronny Martens and Tim Trachet. All rights reserved. No part of this publication may be reproduced, stored in a retrieval system, or transmitted in any form or by any means, electronic, mechanical, photocopying, recording, or otherwise, without prior written permission of the publisher, except in the case of brief quotations embodied in critical articles or reviews. Inquiries should be addressed to Prometheus Books, 59 John Glenn Drive, Amherst, New York 14228-2197, 716-691-0133. FAX: 716-691-0137.

01 00 99 98 97   5 4 3 2 1

Library of Congress Cataloging-in-Publication Data

Martens, Ronny.
  [Astrologie, zin of onzin? English]
  Making sense of astrology / by Ronny Martens and Tim Trachet.
     p.   cm.
  Includes bibliographical references and index.
  ISBN 1-57392-218-8 (alk. paper)
  1. Astrology. I. Trachet, Tim. II. Title.
BF1708.8.D8M3713   1998
133.5—dc21   98-3528
                                                                        CIP

Printed in the United States of America on acid-free paper.

CONTENTS

	Acknowledgments	7
1.	Introduction	11
2.	The Starry Sky	24
3.	The Zodiac	42
Intermezzo I.	The Age of Aquarius	74
Intermezzo II.	The Eysenck Case	78
4.	The Astronomical Planets	82
5.	The Astrological Planets	93
Intermezzo III.	The Planets in the Horoscope of A. S. Trologer	108
6.	The Houses	112
Intermezzo IV.	The Principles of the Division of the Houses	138
Intermezzo V.	The Houses in the Horoscope of A. S. Trologer	144
Intermezzo VI.	Weird House Situations in Arctic Horoscopes	148
Intermezzo VII.	The Skeptics and the Mars Effect	157
7.	The Aspects	166
Intermezzo VIII.	The Aspects in the Horoscope of A. S. Trologer	182
8.	Astrology and Psychology	186
Intermezzo IX.	Cosmic Influences	207
Intermezzo X.	The Moon and Life on Earth	219
9.	Astrology: Past and Future	226
10.	Criticism in a Nutshell	245
11.	Conclusion	254
	Postscript	262
	Bibliography	263
	Index	273

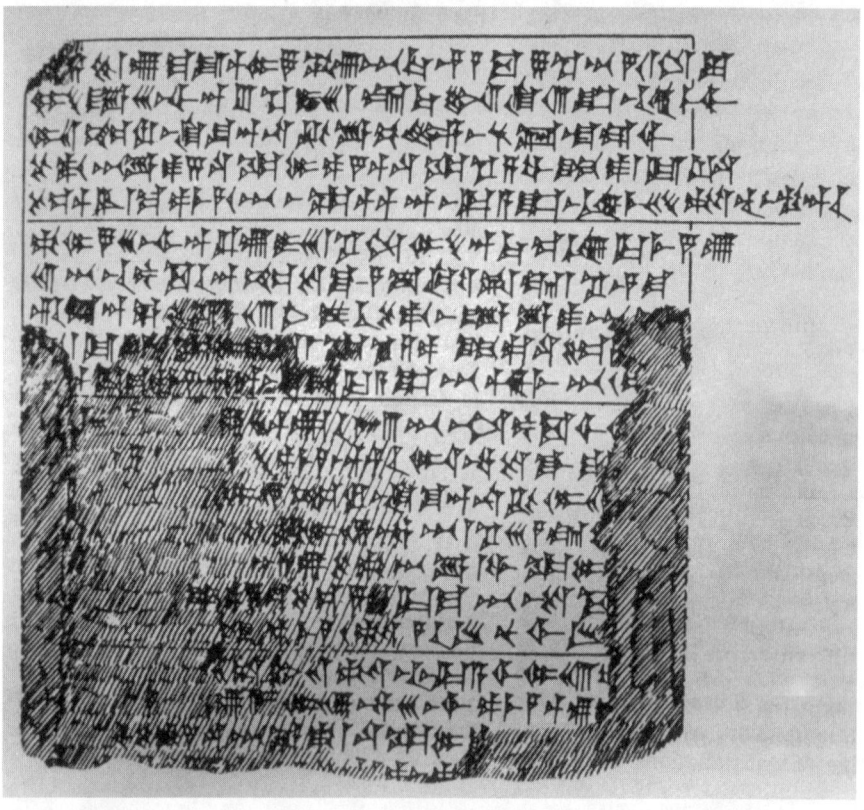

This cuneiform text, which can be found in a museum in Berlin, contains the oldest known mention of the twelve signs of the zodiac. In line 5 it says "Jupiter and Venus in the beginning of Gemini, Mars in Leo, Saturn in Pisces. Twenty-ninth day: in the evening Mercury is located in Taurus." These positions agree with April 419 B.C.E.

ACKNOWLEDGMENTS

This is not an astrological handbook, nor a book in which the relations that are supposed by some to exist between horoscope and personality are discussed, but rather, a book *about* astrology.

Each bookstore of any size nowadays has tens or even hundreds of volumes about astrology. Newspapers provide us not only with "horoscopes," but also with hundreds of advertisements of astrologers offering their services. There are specialized stores, publishers, organizations, and periodicals about astrology. Yet astrology remains something marginal. Everywhere courses in astrology may be offered, but those are only private courses; there are no official or government-supported schools of astrology and astrology is not taught at the universities. There is no place for astrology at accredited academies and scientific institutions. Something called "medical astrology" exists, but as far as we know hospital staff does not consult the horoscope of a patient to determine what has to be done, and medical-astrological consults are not reimbursed by health insurance systems. According to some, more and more managers select their personnel by means of horoscopes, but astrology is not used by government services for career counseling or for job hunting. Astrologers make predictions about upcoming events in the world, about political developments, natural disasters, and economic trends, but one does not find them in centers for policy study or intelligence services, nor in meteorological institutes, seismological services, or in bureaus for economic planning. Astrology does not have any official standing or recognition, no matter how popular it appears to be.

This schizophrenic situation does not make it easy to form a well-founded opinion about the sense or nonsense of astrology. Most astrological books provide very few, if any, arguments for the justification of astrology; and those that try are the exceptions. The number of books that criticize astrology is even smaller.

Books "in favor" are almost exclusively pleas in self-defense by the astrologers themselves. Books "against" are mostly written from a scientific point of view; the basic argument usually being that astrology is scientifically incorrect and therefore just cannot be true. However, the latter argument does not impress the general public very much; after all there are plenty of people who have the experience that astrology *works*.

Our approach is somewhat different. In this book we want to provide information which should enable the reader to make a judgment about the validity of astrology. We do this by explaining the different parts of the astrological system and by providing appropriate critical remarks on each of them.

We know that a number of people will not be thankful for this book (this was at least the case with the Dutch edition). Some opponents of astrology consider it a waste of time to pay any attention to the subject. We don't think so, the more so because, as was already mentioned, so many books are published about astrology that lack any critical note.

On the other hand, some proponents of astrology think that only people who believe in astrology have the right to talk about it. But that stance will not prevent those of us who study astrology from writing what are in our opinion sensible things about it. Astrology claims things about objective reality and it should be possible to check these claims, even by people who do not believe in it.

For that matter, we have no prejudice against astrology as such. If astrology does indeed work, then determining that would, in our opinion, be exceptionally useful and interesting for humanity. But whether astrology works or not is exactly what the facts have to decide. If those facts are missing or are invalid, then astrology cannot claim the benefit of the doubt. If someone claims that he flew around on a flying horse, then he has to prove that statement. As long as he is unable to do that we see no reason to believe in flying horses.

Our interest in astrology grew out of astronomy. Some astrologers argue that astrology has nothing to do with astronomy and that all criticism from that side should be rejected.* We do not share that opinion, however. Astrology as a system works with "cosmic influences" and claims that a meaningful relationship exists between the position of some celestial bodies and human experience. Where "cosmic influences" of any kind or celestial bodies are mentioned, we think that taking into account what science—in this case astronomy—has to say about those influences or objects is important. Why then, should the astronomer not have the right to make his remarks about astrology? On the other hand, we agree that a purely astronomical view of the subject is too limited. Not only should the existing astronomical knowledge be taken into account in the evaluation of astrology, but so should its histor-

---

*The difference between astronomy and astrology is discussed in chapter 1.

ical heritage and psychological aspects. For that reason this book is not limited to a purely astronomical critique of astrology.

The astrological point of view often claims that the cause of the problem (i.e., the non-acceptance of astrology by the scientific community) lies with modern science, which is presumed to reject whatever does not fit in its worldview. The discussion about the sense or nonsense of astrology then usually quickly degenerates into a discussion about the foundations and value of science. This discussion of the philosophical basis of science, however, is in this case beside the point. We prefer to approach the subject from an empirical point of view, and as such we do not want to force an exclusively scientific worldview on the reader. We do appeal, however, to the reader's common sense and critical faculties.

Some people consider all criticism as a direct attack. Why not leave the astrologers alone? Aren't they allowed to have their own opinion? Of course they are, but that should not prevent others from passing a sound judgment and searching for the validity of the claims. And if things do not square, then the public has the right to know, whatever the consequences. Tolerance is not the same as indifference. Research should be done as objectively as possible, but that does not necessarily mean that the conclusions are neutral or without consequences.

This last premise causes the tone of the book to be ironic at times. We cannot avoid mentioning ridiculous facts, and sometimes we prefer laughing to crying.

We tried very hard to be complete. The subject was considered from as many angles as possible. We collected information that seldom or never reaches the public, information that many astrologers *themselves* do not know or do not want to know. To render all the facts and arguments, however, would have been too much for one book, but what is presented here should be sufficient for the reader to form an opinion about the sense or nonsense of astrology. We think that what we omitted would really add nothing to the case, nor would it change the final judgment. We honestly tried not to leave a single essential argument undiscussed, which is not always the case in the discussion of these kinds of subjects.

This book has had a long history. Everything started in 1976 when some people who were interested in astronomy started a working group for the critical study of—among other things—astrology. The group decided to compose a pamphlet about astrology. When the draft was ready, it turned out to be much too long for a pamphlet. A shorter version was distilled from it for use as a pamphlet, but the original manuscript remained in the closet for years. Pressure from people who knew about the existence of the manuscript led to the decision to expand it into a book for a wider audience. This required a thorough reworking; after all, the original manuscript was meant for someone who was somewhat familiar with astronomy. Moreover, we had meanwhile collected a lot more information. By 1988 the text was ready, but for a number of different reasons publication was postponed. When the book was finally published, the text was adapted again in accordance with the newest developments. The same happened in the case of the present English edition.

Finally some words of thanks. We are very grateful to Marie Prins for the English translation of this book. This newest version contains some corrections and updatings recommended by our friends Jean Meeus and Jan Willem Nienhuys. We also thank Paul Kurtz and Prometheus Books, who made this English translation possible.

R.M. & T.T.
Ghent/Brussels, April 1998

1

INTRODUCTION

Astrology

Astrology

Horoscope

Zodiac

Signs

Your future and the stars

I'm a Libra

The abovementioned terms and phrases may well sound familiar to most of us. After all, don't many people regularly read their horoscopes in the newspapers or magazines? And doesn't just about everybody know her or his "sign"? Or maybe someone among your acquaintances occasionally consults an astrologer when he or she has serious problems? And is very satisfied with the services rendered and can recommend the astrologer strongly to everybody?

In spite of the familiarity of these lines, astrology is for most people a largely unknown quantity. Until the middle of the 1960s, astrology was a "damned" subject, something about which one did not speak and about which a normal person should shrug his shoulders. But, by the end of the decade, astrology, together with quite a few other "alternative" ideas, reappeared and gained in familiarity among a large part of the population. In the middle of the 1970s this interest reached a peak; interviews with astrologers

The famous zodiac of Dendera, a sculptured Hellenistic zodiac in Egyptian style, dating from about 50 B.C.E.

appeared from time to time in just about every magazine, the horoscopes of well-known public figures were published and provided with commentary, predictions based on "the stars" found an avid audience. Newspapers and magazines that until then did not have a horoscope section, began running one. Astrology was "in."

At the dawn of the (supposedly) more sensible 1990s people were losing some of their interest in alternative ideas, including astrology, but meanwhile the foundation was laid for the familiarity of the commoner with astrology. Astrology has become a less "damned" subject, and he who nowadays starts to talk about it does not have to be afraid of being laughed out of the room. In some circles it even looks good to mention this subject during a conversation, no matter how little one knows about it. If one then mentions that he has his doubts about it, he ought to give astrology at least the benefit of the doubt: "You know, there is more between heaven and earth. . . ." The acceptance of astrology has partially removed it from the area of social and pseudointellectual taboo: It is again permissible to talk about it. The subject has been discussed in the media, so it is no longer seen as a weird or outlandish phenomenon but as a generally accepted social topic. Astrology has become "normal."

A large part of the population is very familiar with astrological terms and expressions. But quite a few people—a minority we hope—do not even know the difference between astro*nomy* and astro*logy*, between an astronomer and an astrologer. The suffix "-logy," as in biology, psychology, and geology, grants astrology a scientific touch. It is therefore not at all surprising that many people consider astrology to be a real science that is on equal footing with the "-logies" just mentioned. And of course, the astronomers especially are not too happy with that. As an aside, astro*nomy* is the science of the stars, the scientific study of the universe and everything that comprises it. Astro*logy* is astromancy, divination by the stars, connecting human characteristics and ventures with heavenly events. An astro*nomer* studies the stars, an astro*loger* casts horoscopes. And casters of horoscopes are, according to the astro*nomers*, only charlatans and crooks and astro*logy* is pure nonsense. But, of course, you already knew all that.

The form in which astrology is preeminently present in daily life is the well-known section in newspapers and weekly magazines. In these sections a prediction or some good advice is given for each sign of the zodiac that, if one should believe the composers, is particularly applicable for that day or that week for all those who were born "under" that particular sign. Because those sections are very brief, their pronouncements are very vague. As they are printed alongside the comics, it can safely be assumed that they should be taken with a grain of salt. Here astrology is clearly intended as a short moment of amusement.

But even suggesting that this section should not be taken all that seriously, astrology itself is nevertheless ancient knowledge in which, according to rumor, even now prominent people believe. Can one throw this centuries-old knowledge out without much ado, or is there something to it? Is it just an innocent pastime that nobody dares to admit she considers important—"I read my horoscope from time to time, but I don't believe in these things, you know . . ."—or do those short sentences contain a kernel of truth, after all?

It is a pity that most people do not delve deeper into this question. One gets the impression that they are indifferent to the value of these sections. The "horoscope" is read in passing, one smiles at the advice "to be careful of your financial situation and don't tackle affairs too hastily," but life goes on as usual. Five minutes later the predictions are already forgotten. Or are they?

If one does dig somewhat deeper into astrology, one concludes that these few lines in the papers do not give a complete picture of the subject. Astrology is more than a horoscope section; that section is actually a very unimportant part of the whole. The "real" or "serious" astrology—the use of this term by the astrologers themselves automatically implies that the newspaper horoscope is not serious, of course—consists of a rather complicated set of rules which an astrologer uses to determine, on the basis of certain data, the relation of an individual to the "stars." This is completely different from the general pronouncements in the paper which should be valid for a large part of the population.

It has already been mentioned that the opinions as to the validity of astrology vary. Some have an unshakable trust in the art and regularly consult an astrologer. They hope to get from him more certainty about "what the stars are saying" about their life and future, about their chances for success, possible marital problems, raising the children, financial prospects, and many other things. In these circumstances astrology is not a game anymore; for those involved it has become a deadly serious question. They put their trust (and money) in the astrologer and attach so much importance to his or her pronouncements that in some cases no important decision is made without consulting the horoscope. Such believers in the art are in good company: Wasn't the agenda of former president Ronald Reagan drawn up after consulting an astrologer? And didn't he have himself sworn in as governor of the State of California at a time that the astrologer considered auspicious?

Someone convinced of the validity of astrology is not obliged to put his or her fate into the hands of a stranger—the astrologer. Many start by studying astrology themselves, applying its rules and prescriptions and "casting" horoscopes of friends and acquaintances. And if that goes well and they have acquired a sufficient amount of "experience," they can be admitted to the limited circle of "serious" astrologers. Maybe some of them will even start providing astrological consultations as an additional source of income.

But not everybody has such a high opinion of astrology. Some people think that everything involved with "fiddling with a horoscope" has to do with downright nonsense that should preferably disappear from this world as soon as possible. You will find almost all astronomers among them. It is therefore predictable that, if both parties meet, the argument can become very heated and sometimes even heavy quarrels cannot be avoided.

Astrology has many faces. There is *popular astrology*, which finds its expression in the horoscope sections of newspapers and magazines, in necklaces with the signs of the zodiac, in telling each other one's birth-sign, etc. Besides this there is *serious astrology*, mentioned before, which is mostly occupied with casting and interpreting the horoscopes of individual persons.

Whereas everybody recognizes the expressions of popular astrology without much trouble, people are much less familiar with the serious variant. The man in the street hardly recognizes a horoscope (and we mean a real one, not one in the newspaper), let alone knows what an astrologer does with it.

To explain the difference between the "real" astrology and its popular variation, we shall take a look at the former.

Types of Astrology

The preeminent symbol, the "magic word" of astrology, is the *horoscope*: a kind of map of the heavens on which, in a very schematic way, the positions of the Sun, Moon, and planets are shown. The positions of these heavenly bodies are not arbitrary; they are the positions the planets occupied at a certain moment. To this a number of typically astrological factors are added, such as the signs, the astrological houses, and the aspects, to restrict ourselves to the most important ones.

Complicated rules, some of them centuries old—astrology really is ancient—should enable the astrologer to distill some pronouncements from the resulting tangle of astral positions and factors. The principal objective is to lay connections between "the cosmos" and things on Earth about which information or direction is desired.

Popular astrology, to return once more to that, is strictly speaking a degenerate form of the "real thing." The larger part of serious astrology is thrown overboard and only the simplest element, the "sign," is retained. These signs are what people know. Some erroneously confuse them with constellations, but there is, however, very little connection between these signs and the real constellations. Popular astrology is a very diluted extract of the old traditional knowledge and therefore the resemblance between the two is minimal. For that reason the practitioner of "serious" astrology usually shrugs his shoulders over it. Almost all astrologers consider the horoscopes in the newspapers completely worthless. Just consider for yourself: Something consisting of four lines that should be applicable to one-twelfth of the world population? Whom are you kidding? But still, some of those "serious" astrologers are the suppliers of these newspaper sections.

The "real" astrology can in its turn be subdivided into different parts or specializations. Depending for what purpose the horoscope is cast, astrology can be divided into natal astrology, medical astrology, horary astrology, mundane astrology, and predictive astrology.

Natal astrology studies the horoscope that was calculated for the moment of someone's birth. In that chart the positions of the Sun, Moon, and planets are drawn as they appeared at that particular moment. On the basis of this chart the personal characteristics of the subject are determined. Here the emphasis is on the psychology and character of the person, and also on the general tendencies that could develop during his or her life. This form of astrology is the most practiced of all. In fact, the word "astrology" is often synonymous with "natal astrology."

Medical astrology occupies itself with the health of the owner of the horoscope. The horoscope is not only consulted to determine the course of an illness, but also to reach a diagnosis (and therefore to indicate the nature of the illness) and to find the astrologically most strongly indicated medication. According to medical astrology it should be possible to find out from one's horoscope to which illnesses someone is most susceptible so that preventive measures can be taken.

Horary astrology is a special kind of astrology that does not take the time of birth of the individual as its starting point, but rather the time of an event: traditionally the moment at which the client asks the astrologer a specific question. The moment the question is asked is in this case considered to be the symbolic "birth" of the problem (or of its solution). The older, Latin name for this practice is "*interrogationes.*" This technique is supposed to answer questions such as "Is this moment favorable for this investment?" "Can I take the risk of making that trip?" "What is the best choice in this case?" "Where should I look for a solution to this problem?

Then we also have *mundane* or *world astrology*, which studies the fate of countries or nations. The practitioners of this branch appeal to the analogy between the birth of a person and the foundation of a state. In the same way that an individual has a natal horoscope which shows her or his traits, a country possesses a foundation horoscope. That horoscope is supposed to determine certain fundamental characteristics of the country in question. Such horoscopes are consulted particularly in times of international tension or political crises.

"Looking into the future" or *predictive astrology* is probably what appeals most to the layperson. Each type of astrology mentioned above can be used to make predictions: someone's future experiences, illnesses and their courses, how an enterprise will turn out, or how the stock market will develop. On the personal level the ultimate purpose consists of predicting very accurately the course of one's life, up until and including the moment of death. With some very energetic astrologers the predictions reach even further, into the hereafter.

Although predictive astrology appeals most to the imagination of the outsider, this form of astromancy succeeds far less with the practitioners than one would expect. The majority of astrologers are occupied almost exclusively with "casting" natal horoscopes and extracting psychological advice from them. According to solid astrological principles such a horoscope should be more than sufficient to make the other types of astrology superfluous. After all, all important future events, illnesses, and important decisions, should already be included in the natal horoscope.

In spite of the reluctance of most astrologers to take the path of predictions, there still are some individuals here and there who keep themselves occupied with predictions of election results or with what will happen in the world next year. It is a particularly amusing and instructive pastime to check the facts one year after the prediction.

Apart from the popular astrology in the newspapers, which is considered nonsense by the serious astrologers as well as by the critics, the public at large comes in contact with natal astrology most of the time. Therefore this branch of the subject will take up the larger part of this book.

Foundations of Astrology

Which ideas form the backbone of "serious" astrology? Astrology is essentially a vision of man and his relation to the universe. This vision assumes that there exists a connection between the two, and that the nature of this relationship is such that individual human characteristics and experiences are determined by the state of the universe (a universe limited in practice to the solar system). There are supposed to be moments when a one-way traffic from the universe to an individual—the reverse, that the individual would influence the universe, is not assumed—puts a very important imprint on that person, an imprint that will determine the further course of his or her life. Such a moment is birth: At the baby's first cry, the cosmos is supposed to imprint a lasting mark on the newborn, a mark that is decisive for his character, the main lines of the course of his life, and so on. One should not take the words "imprint" and "mark" too literally. Not a single astrologer can explain how the application of such an imprint takes place. How sagacious of the universe to provide a suitable constellation for every newborn baby around the time that the doctors expect its birth!

In order to prevent any misunderstanding, it is useful to indicate exactly what we mean when we use the word "astrology," because it can refer to two related concepts.

On the one hand the term is used to indicate a *general opinion* that Earth and humanity are influenced by the cosmos. In this case one remains very vague when it comes down to describing the nature of these effects on humanity. There is not very much that can be brought in against this idea; it is a fact that humans live on a certain planet somewhere in the universe and, by definition, are part of it. They receive warmth and light from the Sun, their social activities are determined by the changes between day and night, the weather and the growth of plants change with the seasons. The Moon with its ever changing phases determines the calendar of many cultures (think of our month) and together with the Sun it causes the tides. It is therefore clear that the existence of cosmic influences can hardly be denied. It is better not to use the word "astrology" in this context because of the vagueness concerning the influence on the *individual* human being.

On the other hand, the word "astrology" is also used to indicate a *certain, well-defined system,* which not only assumes that man is influenced by the cosmos, but which also claims to know the nature of those influences and to be able to determine their effect on the individual. That system is therefore much more detailed than the previous philosophical thesis. And it is this system, or rather these systems, which are meant if we use the word "astrology" from now on. Let the reader judge by himself: What does he think of upon hearing the word "astrology"? In all probability "horoscope" or "I am a . . ." (fill in the name of a sign) comes to mind. These expressions are part and parcel of the system, not of the aforementioned vague philosophical idea. From now on when questions are asked about the validity of "astrology," this technically elaborate system is meant.

The Astrological Consult

What exactly happens when someone consults an astrologer? To begin with, the astrologer asks the client the date, place, and exact time of her birth. These data provide the material for the calculations which will lead to the construction of the horoscope. These data also determine the strictly personal character of the horoscope. Other people are born at a different time and/or in another place, so as a rule the horoscopes of different people differ drastically.

On the basis of these birth data the astrologer will now set to work and "cast" the horoscope. This is a schematic map of part of the firmament as it looked at the moment of birth. The modern astrologer does this simply by entering the provided data into his computer and after a few seconds a ready-made figure, often beautifully drawn, is generated. A less well-to-do colleague or one who works more traditionally has to resort to checking tables on which the desired astrological data for each day are written. After some simple arithmetic the results can be drawn into the horoscope figure. Contrary to what some astrologers like to claim, this stage of the work is actually quite simple for someone who can read a table and who knows the four major operations of arithmetic (addition, subtraction, multiplication, and division).

Now comes the most difficult part: The horoscope has to be *interpreted*. People do not go to the astrologer to receive a complicated picture, but to obtain advice about their personal problems or a glance at their future. In order to do that the astrologer has to explain the horoscope. From the drawing and with the help of age-old rules and traditional relationships, he tries to describe the personality of the owner. According to astrology the place of each astrological factor (which we will discuss later) and its position with respect to the other factors give insight into certain character traits. And as hardly any two horoscopes are alike because the exact positions of these factors and their relations to each other change from birthplace to birthplace and in the course of time, the interpretation of the resulting horoscopes has to be different. That is why the astrologers put such an emphasis on the unique character of both the horoscope and each individual person.

We hope that after this short survey it will be clear that the real personalized astrology is something quite different from those two or three lines in the newspaper. Whereas the latter only give vague catch words, the interpretation of a personal horoscope can quite easily run up to five pages—and some astrologers are able to make it much longer.

And what do you find in such a piece of astrological literature? It is an attempt to give a description of the owner of the horoscope: her personality traits and characteristics, as well as her relations with other people. General tendencies that determine one's life will also be mentioned, such as whether one will know many financial problems, how the relations with the opposite sex will be, in which direction the general sphere of interest lies, how one will develop professionally, which place one will occupy on the social ladder, and other information of that kind. The person will be astrologically dissected to the bare bones; nothing remains hidden. However, for those who only consult an astrologer to get an answer to a single question, the interpretation can obviously be much shorter.

If everything turns out better than expected, the client goes home satisfied, conjectures are confirmed, plans already made will be carried through or be thoroughly reconsidered, low points in a relationship will take a turn for the better after all, this or that transaction can be thought over quietly. And a satisfied customer also makes a satisfied astrologer.

Past and Future

All through history astrology has been a controversial subject. In the west it was condemned by the Church, but at the same time some popes and other prominent princes of the Church kept a personal astrologer. Kings had court astrologers in their service, while some universities fulminated against this pagan superstition. Then again, other universities had chairs in astrology.

It was not until the seventeenth century that astrology disappeared from the intellectual stage. Astronomy had demoted Earth—ever considered the center of the universe—definitively to a minor companion of the Sun. In that new worldview, which appealed more frequently to science to explain observed phenomena, there was less and less need for the weird influences of astrology. This, indeed, meant the end of astrology as a respectable subject for scholars, but did not yet imply that astrology had disappeared from the face of the Earth, no matter how much some would have liked that.

During the eighteenth and the first half of the nineteenth century, the time of the Enlightenment and various revolutions (the American, the French, and the Industrial), the influence of astrology declined even further; at most it belonged to folklore and the yearly almanac. But roughly during the last quarter of the last century the tide started to turn. A renewed interest for the subject came into existence, particularly in the English-speaking countries. From then on the interest in astrology started to spread slowly over the rest of the Western world. Depending on time and place it experienced periods of more or less success. The last zenith of its success in the Western world came at the end of the 1960s and in the 1970s. Astrology became immensely popular, particularly among younger people. Astrologers were regularly interviewed by magazines. An astrological book by Linda Goodman, *Sun Signs*,* became a bestseller and "professional" astrological literature could be bought at newspaper stands. Since the 1980s the tide seems to have turned slightly, at least as far as the interest of the public is concerned. But, looking at history, this could well be a premature conjecture.

Criticism

In spite of the success astrology has had in recent decades, there nevertheless appear to be people who are suspicious of this "thousand-year-old" wisdom. Is this, as the astrologers contend, the result of a state of mind which is unable or unwilling to adapt to the new "proofs" for the relationship between humanity and the cosmos? Are critics by definition of ill will? Are the expressed criticisms

---

*(New York: Taplinger Publishing Co., 1968)

a testimony of deep-seated prejudices and a lack of open-mindedness? Or are there valid arguments which substantiate the doubts about the validity of astrology? Does there exist something like well-based criticism?

There are more than enough books in which the basics of the astrological system are explained. On that level, astrologers have nothing to complain about. However, it is much more difficult to find something that explains the existing criticism of astrology. Some astrological works devote a couple of paragraphs to it, but for understandable reasons that "criticism" never touches the heart of the matter nor explains the real arguments.

It is the intention of this book to look at astrology from a critical point of view. The method that will be followed is not the simplest one, but we think it is the most interesting and the most complete one. The guiding principle for the research into the truth behind astrology is that responsible criticism on a subject can only be exercised when one is well acquainted with the subject. It is a pity that all too often some of the arguments offered against astrology miss the point because they do not start from what astrologers really claim, but from what the opponent *thinks* (or would like to think) that the astrologers are claiming. And, as a matter of fact, that does not have to be the same thing. That way the argument is perhaps an easier read, or it appeals more to the layperson, but as soon as the nonastrologer comes into contact with the real astrology, the argument collapses like a house of cards.

The only remedy for it is to make sure that you know what astrology does. Know, at least along the main lines, how a horoscope is cast, which factors the astrologer uses, and how these are calculated. The disadvantage of this approach is, of course, that the reader is first served a piece of (technical) astrology. This may make the criticism in some places look rather like a handbook of astrology . . . and it goes without saying that that is not our intention. The advantages of this method, however, sufficiently outnumber the disadvantages. A better picture of the astrological practice is obtained and the value of the arguments against astrology can be judged more clearly because more background information is provided. Also, the more technically oriented criticisms (the arguments that criticize the very building-blocks of the horoscope) can be presented. In short, criticism of astrology does not only come from the outside, but also from the inside.

That is why we advise the reader to take the trouble to go through the more technical sections of this book. We hope that after reading these sections he will be able to form a solid judgment about the validity of the astrological claims. Whether he still accepts or rejects astrology is of lesser importance, as long as the reader knows *why* this or that point of view is taken. Nothing is as dangerous as an unconsidered prejudice.

22 Making Sense of Astrology

Aderlaßmann und Behandlung von Kranken (1499).

The *melothesia* was an astrological theory which connected certain body parts with signs and planets. Later this idea was pictured in the shape of an "astrological man," which was among other things used to determine the suitable organs and moments for blood-letting. This picture is from 1499.

Introduction 23

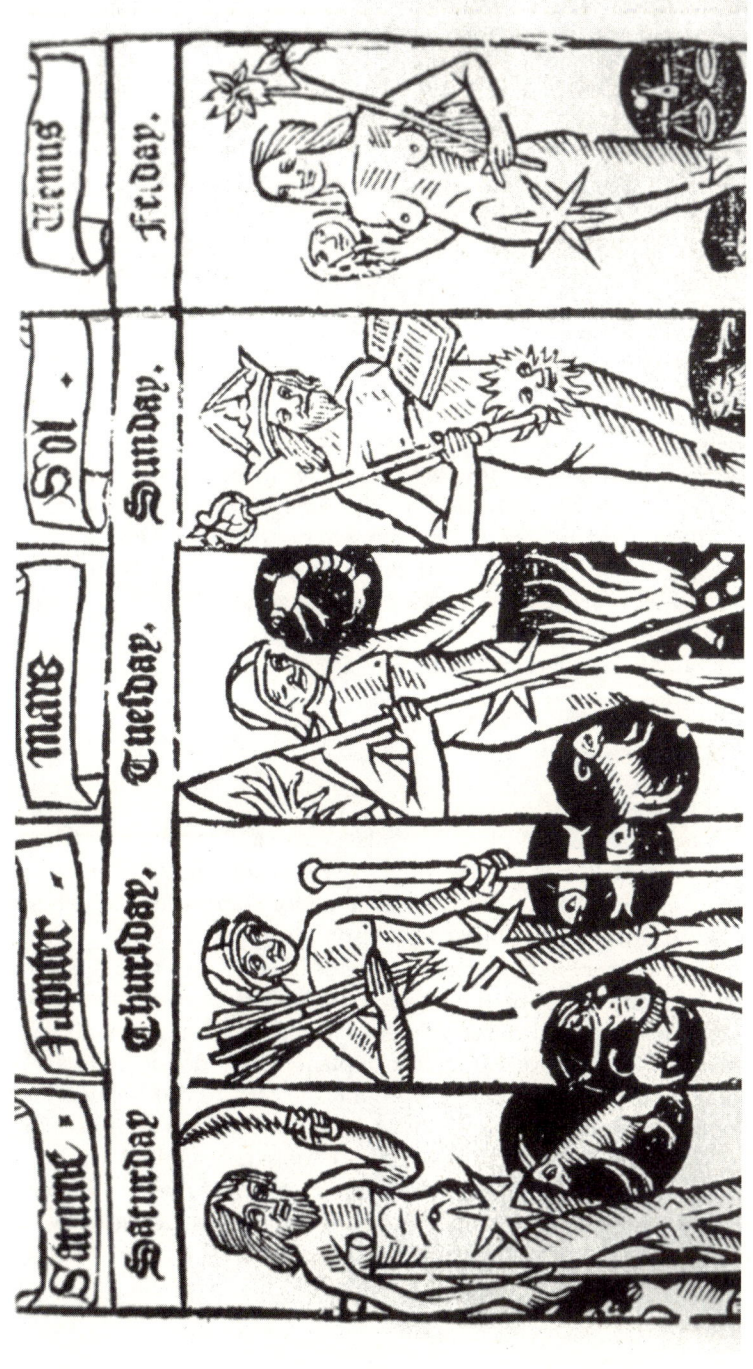

The planets and the signs connected with the days of the week, as shown in this medieval print. For Sunday and Monday, things are clear enough. Saturday comes from Saturn. For the other days the Germanic languages used the names of the equivalent Germanic gods: Mars for mardi in French becomes Tiu for Tuesday in English; Mercury (mercredi)—Wodan (Wednesday); Jupiter (jeudi)—Donar (Thursday); Venus (vendredi)—Freya (Friday).

2

☉ ♆ ☿ ♌ ♋ ♂ ♃ ✶ □ △ ⊼ ☍

THE STARRY SKY

Before we occupy our minds with the art of casting horoscopes it might be interesting to run through the astro*nom*ical data (data based on the *science* of the universe). All in all, astrology has something to do with whatever happens in the sky, although it is very doubtful if the astrologer who pores over his tables or who lets his computer do the work for him would be able to recognize a planet between the stars. For the most part, contemplation of the "cosmic connection" takes place in-house.

We Take a Point of View

When nowadays one reads a book about the solar system and the place of Earth within it, the author as well as the reader often have—unconsciously—a mental picture of the Sun around which the planets turn in more or less circular orbits. One "sees" in his imagination the solar system "from the outside." That image is only partly correct, as everybody seems to underestimate the distances badly. And such a mental picture gives no hint at all of the important effects that arise when the observer is not located outside the solar system anymore but is *on* one of those planets. He then sees everything from a planet which not only turns on its axis, but which at the same time moves around the Sun. And this combination of movements causes the celestial paths of the other planets, which in their turn orbit that same Sun, suddenly to become a lot more complicated.

If we want to understand the origin and the meaning of the astrological elements, then we have to put ourselves into the place of our ancestors, who still held the conviction that Earth was flat, that it was the center of the universe, and that everything turned around it. We should look at whatever happens in the sky with their eyes, not at the real causes that we now know are important, but at the phenomena as they appear to us. We now know well enough that Earth orbits around the Sun and the Moon around Earth, but if we follow the movement of both celestial bodies in the sky, then there is nothing which points to that important difference. Our eyes show us clearly that both turn around Earth (properly speaking, about ourselves), while our daily experience teaches us that Earth stands still rather than that it turns.

It was with this view of the universe that astrology arose and developed. It is obvious then that we must now look at what is happening in our cosmic surroundings with the eyes of an observer on Earth.

A First Orientation

Let us then (in our imagination or not) go outside for a moment into an open field, from where we can have an unobstructed view of the horizon. With a little bit of fantasy we see ourselves standing in the center of a large circle formed by the horizon. Above us is the sky, which covers us as a gigantic hemisphere to the horizon. We can even imagine that hemisphere runs on below the Earth. Thus we find ourselves in the center of a gigantic "cosmic dome" which is closed off by the horizon.

Changes with Time: Day and Night

When we look at that celestial dome for some time, we see a number of noticeable changes.

The most remarkable change is the following of day and night. No matter how cloudy the sky may be, the successive periods of light and dark are always striking. Nowadays even the smallest child knows that this is caused by the fact that Earth turns around on its axis, but because we want to put ourselves on the point of view of our ancestors, we attribute this to the revolution of the Sun around Earth. For that matter, in our modern language we still refer to that: after all, we say that the Sun is rising, and not "this place on Earth is turning toward the Sun."

As an observer in the open we see the Sun rising in the east in the morning and at noon it reaches its highest point in the southern sky. From then on the Sun goes down: It comes closer to the horizon and in the evening it sets in the west. We can imagine the Sun continuing its way under the horizon until it reaches its lowest point in the north. After that it climbs toward the eastern horizon to start a new day (figure 2.1).

26   Making Sense of Astrology

Figure 2.1

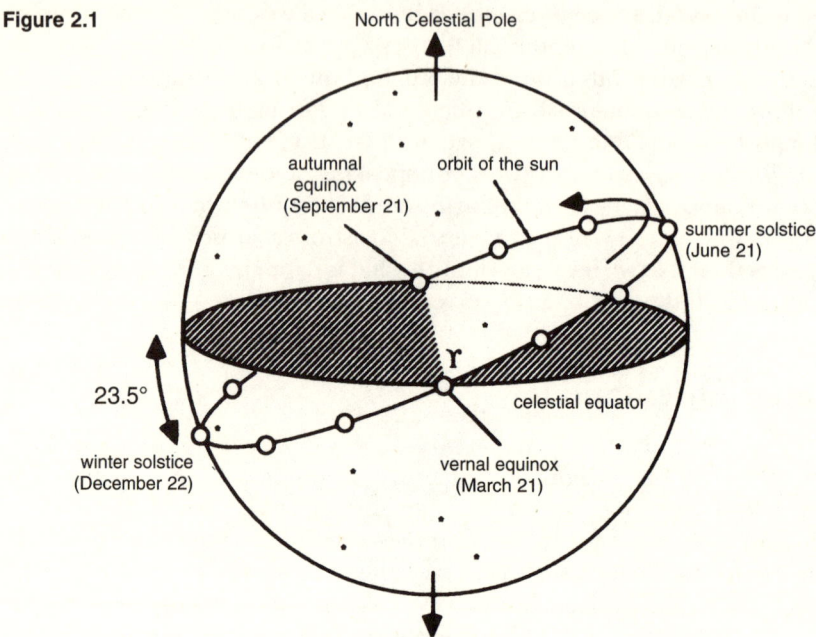

Figure 2.2

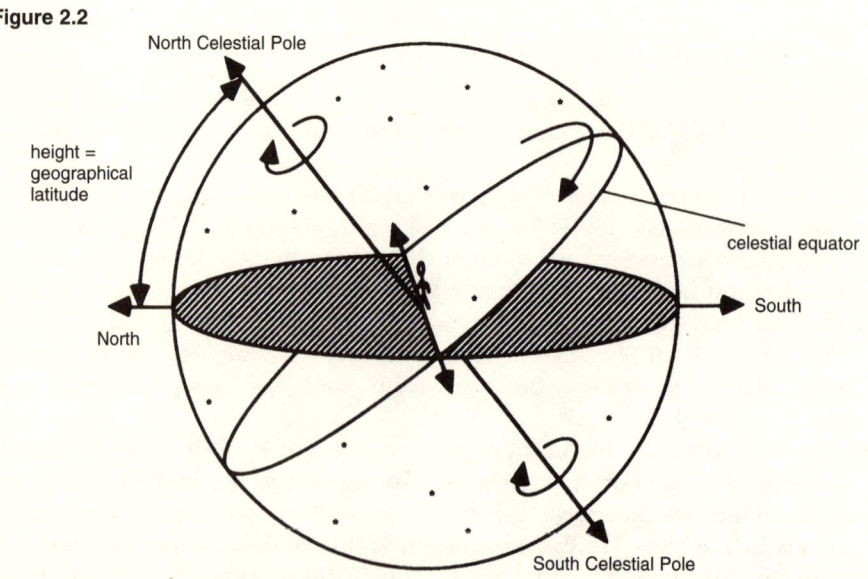

But it is not only the Sun that moves in the sky. If we continue our observations after sunset, we see the stars appear once it is sufficiently dark. If the time is right we can also observe the Moon either as a small crescent visible in the west immediately after sunset, as a more or less half-way lit disc in the south, or as the full Moon rising in the east. After a short time it becomes clear that the Moon and the stars also move along the firmament in the same direction as the Sun: The small crescent of the Moon disappears after a few hours under the western horizon, while a rising full Moon remains visible all night in the south, moving slowly to the west and setting there in the morning.

These observations give the impression that the whole celestial sphere turns around the observer, dragging the Sun, the Moon, and the stars along. During a short period of observation, for instance one single night, one might even think that the Moon hangs fixed between the stars and that it is only the celestial dome that moves.

It is but a small step to expand this nightly observation to the daytime: The Sun is also located, just like the Moon, between the stars, but its bright light prevents us from seeing the stars during the day.

The picture that we—at this stage of the explanation—have of the sky is that of a hollow sphere in which we find ourselves at the center and which makes one complete turn in one day. The Sun, the Moon, and the stars are located on the inside of the sphere.

The direction in which the Sun, Moon, and stars move makes it clear that the axis of the turning celestial dome points to the north (figure 2.2). As in geography, which refers to the two points around which Earth turns as poles, the two points around which the sphere of the heavens turns are called the *celestial poles*. The one in the north is, obviously, called the north celestial pole and that in the south, the south celestial pole. The latter is, of course, not visible to people living in the northern hemisphere, because it is under the horizon. Although it was not always the case, there is now a fairly bright star not far from the north celestial pole, which makes finding that pole quite easy. For obvious reasons this star is called Polaris, the North Star. For the south celestial pole the situation differs: There is no noticeable star or constellation in the neighborhood, so this pole is a little bit lost between dim stars. Too bad for those down under.

The imaginary circle that cuts the celestial sphere into two equal halves with respect to these poles is called the celestial equator, just as the analogous circle that divides Earth is the geographical equator.

Let us look now at what happens when we make a trip from our home, which for most readers will be in mid-northern latitudes. If we travel south, we see that around noon the Sun there stands higher in the sky than at home; at latitudes near the equator it can even stand right above us—at the zenith. If we continue our voyage to the south and, for instance, arrive at the Falkland Islands, then at noon the Sun will stand there lower on the horizon again (just about as low as was the case at home), but now in the *north*. Of course, this is the logical result of the spherical shape of Earth. At the same time we notice that during our voyage Polaris gets closer and closer to the horizon: At the equator the two coincide, and on the Falkland Islands Polaris is no longer visible, since it is located below the horizon. Instead the south celestial pole stands above the horizon.

If we go north from home, exactly the opposite happens: As we travel to *higher* latitudes, the Sun will stand ever *lower* above the horizon, while at night Polaris has to be looked for higher and higher in the sky. On the North Pole Polaris stands at the zenith.

These are all simple astronomical concepts, but they will play an important role in the consideration of the astrological houses, which is discussed in chapter 7.

The Movement of the Sun

If we follow the starry sky over a longer period of time, we see that the view gradually changes night by night; a shift takes place, causing other groups of stars to become slowly visible. Stars that were, on a certain evening, barely visible in the west, can no longer be seen after a number of days, while in the morning, just before sunrise, new groups of stars gradually crop up. It almost looks as if the celestial dome each day turns a little bit farther than we would expect. In the long run this effect becomes more and more striking: After three months at sunset all stars which formerly stood in the south (or above our heads) have disappeared.

There is only one possible explanation for that phenomenon: Since day and night are caused by the movement of the Sun around Earth (that is the point of view we took) and the zone with stars that are visible at night shifts, then this means that the Sun itself must move between the stars in an easterly direction. After one year (a little bit more than 365 days) the Sun has then returned to its starting-point among the stars.

Therefore, we conclude that the Sun moves along its own orbit among the stars. As observers on Earth we see that orbit as a circle with ourselves at the center, the same center as for the circles that form the horizon and the celestial equator. All three are "great circles" (circles that divide a sphere into two equal parts). Let us take a closer look at the most important differences among these three great circles:

- The *horizon* is for us a fixed circle, which does not change either during the day or during the year. A point on the horizon is fixed as long as we do not travel.

- The *celestial equator* is a circle that has a fixed orientation among the stars, but which makes one revolution in about one day. (The actual duration of a revolution is 23 hours 56 minutes; the difference from 24 hours is caused by the proper movement of the Sun. This is easy to check: 24 hours divided by 365 days is slightly less than 4 minutes per day.) The inclination of the celestial equator with respect to the horizon remains constant for a given latitude on Earth. For a place in the Netherlands or Canada at a latitude of 51.5° North the inclination amounts to 38.5° (the inclination is calculated by subtracting the geographical latitude from 90°, in this case that will be 90° − 51.5° = 38.5°; see also figure 2.2). For Washington, D.C., at 38.5° North this is 51.5° and for Miami, Florida, at 25.5° North it has increased to 64.5°. At the *terrestrial* equator the celestial equator is perpendicular to the horizon (90° − 0°) while at the North Pole it lies "flat" and coincides with the horizon.

According to geometry two great circles intersect at two points diametrically opposite each other. This is also true for the horizon and the celestial equator. They intersect in two points: one in the east and one in the west. At any given moment we see exactly one half of the celestial equator above the horizon (figure 2.2).

- The annual *path of the Sun* between the stars or the *ecliptic* also forms a great circle in which the observer stands in the center. This circle differs from the celestial equator. Just as the celestial equator makes an angle with the horizon the orbit of the Sun makes a fixed angle with the celestial equator (figure 2.3). That angle amounts to about 23.5°, which has important consequences for the position of the Sun with respect to the horizon during the year. Let us therefore return for a moment to the description of the movement of the Sun during the day.

It was already mentioned that the height of the Sun at noon is dependent on the place on Earth (more exactly, on the geographic latitude) from which we are observing. Additionally, this height is dependent on the position of the Sun in its orbit, and that position changes every day. Because the orbit of the Sun makes an angle with the celestial equator, we can imagine that the Sun "swings" around the celestial equator during the year (figure 2.4a). This causes the height of the Sun above the horizon at noon to change during the year. At our latitude on about March 21 the Sun is located on the celestial equator, which has an inclination of 38.5° with the horizon. After that date the Sun climbs a little higher in the sky each day; it moves in that part of its orbit that is located above the celestial equator (figure 2.4b) until, about June 21, a maximum height of about 62° is reached (23.5° above the celestial

30   Making Sense of Astrology

Figure 2.3

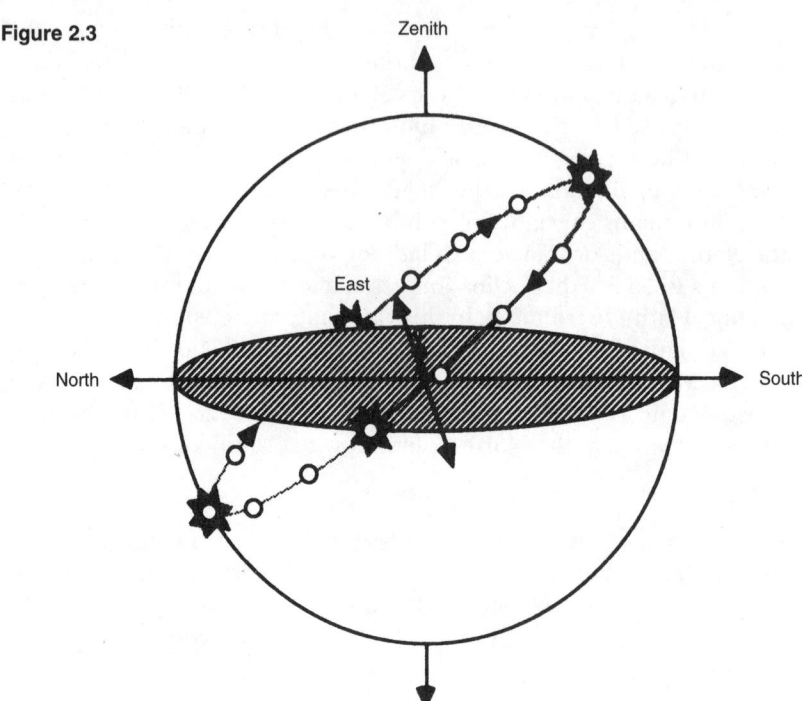

equator, which in turn is located at 38.5°). At noon the Sun is now much higher in the sky (in figure 2.4b the daily movement on that day is drawn in a dotted line). We notice this, for that matter, in the changes in the weather: It is getting warmer and the spring makes way for the summer. After June 21 (the summer solstice), the height of the Sun decreases, and by about September 23 it has already fallen back to 38.5°. The Sun then stands again at the same height as the celestial equator. It is also getting cooler; fall and winter are coming. From then on the Sun is moving in that part of its orbit that lies "under" the celestial equator. This descent continues until December 22, by which time the Sun has arrived at its lowest point (the height of the Sun then amounts to 38.5° − 23.5° = 15°). It gives less light and heat: It is winter. After that the ascent starts again to reach March 21 of the next year.

In figures 2.3 and 2.4b it can clearly be seen that the celestial equator and the orbit of the Sun intersect at the Sun's location on about March 21 (the beginning of spring) and on September 23 (the beginning of autumn). These two points are the *vernal equinox* and the *autumnal equinox*, because day and night are of equal length at these times. The vernal equinox is generally taken to be the starting point of the celestial equator as well as of the orbit of the sun. More will be said about this in chapter 3.

Together with the height of the Sun the length of the day also changes. At the beginning of spring and of autumn day and night last equally long. The Sun is then located on the celestial equator and on these days rises exactly in the east and sets exactly in the west. Exactly half of its daily orbit is located above the horizon. When the height of the Sun increases, the route that we see the Sun take in the sky shifts a little to the north. The part of its daily movement that we are able to see then is consequently larger than half of its daily orbit, so that the days last longer. The Sun rises somewhat earlier in the morning and sets somewhat later at night (figure 2.4a).

This lengthening of the days continues until June 21, the longest day of the year. From June 21 through December 22 the reverse is true: Between those dates the Sun rises and sets more to the south. The visible part of the daily orbit of the Sun is then shorter, and so are the days.

The Moon

Now that we already have some notion of the movement of the Sun in the sky, we can treat the movement of the Moon quickly.

The Moon is a satellite of Earth, which means that the Moon really orbits Earth, in contrast to the Sun. Just like we did with the orbit of the Sun, we can imagine the orbit of the Moon as a great circle in the center of which we, the observers, are standing (this time with more justification). That circle does not coincide completely with the orbit of the Sun, but makes an angle of about 5° with it. When we combine this with the foregoing, the picture becomes somewhat more complicated: The celestial equator forms an angle with the horizon, the orbit of the Sun forms an angle with the celestial equator and rotates with the latter, and the orbit of the Moon in turn forms an angle with the orbit of the Sun (but that is where it ends, fortunately, there is nothing else yet that forms a constant angle with the orbit of the moon).

The most striking thing about the movement of the Moon in the sky are its phases. Since the Moon needs slightly less than a month to complete its orbit, as opposed to a year for the Sun, the relative positions of the two celestial bodies change from day to day. In addition, the Moon does not radiate light by itself, but reflects the light of the Sun, which causes the lit part that we can see to change quickly. When the Moon and the Sun appear close together (the real distance is almost 150 million kilometers) we have the New Moon: The Moon is too close to the Sun to be visible, and, moreover, the lit part is turned away from us. The Moon then sets together with the Sun. One day later the Moon has shifted quite a bit to the east, and we can see it at night as a

32 Making Sense of Astrology

Figure 2.4a

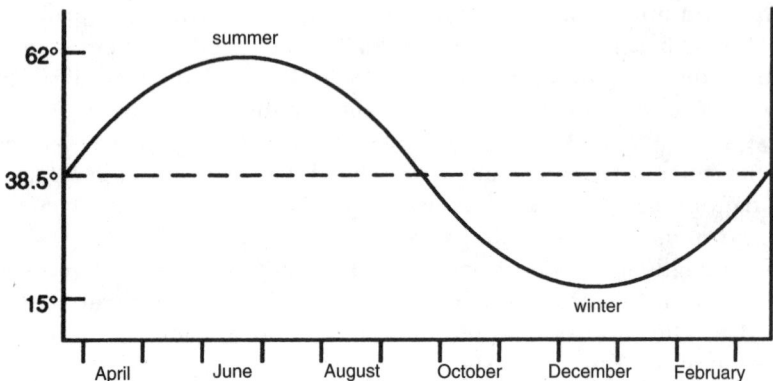

The changes of the maximal height of the sun throughout the year at 51.5° North latitude. The dotted line indicates the height of the celestial equator.

Figure 2.4b

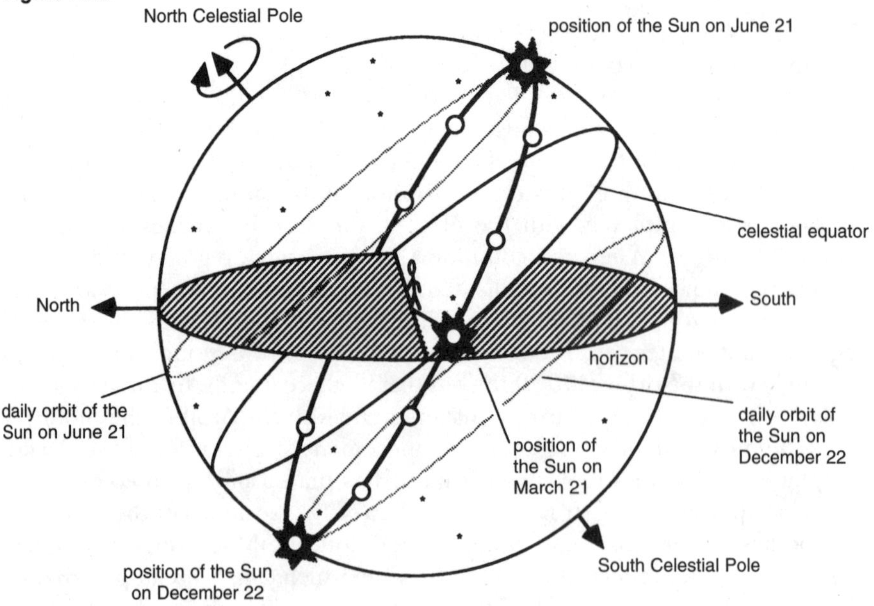

narrow crescent if the horizon is cloudless. Each succeeding night the distance has increased, so that the crescent Moon becomes larger and the Moon sets later. After about a week the Moon is half illuminated: It is the First Quarter. At sunset it now stands in the south. The increase in size of the lit part continues until the Moon, after two weeks, is full: It then stands exactly opposite the Sun and rises in the east at sundown. This brightly lit disc, on which some vague spots can be seen with the naked eye, is now visible all night.

From then on the size of the lit part decreases. After another week, during the Last Quarter, half of the Moon's disc is dark. What is still lit then transforms into a crescent which decreases every day. The Moon is now only visible in the morning above the eastern horizon, just before sunrise. Four weeks after its first appearance it has become invisible again.

The orbits of the Moon and the Sun also intersect at two opposite points, which are often called *nodes*. At these nodes something interesting can happen: When the Sun appears in one of these points simultaneously to the New Moon, then the Moon is also at that point, therefore it comes to stand in front of the Sun and darkens it. On Earth we then see a *solar eclipse*.

This is an utterly remarkable natural phenomenon. Because of a freakish coincidence we find ourselves now in a period of the history of Earth—and this history extends over more than 4 billion years—in which the Moon is standing just far enough from Earth that, seen from Earth, it appears just as large in the sky as the Sun. This has not always been the case: Hundreds of millions of years ago the Moon stood much closer by; it still moves away from Earth with the fantastic speed of a few centimeters per year. Had the Moon been smaller, or stood it farther away, it could never completely cover the Sun, so that a solar eclipse would never be total. The Moon would simply pass over the sun's disc, a not too spectacular event during which the Sun would not lose much of its brightness. In the opposite case, if the Moon were closer to the Earth or were larger, a total eclipse would not only occur more often, but would also last longer and be visible over a larger area of Earth. One might ask oneself if the general fear of our ancestors of such a spectacle would then have been greater or smaller. That fear is indeed still present in many places on Earth.

Nowadays only the fiercely radiating disc of the Sun is darkened (far from all eclipses are total; there are also partial eclipses, during which the Moon covers only a part of the Sun's disc, so that part of the sunlight remains visible). The areas around the disc, the "atmosphere of the Sun" or corona, become visible. The eclipsed Sun shows a beautiful aura of which the form and the structure can vary quite a bit. This alone is reason enough for astronomers to plan years ahead of time to be in the area in which the phenomenon will occur.

The fact that the size of the Sun and the Moon in the sky have to be so exactly tuned to each other for a total eclipse to take place has as a result that such a phenomenon is only visible in a limited area of Earth. The width of the shadow of the moon that slides over the surface of Earth amounts to at most two hundred kilometers or so. This shadow moves at about 15 kilometers per minute across Earth, so that at a given place the total eclipse lasts only several minutes. If you find yourself outside this area you will see that only a part of the disc of the Sun is blacked out by the Moon. This is also easy to understand: If you find yourself farther north on Earth then the Moon is standing somewhat lower than the Sun and will not cover it completely. From that point of observation the lunar orbit will be shifted a little with respect to the Sun, and the total eclipse will be missed.

In addition to solar eclipses there are also lunar eclipses. In that case the Moon is blacked out by the shadow of Earth. That can only happen when Earth is located between the Sun and the Moon and when these two are in the neighborhood of a node. If they are too far removed from a node, then the Moon moves under or over the shadow of Earth. Because the Earth's cone of shade is much bigger than that of the Moon (because Earth is bigger), a lunar eclipse lasts much longer than a solar eclipse. Moreover, the lunar eclipse is visible from a large area: Whoever can see the Moon also sees the eclipse. The phenomenon is far less spectacular than a solar eclipse: The part of the Moon that gets into the shade becomes reddish and decreases in brightness but remains faintly visible. It can take more than one hour before the Moon leaves the shade.

The area in the sky where eclipses can occur remains limited to the nodes. The lunar orbit, however, does not have a fixed place between the stars: The nodes shift slowly with respect to the orbit of the Sun. In roughly eighteen years (a period called *saros*) the nodes—and with them the places where eclipses can occur—run through a complete cycle along the solar orbit. Because eclipses can occur on any point of the solar orbit, this orbit is called the ecliptic.

The Planets

The Sun and Moon are the most striking objects which move in the firmament. Far less striking are other celestial bodies which rotate around the Sun and which play an extremely important role in astrology: the planets. Everybody has heard about them, but who has actually seen them?

The planets are not at all that noticeable in the sky. They look like common stars which are a little bit brighter than the stars in their neighborhoods. One has to keep track of the part of the sky in which they can be found for somewhat longer time before noticing that there is something unusual about these light sources: They move between the stars. It is not a rapid movement like that of the Moon, but rather a slow crawl. Depending on the planet one needs several days or even weeks to note clearly any changes in position. Because of their movement, the planets are sometimes called wanderers. Our word "planets" is, as a matter of fact, derived from a Greek word with exactly the same meaning: a cosmic rambler between the stars.

Five planets are visible in the sky with the naked eye and therefore have been known from ancient times. They are, in order of their distances from the Sun, Mercury, Venus, Mars, Jupiter, and Saturn. Seen from Earth their movements show large irregularities; but more about that in chapter 4.

Mercury and Venus are closer to the Sun than Earth, that is why we always find them in the neighborhood of the Sun. Therefore very little imagination is needed to interpret their movements as orbiting around the Sun. Because they are always found near the latter, they also need a year on the average to run their course among the stars. The time in which they move once around the Sun is, however, much shorter: 88 days for Mercury and 225 days for Venus.

Mercury, the planet closest to the Sun, is usually difficult to observe. Venus, on the other hand, can be an extraordinarily striking appearance at twilight: a bright white object that outshines every "common" star. Because of its movement around the Sun it is alternately visible in the evening and in the morning, which through history has given it the names of "morning star," "Lucifer," and the "herald of light" who announces daybreak.

The planet that the layman knows best (at least by name) is without doubt Mars. The appearance of this planet varies quite a bit. At midnight it sometimes stands as a very striking orange-red point of light sparkling among the stars, while at other times it is difficult for an experienced observer to find it. In the course of history its complicated movement has brought many an astronomer almost to the edge of despair.

The planets Jupiter and Saturn attract less attention. Both show a constant brightness and, because of their large distances from the Sun, they move much more slowly in the sky than the previously mentioned planets. Jupiter needs about twelve years to run once through its course, Saturn takes almost thirty years.

We see the planets only in a rather narrow strip in the sky which lies around the ecliptic (the solar orbit). That is because all the visible planets move in roughly the same plane as the Sun.

Up until now we have talked about the visible planets. However, invisible planets exist. By "invisible" we mean that these planets are not visible with the naked eye due to their low brightness. These are Uranus, Neptune, and Pluto, and they were only discovered after the invention of the telescope (although certain astrologers would have liked to see this differently).

These last three planets are still farther removed from the Sun than Saturn and move even slower among the stars. The time they need to traverse their orbits once is therefore much longer: Pluto, the farthest of the as yet known planets, requires almost 250 years. They are "wanderers," but they certainly roam very slowly indeed.

Between the orbits of Mars and Jupiter a large number of minor planets are found in what is known as the asteroid belt. The largest of these has a diameter of barely a few hundred kilometers, the smallest we probably have to imagine as some oversized rocks. They sometimes run along very unusual orbits. Once in a while it happens that they closely approach Earth, although this still means some millions of kilometers away. This small grit was also discovered only after the invention of the telescope.

In addition to the large and the small planets a number of other celestial bodies turn around the Sun. The most striking are the comets. Who doesn't remember the recent rage about Comet Hale-Bopp? The research in 1986 regarding Halley's Comet was crowned by a successful spaceflight that clearly confirmed that a comet is a very small object (only a few tens of kilometers large) that spews a large quantity of dust and gas into space, forming the striking tail of the comet. Under favorable conditions the comet can be very impressive in the sky. Because they turn up so unexpectedly—each year new comets are discovered—they created much fear among our ancestors. Even now many people are not fascinated by such a phenomenon for scientific or aesthetic reasons: Even as late as 1997, when Comet Hale-Bopp was visible, there were still people who expected the end of the world (recall the Heaven's Gate cult!).

Another astronomical phenomenon that is often misunderstood by laypersons are the so-called falling stars or meteors. Meteors are not stars at all—real stars are not in the habit of falling—but small pieces of stone and grit that pass through our atmosphere and burn up in its higher layers. This combustion causes a short flare-up which is observed as a "falling star." Sometimes the grit is on the large side and a piece of it hits the surface of Earth, where, if it is very large, it may form a crater. Some years ago in the Unites States such a piece fell straight through the roof of a house. Fortunately there were no injuries from this gift from heaven.

Stars and Constellations

After this concise review of our solar system (note that we did not say anything about the many moons that revolve around the planets) we can look for a moment at its place in the cosmos.

As is well known, our Sun is a very average star among hundreds of millions others. There are stars in all colors and kinds: from blue-white giants that radiate hundreds of times more light than the Sun, to red giants that are so big that the *orbit* of Earth would fit inside them without any trouble

The Starry Sky

(imagine Earth revolving inside the Sun!), to dwarves that are hardly noticeable and which give hardly any light. With the naked eye not much is noticeable about that: Most of the stars appear to us to be equally white, except for a few red exceptions like Antares and Betelgeuze. Particularly striking are the large differences in brightness among the stars. This can have two causes: On the one hand one star can be much farther removed from us than the other, and on the other hand one star may radiate more light than the other. Because of that a small, weak star which is closer by will appear much brighter than a star that is far away with a thousand times stronger light intensity. Nowhere are appearances more deceiving than in astronomy.

However large the number of stars appears to be, without the help of a telescope we can, even under the best of circumstances, seldom see more than one thousand stars at the same time (and in practice quite a few less). The total number of stars that is visible with the naked eye in both hemispheres is about three thousand. Because there are only a few stars that are in close proximity of our neighborhood and most stars do not radiate all that much light, we see relatively few bright stars in the night sky. These bright stars are more or less randomly divided over the celestial sphere. But because humans love to give meaning to everything, from earliest times they grouped certain stars in their imaginations so that they could see recognizable figures: the *constellations*. These patterns also made it easier for people to find their way in the sky.

It should be clear that not the least bit of reality is hiding behind those capricious configurations of starts. Constellations are formed by stars that, as seen from our position in space, *apparently* are in each other's vicinity. When you look at night at a landscape that has lots of illuminated roads, you can see that some lights, which are in reality hundreds of meters apart from each other, appear from your perspective to be right next to each other. This is also the case with the stars that define the constellations. Of the seven brightest stars in the Big Dipper, the one that is farthest away (named Alkaid) is four times farther from us than the nearest one. The star Mizar, which appears to be right next to Alkaid, is in reality closer to the Earth than to Alkaid (figure 2.5a). Constellations are purely the products of human imagination, but they are still being used in astronomy. On the one hand these figures are handy for finding one's way in the sky (the Big Dipper, for instance, is a real signpost); on the other hand, the brighter stars, following an old tradition, are still named and catalogued according to their constellations.

The way in which constellations were formed and named differed from culture to culture: The Chinese and the people of the Pacific saw different patterns in the stars than the Babylonians or the Egyptians. The constellations were usually identified with figures from mythology. Nowadays we know of forty-eight constellations that were in use in classical antiquity (a large part of them are of Babylonian origin). But these forty-eight do not span the whole sky. When, from the fifteenth century on, the Europeans started to sail to the tropics and the southern hemisphere, they saw stars there that the Greeks and Romans never mentioned. Some navigators therefore invented new constellations. Later astronomers also went south to complete this work. But in the northern hemisphere additional constellations were also introduced. Sometimes they served as "filler" for less striking parts of the sky (the constellation Giraffe, for instance, covers a large empty area near Polaris where only a few dim stars are visible). With almost every new starchart or atlas (and formerly, because of their magnificent engravings, these were real works of art) the author fixed the boundary of the constellations according to his own insight. In some cases he deviated quite a bit from tradition. For instance, in some atlases pagan names were replaced by christian ones, where the twelve constellations of the zodiac (which will be discussed later) were named after the apostles. To avoid any confusion, in 1927 the astronomers introduced an official division developed by Belgian astronomer Eugène Delporte, who definitively eliminated a number of insignificant constellations, chopped one exaggeratedly large one in several pieces, mapped out the borders in straight lines, and fixed the official (Latin) names, some of which were drastically simplified. In that way the Painter's Easel (Equus pictoris) became a common Painter (Pictor) and the Fox-with-Goose (Vulpecula cum ansere) a common Little Fox (Vulpecula). Among the eighty-eight constellations which have been used since (sometimes one wrongly counts eighty-nine because the constellation of the Serpent consists of two separate pieces) there are still some that are completely unnoticeable and superfluous. They are also very different in size.

Quite a few constellations have obtained the names of animals. The Big and the Little Dipper are officially called Big Bear and Little Bear (Ursa Major and Ursa Minor). And in that way we also have the Hunting Dogs, Lion, Little Lion, Ram, Bull, Goat, Scorpion, etc. In the southern sky appear the Swordfish (Dorado Fish), the Chameleon, Crane, Toucan, Phoenix (the mythological firebird), and so on—a complete astronomical zoo. Most of the ancient names come straight from Greek mythology; for example, the Bull is supposed to be named after the shape that the supreme god Zeus had taken to elope with the nymph Europa.

Many a figure or object from mythology can be found among the remaining stars: Orion, Cepheus, Andromeda, the Twins, Perseus, the river Eridanus, the Arrow, the Lyre (the instrument of Orpheus), the Scales. Somewhat more modern is the Shield, which depicts the shield of the Polish king Jan Sobieski, who in 1683 stopped a Turkish invasion. (More constellations have been proposed for "political" reasons, but mostly without success.) The names of a lot of the southern constellations show clearly that they are of recent origin: There we meet among others the Microscope and the Telescope, the (chemical) Furnace, the Clock, the Air Pump, the Sextant, the

The Starry Sky 39

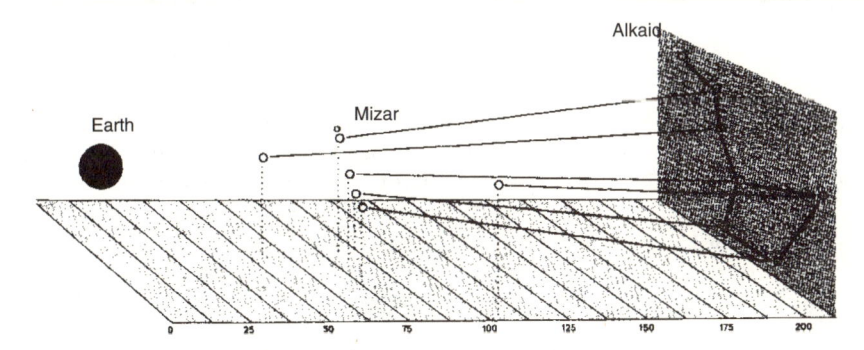

Figure 2.5a. The seven bright stars of the big dipper or the Great Bear, pictured with their real, relative distances to Earth (left). The star Mizar is closer to Earth than it is to the star Alkaid, but projected on the sky (right) the two appear to be close together.

Figure 2.5b. Engraving from *Uranographia* (1801) by Johann Elert Bode: A starchart with pictures of the Great Bear (Big Dipper) and the Lesser Lion. (The seven best-known stars were connected by the authors.)

Compass, the Rule, and the Sculptor's Tool. For these names we can thank the importance that eighteenth-century French astronomer abbé Nicolas-Louis de Lacaille attached to the scientific instruments of his time when he first mapped out certain areas of the southern sky. According to some people these names are more witness to the lack of imagination of this scientist and they deplore that this name-giving has remained in existence to the present.

The arbitrariness of this classification is not so surprising if one realizes that only a handful of constellations have a striking or recognizable form. We will return to this, as well as to the important but often neglected difference between constellations and signs of the zodiac.

Deeper into the Cosmos

But now, back to the stars. The brighter stars are more or less equally distributed over the sky. If we fix our attention however to the dimmer stars, we notice that the distribution of these is less regular. A very large number turn out to be concentrated in a wide strip in the sky: the *Milky Way*. This rather vague smear to the naked eye, the real nature of which was only discovered after the invention of the telescope, consists in reality of a gigantic collection of stars that are spread over a flattened disc. Because our Solar System is located within this disc, we see it as a strip in the sky. Such a collection of stars we can consider as a kind of "island of stars" in the cosmos.

Besides common stars we also find several other objects: dust and clouds of gas in which new stars are born (nebulae), stars of which the brightness changes regularly or irregularly, remnants of exploded stars that like a balloon expanded around the remainders of their stars, collapsed stars which are only a few kilometers in diameter and rotate very quickly around their axes. Stars are not always single, sometimes two or more stars orbit each other, sometimes stars form a more or less stray group. The Pleiades or Seven Sisters in the constellation of the Bull is a magnificent example: This star cluster is easily visible with the naked eye and looks a little bit like a miniature version of the Big Dipper. In contrast to the stars in a constellation the stars in a star *cluster* are indeed close together and they have a common history. In addition to open star clusters like the Pleiades, which have tens or hundreds of members, globular star clusters also exist, in which several hundred thousands of stars are located close together.

Our Milky Way is not alone: There are millions of other "milky ways" or galaxies, some of which are larger than ours and others that are smaller. One has to imagine these systems as distributed just like we see the stars: one farther away than the other, one brighter than the other, and the farther away they are (millions of times farther than the stars that we can see) the dimmer they appear to be and the more difficult it is to observe and study them. And just as certain stars are found in clusters it turns out that galaxies are also.

And that is where our discussion ends (for the time being). These clusters of galaxies are the largest structures we know in the cosmos. Of these hundreds of billions of stars that roam the universe an average, unnoticeable star is our Sun, a piece of dust in the infinity, an atom in the unimaginable, and yet so extremely important to us.

3

THE ZODIAC

In the introduction we gave a short description of the activities of an astrologer and the way in which she "casts" a horoscope. Up until now it was not necessary to know more about the construction of the horoscope, but because in this and the next chapters each part of it will be examined in more detail, a review of it now becomes urgent.

The Astrological Elements

Taking a closer look at the astrological elements gives not only a better insight into what astrology is in theory and in practice; it will also clarify a part of the technical astrological vocabulary. Let's admit it, a sentence like "Mercury is the Lord of the Ascendant and his place in House VIII points to careless action, particularly as there is also a square with Saturn" does not excel in clarity for the nonadept.

The horoscope consists of a number of parts. How many of them there are is not exactly determined; some astrologers use factors that their colleagues reject categorically. Yet it is possible to find a common denominator which is applied by the majority of the astrologers. These common "separate parts" of the horoscope follow:

- *The zodiac*, a twelve-part division of the sky in the neighborhood of the ecliptic (the orbit of the Sun). In the astrological vocabulary these twelve parts are called *signs*. We can imagine these signs as being attached to the stars: for the observer they rotate with the stars around

Earth. The current chapter is devoted to a critical examination of the zodiac.
- *The planets.* In astrology, the Sun and the Moon are reckoned among the planets; they are used in the same way as the eight astronomical planets that orbit the sun. As was explained in the previous chapter, those celestial bodies can always be found in the sky in the neighborhood of the ecliptic and therefore in the zone shaped by the signs. These planets will be the subject of further examination in chapters 4 and 5.
- *The houses.* Just like the signs of the zodiac, the houses are a division of the celestial dome, but this time it is a division that is "fixed" to the horizon. The houses, therefore, in contrast to the signs, do not move with the stars. They will be discussed in chapter 6.
- *The aspects.* These are the angles that certain factors (the planets, certain houses) in the horoscope make with each other. They are discussed in chapter 7.

An astrological system that is mainly based on the use of these four elements is sometimes described as "classical astrology." "Classical" is here understood in the sense that these elements have been in use since classical antiquity (the ancient Greeks and Romans). Once in a while there is some astrologer who "discovers" a new system and who throws out one or more of these parts, or who adds a new one, but as a rule such an "improvement" does not have very much success with his colleagues. What happens more often is that an astrologer "reforms" one or more of the existing elements and proposes an alternative definition of it. We will meet quite a few examples of that phenomenon.

Because the four elements of classical astrology appear in just about all the systems now in use, we will occupy ourselves mainly with these elements. It is not necessary to involve the lesser known elements of astrology in this critical examination, primarily because there are too many of them, so that even a superficial discussion would fill too many pages. Moreover, each of them is used by so few astrologers that most of the astrologers consider criticism of them as beside the point. Therefore, following their advice, we will save ourselves the trouble.

The Astronomical Zodiac

In the previous chapter the rotation of the celestial dome and the movements of the Sun, the Moon, and the planets on that dome were described. An important element in this discussion was the orbit of the Sun or the ecliptic.

The zone in the neighborhood of the ecliptic, in which we see the Moon and the planets move, we call the zodiac. We can imagine this as a wide band stretched around the celestial dome and cut in half by the orbit of the Sun. The constellations that are found in this zone are called the *zodiacal constellations*.

The zodiac is divided in twelve equal parts. Because a circle has 360 degrees, each part contains 30° (360°/12). It is with these twelve pieces, called *signs,* that the astrologers work. These are *not* the constellations, a concept that is often mixed up with them, as we shall see. Signs are not a purely astrological notion: Up until the last century they were also used in astronomy to indicate the location of the planets. Modern astronomers, however, just calculate from 0° to 360° on the ecliptic.

In order to indicate a position on a circle it is necessary to select a starting point on that circle. In astronomy the vernal equinox, the sun's location at the beginning of spring, is used. (More exactly, the intersection of the celestial equator with the ecliptic, and in particular that intersection where the Sun moves from the southern hemisphere to the northern one, is used [refer to figure 2.3]).

By taking the vernal equinox as the beginning of the zodiac the latter is connected with the seasons; this zodiac is therefore also called the *tropical* zodiac. From the vernal equinox, in the direction of the "annual" movement of the Sun in the sky, twelve astrological signs are delimited. In order to remember this dry mathematical distribution better, the ancients gave each sign the name of the constellation that was "behind" it.

The first sign, the first 30 degrees, coincided roughly with the constellation of *Aries* and so was named after it. Then follow *Taurus* (30° – 60°), *Gemini* (60° – 90°), *Cancer* (90° – 120°), *Leo* (120° – 150°), and *Virgo* (150° – 180°). With these we have run through half of the zodiac and we find ourselves exactly opposite the vernal equinox. When the Sun reaches this point, fall starts. The next six signs are *Libra* (180° – 210°), *Scorpio* (210° – 240°), *Sagittarius* (240°–270°), *Capricorn* (270° – 300°), *Aquarius* (300° – 330°), and finally *Pisces* as the last one (330° – 360°). So we have arrived again at the vernal equinox (figures 3.1a and b).

As we have already pointed out, signs and constellations are not the same thing. The constellations are by definition formed by a pattern of stars and their sizes are different from constellation to constellation. The signs, on the other hand, are pure geometrical figures; they are all exactly 30° long and their places in the sky depend only on the position of the vernal equinox. That is also why constellations never coincide completely with the sign of the same name.

However, there is a second reason why the signs ought not to be confused with the constellations. The agreement between the two, as it existed at the time astrology arose, was only a temporary phenomenon. In the course of the centuries the vernal equinox shifts slowly between the stars, an effect that is called *precession*. The cause of it is a change in the direction in which Earth's axis of rotation points. The celestial equator, which is perpendicular to this axis, shifts with it, as a result of which the vernal equinox, which is the inter-

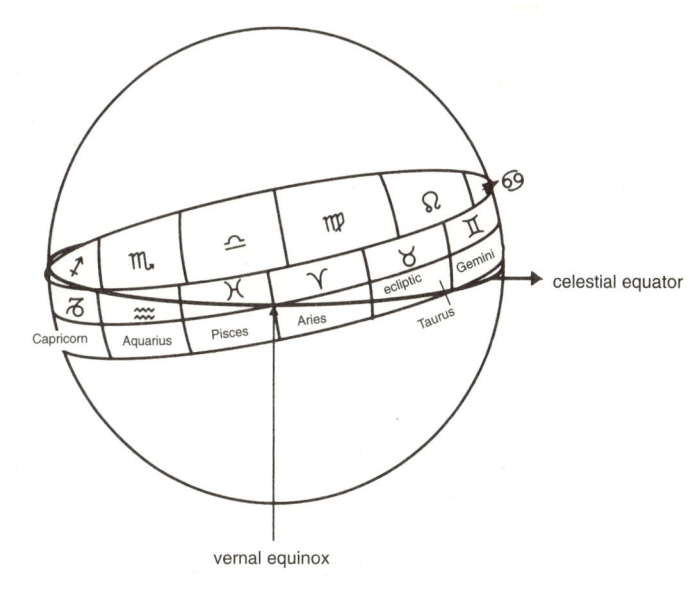

Figure 3.1a. The zodiac on the celestial sphere (compare with figure 2.3).

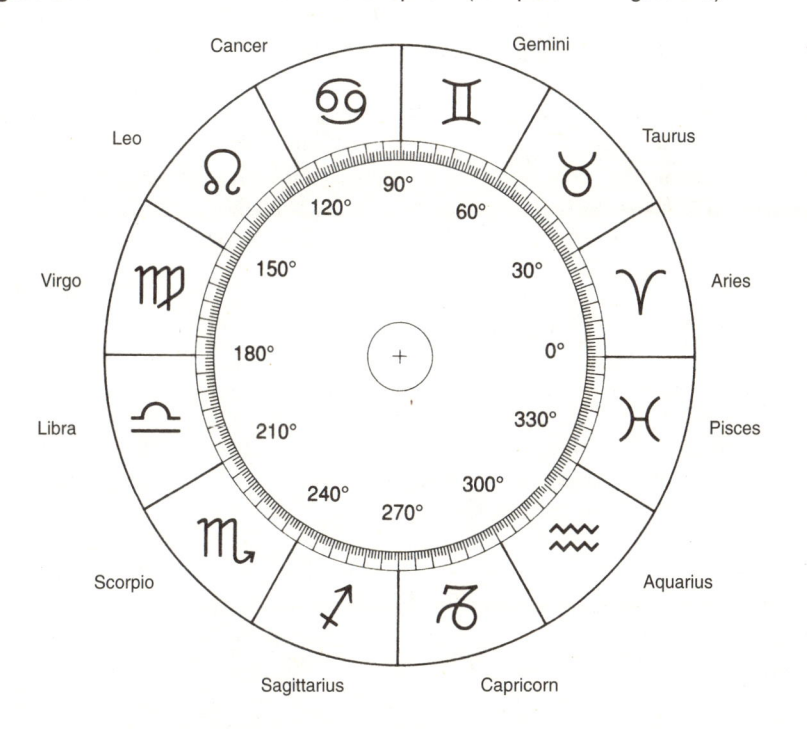

Figure 3.1b. The zodiac in the horoscope (top view of figure 3.1a).

section of the changing celestial equator and the unshifting ecliptic, moves between the stars.

This shift is not all that large, but after 2,000 years it amounts to a full sign. As a result of this now at the start of spring the Sun is located in the *constellation* of Pisces (the Fishes) while, by definition, it then enters the *sign* of Aries. The signs, therefore do not coincide at all with the constellations of the same name (figure 3.2). This should make it clear that the astrological zodiac has nothing to do with the stars; stars, as a matter of fact, never played a very important role in astrology. As an aside, the term "star-sign" which is sometimes used by laypeople, does not exist in astrology.

The signs have nothing in common with the constellations, except for their names. But even then the twelve well known zodiacal symbols should be used exclusively for the signs (the constellations have official abbreviations of their Latin names). For example, the official Latin name for the the constellation of the Scorpion is "Scorpius," but as a rule astrologers indicate the equivalent sign with "Scorpio" (in Latin both words were used).

Therefore never talk about constellations if you mean signs. Do not talk about "the twelve constellations" (as if there were only twelve—remember, there are eighty-eight of them). For an astrologer a clearer proof of astrological ignorance is hardly imaginable. Although since most people know more or less what a constellation is, but never heard of an astrological sign, one finds a fair number of astrological sections in newspapers and magazines which refer to the stars. Headings like "Your Constellation for Today" are not uncommon, particularly in Dutch- and French-speaking countries. Astrologers sometimes even give the impression that they do not know the difference all that well: For instance there was a series of astrological books available in the stores with titles like *Your Constellation Is.* . . . Talk about confusion (or astrological ignorance?)!

The Astrological Zodiac

The importance of the signs in astrology is not so much due to the fact that they divide a region in the sky, but that they are supposed to have certain *properties*. The sign of Aries, for instance, is in the eyes of an astronomer only a small piece of the sky that encloses the ecliptic between 0° and 30°, but for the astrologer it is much more: Aries stands for activity, entrepreneurship, energy, militancy. The sign of Taurus has such characteristics as practical inclination and economic activities; Leo expresses leadership; Libra looks for equilibrium and harmony, is artistic; and so on. A list of the properties of all twelve signs is given in table 3.1.

How we should exactly imagine the cause for the characteristics of the signs is quite unimportant for the astrologer. Some of them talk about a kind

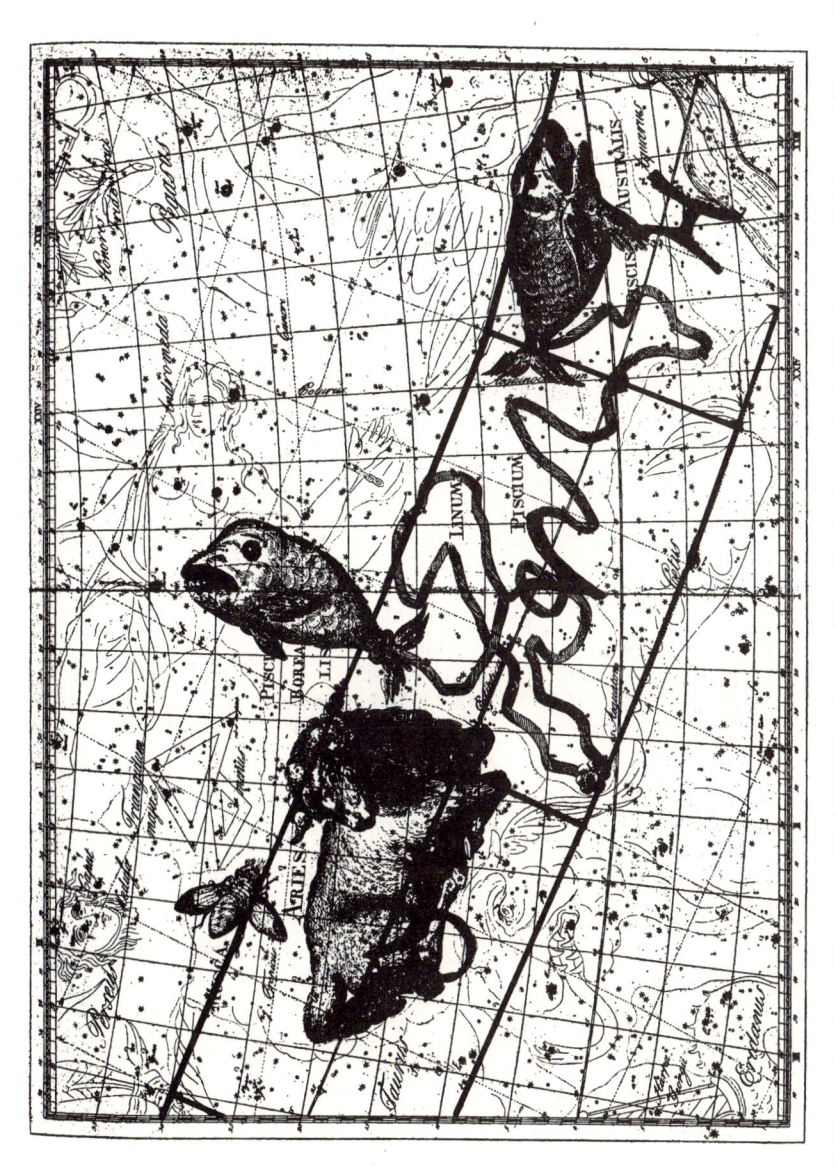

Figure 3.2. Engraving from *Uranographia* (1801) by Johann Elert Bode: A starchart with pictures of Aries and Pisces. (The zodiac and the signs were drawn by the authors.)

Table 3.1: Short Survey of the Characteristics of the Signs

Latin Name	English Name	Symbol	Characteristics
Aries	Ram	♈	Energy, activity, entrepreneurship
Taurus	Bull	♉	Materialism, practical sense, perseverance
Gemini	Twins	♊	Communication, social activities
Cancer	Crab	♋	Social work, caring professions
Leo	Lion	♌	Authority, leadership, vitality
Virgo	Virgin	♍	Scientific, analytical ability
Libra	Scales	♎	Artistic, sense of equilibrium, mediation
Scorpio	Scorpion	♏	Sex, medicine, science, intensity
Sagittarius	Archer	♐	Sports, idealism, religion, philosophy
Capricorn	Goat	♑	Ambition, politics
Aquarius	Water Bearer	♒	Humane, intuitive
Pisces	Fishes	♓	Dreamer, altruistic

of "influence," some sort of radiation that is supposed to originate from these sectors of the sky; others stick to "reflections" of the effect of the seasons on Earth, while still others believe it has to do with pure symbols without any physical reality. But most astrologers are indifferent to the why and how; they just accept the traditional properties and do not bother with it any further.

According to astrology not all signs in the horoscope are equally important. Certain signs and their properties are more dominant when they are found at an important place in the horoscope. The sign that was rising in the eastern sky at the moment of one's birth, the so-called *Ascendant,* and the sign in which the Sun then stood, the *sun-sign,* in particular, are of prime importance. The former plays a decisive role in the determination of the character of the owner of the horoscope. The sun-sign, although considered to be of lesser importance, is the best known, after all, it is this sign to which laypeople refer when they talk about "their" sign or "their" horoscope. One does not have to look very far for the reason for its popularity: because the Sun moves slowly through the zodiac, it remains for about a month in the same sign. It is therefore sufficient to know the date of birth in order to know which was the sun-sign.

It is much more difficult to determine the Ascendant. The celestial dome—and therefore the zodiac—revolves once a day on its axis, as a result of which each sign will become the rising sign (the Ascendant) for only about two hours. Moreover, the moment of the day when a sign rises changes during the year. This is easy to understand if we consider the situation around sunrise: At that moment the sun-sign is the Ascendant, but because of the movement of the Sun in the zodiac this sign will change during the year. How to determine the rising sign will be discussed in Intermezzo V.

Figure 3.3. Divisions of the zodiac.
Groups of signs with respect to Aries:
— positive, masculine signs (hexagon): Aries, Gemini, Leo, Libra, Sagittarius, Aquarius
— fire triangle: Aries, Leo, Sagittarius
— cardinal signs (square): Aries, Cancer, Libra, Capricorn

In this short astrological discussion we should mention a number of often-used divisions of the zodiac. The twelve signs are located on a circle, the ecliptic. Now, arithmetically speaking 12 is a very interesting number: It can be divided by 1, 2, 3, 4, 6, and 12 and therefore it is very easy to draw a triangle, a square, and a hexagon in this circle in such a way that the points of these polygons connect certain signs with each other. The groups obtained in this way have, according to the astrologers, certain characteristics in common. In this way the signs that are located on a triangle are connected with the ancient (Greek) natural elements of *fire, earth, air,* and *water*. The signs Aries–Leo–Sagittarius form the fire triangle (figure 3.3); Taurus–Virgo–Capricorn form the earth triangle; Gemini–Libra–Aquarius the air triangle; and Cancer–Scorpio–Pisces the water triangle. This division deviates from what the names of the signs would make one to expect: Aquarius (the Water Bearer) is an air sign and Scorpio (the Scorpion) is a water sign.

The division according to the squares speaks much less to the imagination. The astrological terminology speaks here of *cardinal signs* (Aries–Cancer–Libra–Capricorn), *fixed signs* (Taurus–Leo–Scorpio–Aquarius) and *mutable signs* (Gemini–Virgo–Sagittarius–Pisces).

The final geometrical groups in this series are formed by the inscribed hexagons; these are the *positive* or male and *negative* or female signs (clearly a relic of ancient ideas about women!). The positive signs start with Aries, the negative ones with Taurus. That is why Taurus (the Bull) is female in this distribution.

In the modern terminology that astrologers love to use, these two characteristics are connected to the psychological conceptions of extroversion and introversion. The former has something to do with being oriented to the outside world, social activities, and so on, while the latter is more associated with being concerned about one's own thoughts and feelings. How much this agrees with reality will be shown in chapter 8.

There are other divisions that are clearly derived from the names of the signs. Pisces (the Fishes), for instance, together with Cancer (the Crab) and Scorpio are "mute" signs, meaning that they "do not have a voice" (they are the only three animals in the zodiac that do not produce any sounds). The same manner of thinking led to placing Gemini (the Twins), Capricorn (the Goat), and Pisces (the [two] Fishes) into the category "double signs" (Capricorn was originally a goat-fish, a mythical animal with the front of a goat and the tail of a fish). This type of division is, however, not used much nowadays.

To finish the discussion of this subject we can mention a division of the zodiac that was used frequently in the past, but which present-day astrologers have all but abandoned: the *decans*. These have their origin in the Egypt of the pharaohs and were very important in the ancient astrology of the Greeks and Romans. According to this system the zodiac is divided in 36 pieces of 10 degrees each (in Greek *deca* means ten, hence the name) and characteristics were attributed to them also, just as to the signs. Because 36 is equal to 3×12

the decans were connected with the signs in such a way that each sign was allotted 3 decans. In antiquity the zodiac was split up even further: characteristics were attributed to each degree of the zodiac! It should have become clear by now that astrology can not only be extended without limits, but also that geometry played an important role in it.

Zodiacal Problems

The zodiac is one of the most important parts of astrology. That is not because without a zodiac no astrology could possibly exist—an astrology without signs is very well imaginable—but because the zodiac forms a frame of reference on which the other points are posted. The zodiac enjoys the greatest familiarity with the public-at-large; the astrological knowledge of the man in the street does not reach much further than the names of the signs. The zodiac is also the first element that is drawn on the horoscope.

In spite of this importance, the astrological zodiac is open to criticism. According to the astrologers there is, properly speaking, no reason for that. It only testifies to the flagrant lack of knowledge on the part of the skeptics. Whether the objections are valid, and whether the opponents of astrology are nitpicking the reader can judge for himself.

The Problem of the Precession

As was already mentioned, the signs do not coincide with the constellations of the same names. If we take into account the explanation that was provided when discussing the signs, there don't seem to be any problems. The signs are plainly attached to the vernal equinox, which is not the case with the constellations. In this way signs and constellations have nothing in common. That they carry the same names is an accident of history; the pieces of the zodiac simply had to be given a name and the Greco-Roman astrologers cannot be blamed for using the names of those constellations that at that time coincided with them. That, at least, is the opinion of quite a few astrologers. It is worth our while, however, to test that assertion critically, because it will be shown that things are not quite that simple.

The zodiac arose from an astronomical necessity: About 2,500 years ago the Babylonians needed a frame of reference to indicate the position of the Moon and the planets between the stars. Due to the development of their astronomy it was no longer sufficient to note that a planet was close to this or that star; a more precise indication was necessary. For that purpose the schematic calendar then in use which divided the year in twelve months of thirty days each was employed. (This calendar is schematic because of the fact that the year does not consist of exactly 360 days.) This schematic year was then connected with the stars: Each ten days of the schematic year had been connected with the first appearance at daybreak of a star or a small group of stars, which boils down to a division of the ecliptic into 36 × 10 "days." That relation with specific astronomical phenomena certainly caused the schematic months to keep pace with the solar year. But it also made it necessary to add a couple of extra days now and then.

Right about this time there had also been a revolution in the mapping of the constellations in the neighborhood of the ecliptic. At first there had been a historical phase in which the zodiac had been divided into eighteen constellations; later this number became fifteen and finally it was reduced to twelve. This development was expedited by the fact that certain stars had already been connected with the schematic year of 12 months × 30 days. What was now easier than to award each month a constellation right away?

A nice plan, but a bit too schematic. The pieces of the zodiac that were connected to the months are, of course, our signs: There are twelve months in a year and therefore twelve signs. A schematic month numbered thirty days, therefore each sign numbered thirty degrees. At the same time the circle was first divided into 360 degrees.

The constellations, however, cannot just be pushed into equal little boxes. Some constellations, like Leo and Gemini, are very much determined by the "figure" that the stars form and that is, of course, not always exactly 30° long. Because of this fact the signs did not always coincide completely with the constellations.

For the Babylonians that did not matter much; the signs were only mathematical constructions that were useful for astronomical calculations. Whenever the "real" position of a planet needed to be determined, the calculations were always converted from the signs to a place among the stars. And because of the very close relationship between the zodiac and the constellations, the zodiac had been oriented in such a way that the signs coincided as much as possible with the constellations of the same names. The zodiac was therefore connected *firmly* with the stars and is therefore called the *sidereal* zodiac (*sidus* means star in Latin).

How then did one get the idea to connect the signs to the vernal equinox? The Babylonian astronomers had barely any interest in the great circles in the sky such as the celestial equator and the ecliptic, and therefore paid very little attention to the vernal equinox. It was the stars and not the seasons that demanded the main part of their attention. As a result, no Babylonian texts that explicitly treat the vernal equinox are known. If the place of the vernal equinox is calculated for that time (about 500 B.C.E.) and the tropical zodiac is compared to the sidereal one, it turns out that the difference between the two was about 3°: The vernal equinox was located at 3° of the sidereal sign of Aries (figure 3.4).

The Zodiac

To make things still more complicated, we could not only look at the place were the real vernal equinox was located, but also where the Babylonians *thought* it was. The starting point are texts which record when, according to their calculations, day and night were equally long (which happens when the Sun is located in either the vernal or the autumnal equinox, as described in chapter 2). It then becomes clear once more that our conceptions are not necessarily the same as those of our ancestors: They used two means of calculation concurrently—in the one system the vernal equinox was situated at 10° Aries, and in the other at 8° Aries.

The last number is particularly important: The Greeks adopted the sidereal zodiac from the Babylonians, together with the vernal equinox of 8° Aries, in the conviction that that was its real location. Greek astronomy, however, differed from Babylonian astronomy because in it the great circles in the sky (celestial equator, ecliptic, etc.) were considered very important. Therefore they carried their calculations out with respect to the vernal equinox, in the tropical zodiac, and not with respect to the stars.

Now, what did such a Greek astronomer do? He used the ecliptic (tropical zodiac) to calculate the position of the planets. Once he had obtained the result, he converted them to positions in the sidereal zodiac in order to find the real place among the stars, and he did this by adding 8° to the result, the difference between the vernal equinox—the starting point of the calculation—and the starting point among the stars.

This was all well and good as long as it was assumed that the vernal equinox was fixed among the stars, so that the difference remained a constant 8°. But around 130 B.C.E. the Greek astronomer Hipparchos discovered that the vernal equinox shifts.

After that discovery it appears that astronomers in general did not know what to do. There where those who simply did not believe it and who went on using the 8° correction. Others accepted some other value (5°, 3°, 1°), while some astronomers/astrologers just dropped the sidereal zodiac. This last practice gained support because the difference between the sidereal and the tropical zodiac became smaller as time went on due to the movement of the vernal equinox in the direction of the beginning of the constellation of Aries (see figure 3.5). When the vernal equinox had arrived there, the twelve divisions of the two systems coincided for all practical purposes, so that the difference between the names of the signs and those of the constellations slowly faded away.

The group of astronomers that completely switched to the tropical zodiac included Ptolemy, the man who wrote the definitive manual of ancient astronomy—and who, besides that, also found time to compose the reference work on astrology, the *Tetrabiblios*. On his authority everybody in the West switched to the new system, so that the sidereal zodiac slowly fell into disuse.

What kind of criticism of astrology can this short historical review provide?

In the first place it should be clear that astrology is not as old as some pro-

54   Making Sense of Astrology

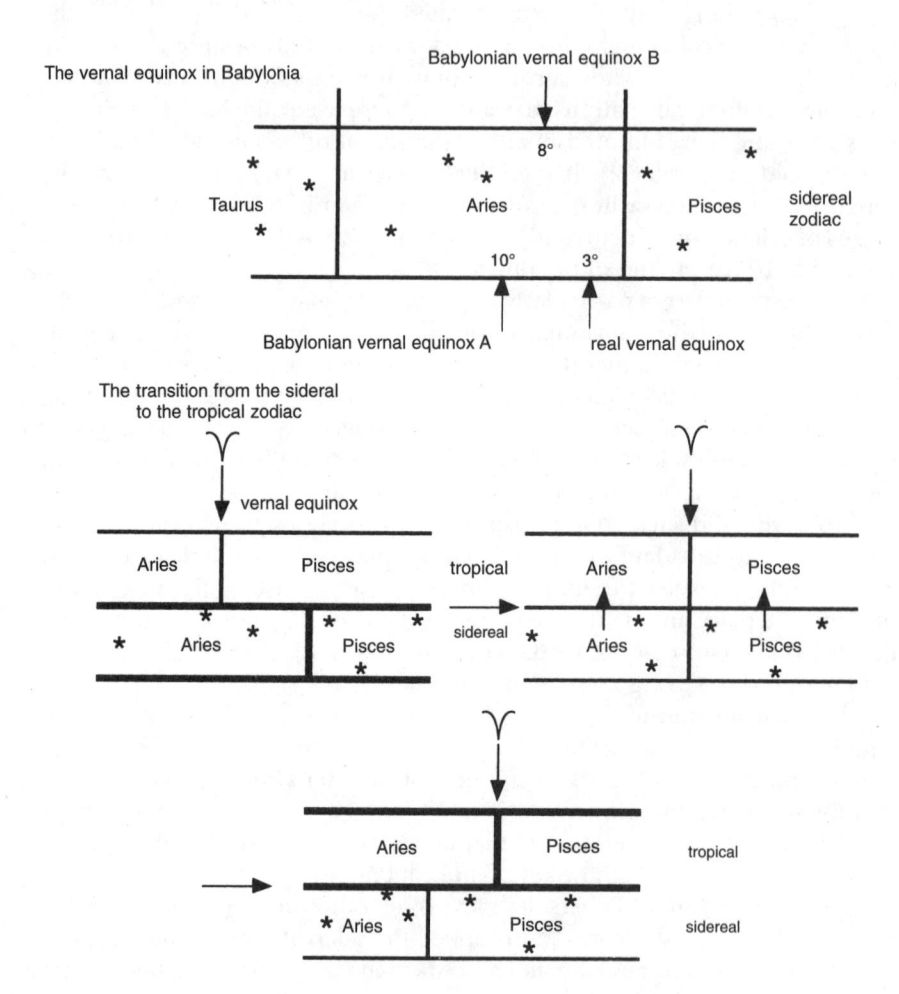

Figure 3.4.
The vernal equinox in Babylonia.
The transition from the sidereal to the tropical zodiac.

The Zodiac 55

Figure 3.5. The shift of the signs with respect to the stars.

The position of the zodiac around 2000 B.C.E.

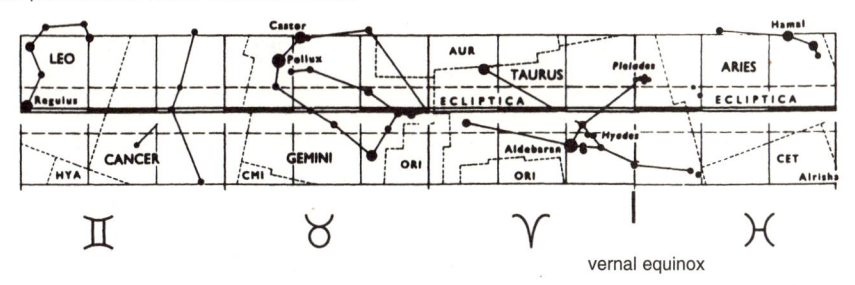

vernal equinox

The position of the zodiac around the beginning of the common era.

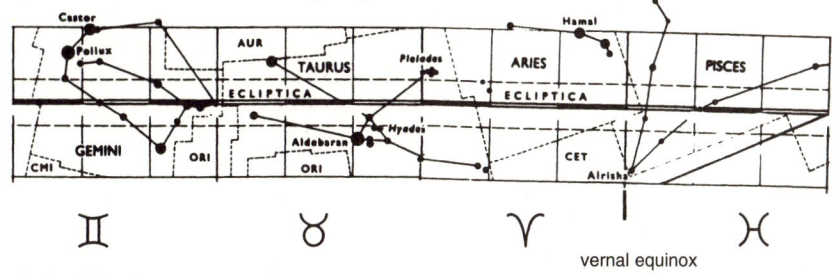

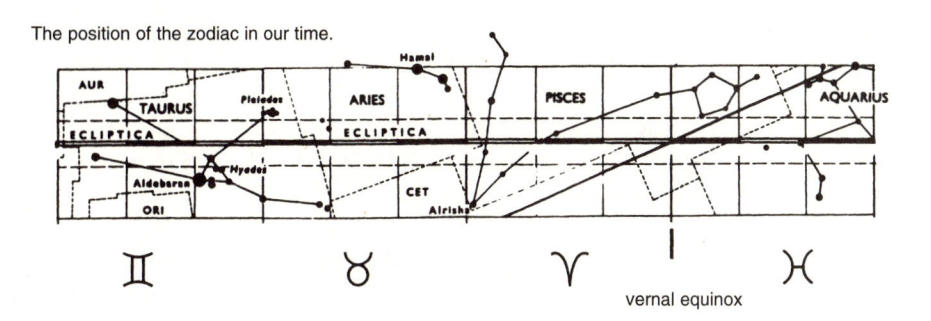

vernal equinox

The position of the zodiac in our time.

vernal equinox

56 Making Sense of Astrology

ponents would have us believe. He who maintains that astrology is tens of thousands of years old makes a monkey of himself; it is clearly impossible to date the period in which astrology arose as earlier than the time when the vernal equinox was situated in the constellation of Aries (the Ram). The historical sources are completely in agreement with this: The zodiac dates at the earliest from about 500 B.C.E. For that matter, the oldest horoscope we know of is also not much older than 400 B.C.E.

In the second place the history of the zodiac shows that it was originally sidereal, that is, fixed with respect to the stars. The idea that the stars have nothing to do with the signs, as the French astrologer André Barbault boldly claimed, would sound rather strange in the ears of a Greek astrologer. The best proof of the opposite is the use of the 8° for the conversion from the tropical to the sidereal zodiac. If the zodiac had always been considered to be fixed to the seasons, why then, were the astrologers the last ones to stick to this fudge factor?

Until the Middle Ages there were astrologers who mentioned the 8° to convert a calculated (tropical) result to the needed final astrological value. Astrologers who work with the tropical zodiac have, therefore, broken with an important basic principle of their "art." The tendency not to ascribe the "influences" any longer to the stars, as had earlier been the case, but to a purely imaginary division of the ecliptic, is therefore properly speaking a historical aberration.

The Origin of the Characteristics of the Signs

A very important question that we can ask the astrologers, and which has connections with the foregoing, is how were the properties of the signs discovered? Why is Aries (the Ram) and not Taurus (the Bull) energetic, impulsive, and active? How does one know that Libra (the Scales) is more artistic than Virgo (the Virgin)?

The answer to that is usually something like "that is known from experience" or "that is the astrological tradition." Such responses are, however, no answers. What "experience" is one talking about? And on what is that so often cited "tradition" based?

If the astrological characteristics are looked at critically, then it is quite clear that these characteristics have not been selected randomly. There is, after all, an undeniable connection between the characteristics and the image of the sign that is supposed to symbolize them.

As an example, take Aries, the ram. That sign is, according to the astrologers, energetic, active, impulsive, sprightly, and violent. That is surely and clearly copied from the animal, the head bent and ready to initiate the attack. Think for instance of the battering-*ram*. The oldest astrological manual that we have, an astrological poem in Latin by a certain Marcus Manilius (about 10 B.C.E.), mentions explicitly that people born under this sign will find their profession in the wool trade! The relationship between rams and wool is rather obvious.

The sign Taurus is slow, persistent, and fertile, like his earthly counterpart. The aforementioned manual even adds that this sign grants the farmer the fruits of the earth, like the bull or ox yoked to the plow.

Gemini (the Twins) is associated with the press (journalists), literature, and books. People who are strongly influenced by Gemini are supposed to make easy contacts and to have a large circle of acquaintances. The connection with the constellation seems at first glance obscure, but after some search everything becomes clearer. The ancient Greeks gave the two brightest stars in that constellation of the Twins names. According to some these were Castor and Pollux, according to others they were Apollo and Heracles, an opinion which in time won out in the ancient world. These mythological figures got along well with each other—social contacts—and Apollo was, moreover, the god of art, literature, and music—in short, cultural life. Hence the Gemini characteristics.

The origin of the characteristics attributed to Cancer (the Crab) is uncertain, but for Leo (the Lion) everything is much clearer. This sign stands for a leader, naturally forceful and eager for power. Confidence and pride are characteristic of him, like what is ascribed to the king of the savanna. The search does not have to reach all that far. If one considers that thick wavy hair also belongs to this sign then the picture is complete.

In this way we can also look at the rest of the zodiac. With some signs the analogy with the characteristics of the image is more than clear. Libra (the Scales) stands for harmony and equilibrium, and therefore also for artistry; Scorpio (the Scorpion) is associated with a sharp character, and the relation to medicine can be explained by means of the poison from the sting. Sagittarius (the Archer) likes sports, a characteristic that is attributed to the centaur (half man/half horse). For other signs it is necessary to go back to ancient ideas to recognize their attributes. Pisces are supposed to be sensitive people, for in antiquity water was connected with feelings. And something similar may account for the caring, mothering Cancer (the Crab). The scientific interest of Virgo is probably connected with the Muses, patron goddesses of arts and science. But for a number of signs the origin of their astrological characteristics is unclear, such as for Capricorn (the Goat) and Aquarius (the Water Bearer).

The principle on which the connection between sign and figure is based is *analogy*. The application of analogy is typical for magical thinking. In this case the assumption is made that in some sense an image has the characteristics of whatever it pictures. The lion is proud, therefore that trait is projected on the constellation of that name. That constellation was then supposed in some sense to symbolize "being proud" in its purest way. Finally this idea was attached to a piece of the ecliptic with a length of 30° that once was located in the neighborhood of the constellation Leo.

To us this way of thinking may well appear rather strange, but in antiquity this was not the case. People then had totally different ideas of how the cosmos was put together (Earth, for instance, was considered to be the center) and about the kinds of laws that prevailed in nature. An important aspect of this thinking was the belief in "cosmic sympathy," a relation that connected strongly divergent things together. The knowledge of the characteristics of one thing was useful to get to know something about things that showed "sympathy" with it (the word "sympathy" is derived from the Greek *syn,* which means together, and *pathos,* which means feeling. Sympathy is therefore literally feeling together, feeling with [something]). The Sun, for instance, the "heart" of the heavenly phenomena, was associated with the human heart and with certain plants. Plants with heart-shaped leaves were then used to treat heart diseases, and the moment of application was determined by means of the position of the Sun. According to the ancient view the cosmos was seen as divided in sympathetic layers.

The largest unit was the *macrocosmos* (literally the "large cosmos" or the "large ordering"), which nowadays we would call the universe. Everything that happened on Earth sympathized with analogous events in the macrocosmos. The appearance of a comet in the firmament or a manifest disturbance of the harmony of the planets brought death and destruction. Solar eclipses—at that time still unpredictable events—were connected with earthquakes and other natural phenomena.

Man was also connected with the cosmos by means of these same sympathies. He himself was a *microcosmos* (literally "small cosmos") and an analogous macrocosmic factor correlated with with each part of his body and his soul. These concepts explain why it was believed that knowledge of the "stars" could provide insight in the condition of man; changes in the macrocosmos after all reflected the course of life. And in order to figure this out the horoscope was the preeminent tool.

Aries, for instance, correlated with the head; Taurus, with the neck; Gemini, with the arms and lungs; Leo, with the heart; and so on to Pisces, which sympathized with the feet. The basic idea here was the count of all body parts of man, from head to toe, in the order of the signs. In medical astrology, the cosmic "condition" of a sign is then connected with the health of the analogous part of the body.

Another important source of analogies was the Greek theory of the elements. This early mixture of physics and natural philosophy assumed that there were four basic elements in nature: fire, earth, air, and water, which were themselves combinations of the characteristics hot, cold, dry, and wet. All that was hot and dry showed an excess of fire, cold and dry was characteristic of earth, wet and cold was, of course, water, and hot and wet was air. All of nature was classified by the philosophers according to these elements. For that matter, that is also the origin of the previously mentioned division of the signs in fire, earth, air, and water signs. However, the "physical" group "fire" included, besides certain signs, also planets (Mars "possessed" an excess of this element), a whole class of plants and animals, some minerals, some regions, parts of the body, etc.

Many characteristics of the astrological elements found their origin in this strange thought pattern, in which unlimited analogies were considered to be useful methods to work with. Now we know that that analogy is not a valid way of thinking to obtain reliable knowledge. Analogy can indeed be used in limited areas, for instance to show something graphically, or it can suggest certain ideas (which then have to be tested by further research), but it can never be accepted as a *justification* for a claim. For the acquisition of knowledge analogy is quicksand, but the foundations of astrology are supported by it.

An astrologer can retort that this criticism is completely beside the point. Is it not possible that the analogy worked the other way around, that the characteristics of the signs were known from experience and that this was expressed by giving the constellations names that symbolized these characteristics?

In order to judge this, one can check how far the constellations of the zodiac agree with the patterns that the stars form in the sky.

To begin with there are "natural" constellations, constellations for which not much imagination is necessary to recognize a certain figure. One of the best examples is Leo: In the pattern of the stars one can clearly recognize a reclining quadruped, but it may just as easily be a dog or cow as a lion or cat. Scorpio is also a good example, particularly the curved row of stars that forms the curved tail with the sting. With some imagination the head of a bull can be seen in Taurus: The brightest stars form a triangle with two bright "protuberances" which form the horns. In a certain sense the same is true of Gemini. The four brightest stars in this constellation form a rectangle; a division in two groups of two stars each becomes obvious.

In addition there are some constellations outside the zodiac with obvious names such as Crux (the Southern Cross), Triangulum (the Triangle), and Triangulum Australe (the Southern Triangle), and one can imagine that the cross of Cygnus (the Swan, also called the Northern Cross) indeed represents a flying bird. In the other constellations one can see just about whatever one wants. Think of Ursa Major (the Big Dipper or Great Bear); some people see a pan, a ladle, or an oxcart in it. A constellation like Orion is certainly striking, but one cannot recognize it right away as a mythological hunter.

Some constellations in the zodiac attribute their names to the season in which the Sun appeared in that constellation or the season in which that constellation became visible again in the morning for the first time. This is, for instance, the case with Taurus. In addition to the fact that with some imagination the head of a bull can be seen in it, it is also one of the constellations in which the Sun is located in the spring and which therefore symbolizes the propagation of cattle in this period. The Virgin—originally an ear of wheat, later a woman who held the ear of wheat (the brightest star of this constellation is still called Spica, "ear of wheat")—determines the time of harvest, while Libra (the Scales) is connected with the sale of that harvest. The Sun is located in Capricorn—originally a goat-fish—at the transition of the dry season to a wetter period. The goat-fish was, as a matter of fact, the symbol of the Babylonian water god, Enki. Aquarius then stands for the rainy season and Pisces was supposed to herald the end of it (the end of winter, when the rivers are full of fish?).

There are quite a few arguments against the thesis that the figures were determined by previously known astrological characteristics:

- The agreement of a number of constellations with an existing pattern of stars or with a seasonal phenomenon.
- Most of the names of the constellations of the zodiac existed before one could talk about astrology. Astrology therefore had nothing to do with the naming.
- The astrological characteristics apparently change with the name of the constellation. For instance Virgo was originally the ear of wheat, later extended to the woman who held the ear (the bright star Spica). The astrological characteristics that are attributed to this sign have more in common with the Greek depiction of the Virgin (a Muse?) than with an ear of wheat.

Another example in this respect is Aries. We have already pointed out the strong agreement between the characteristics of the image and the animal of the same name. Formerly, however, this constellation did not exist! For the Babylonians this group of stars carried the name "Hired Farmworker" or "Farmworker for Pay" (Babylonian ^{mul}LU-HUN-GA). It was clearly a seasonal constellation: When the Sun was in it the winter was over and farmworkers were needed to work in the fields. But the Babylonian clerks clearly considered the name rather long and started to abbreviate it to LU or HUN. According to the assyriologist A. Ungnad, after some time confusion arose as a result of the use of LU. There are several signs in cuneiform that can be read as LU. One of these was supposed to have had the meaning of ram or sheep! The constellation probably changed its name because of a writing error! When astrology arose, the designation "Ram" (the second LU, so to speak) had already become common. And that is why that piece of the sky acquired the characteristics of the quadruped and not those of the drudging farm worker.

It is remarkable that the astrologers do not seem to know this. They take all kinds of trouble to connect the origin of the constellation/sign Aries with flocks of sheep. Of course, this somewhat affects the credibility of their version of the earliest history of astrology.

That names and characteristics are firmly connected in astrology can yet be illustrated on the basis of the *paranatellonta*. This is the ancient technical term for constellations north and south of a certain zodiacal constellation that rise at the same time. In addition to the division of the sky in constellations that are familiar to us, there also existed another division in the centuries before the common era. This division was derived from not only the Babylonians, but also from the Egyptians or the people from Asia Minor (modern Turkey). The Greek astrologers used these constellations, among other things, in horary astrology. And what do we read in the old manuscripts which refer to this? The constellation Crater (the Cup) points to a vintner, a cheerful drinker of wine or a wine-merchant. Under Cygnus (the Swan) bird catchers and bird traders were born. Temple musicians consorted under the constellations of the Flutes and the Cymbals, while Lyra (the Lyre) sires worldly musicians and the Lamp-Bearer determines torchbearers, of course. That analogy is the only source of such similarities was openly admitted by the astrological author Teukros (first century C.E.?): "Together with Capricorn, the Altar or Offering-Table also rises. Its children (all who are born under it) are grocers, traders in meat or butchers." Can this be made any clearer?

Astrological Disagreement (Part I)

The historical examinations above are not of such a nature as to promote our trust in any reality behind the zodiacal signs. It is even worse: There are no historical indications that *observations* ever played a role in the development of astrology. That becomes even clearer when attention is paid to what the astrologers themselves think about the zodiac.

Previously the difference between the tropical zodiac (attached to the vernal equinox) and the sidereal zodiac (attached to the stars) was explained. Because of the precession they move with respect to each other, and in the past 2,000 years the difference between the two zodiacs has increased to roughly a full sign. That the astrologers work with the tropical zodiac would, by itself, be no reason to refer the astrological zodiac to the realm of the fairy tales. Maybe it could be possible (but, considering the above arguments, highly improbable) that the astrological characteristics indeed originate from the tropical zodiac, but that earlier, when the two zodiacs almost coincided, an error was made in ascribing the presumed effects. The use of the sidereal zodiac by the Babylonian, Greek, and Roman astrologers would then be a temporary error, which would not be detrimental to the reality of the tropical zodiac.

That would sound convincing, except that in that case serious difficulties arise. The fact is that something remarkable occurred in the evolution of astrology. In the course of time in the West the switch was made to the tropical zodiac, but in other parts of the world which astrology had also penetrated this did *not* happen!

During the first centuries of the common era the Greco-Roman astrology spread to the Indian subcontinent, where it experienced a great flowering. Even now astrology has many adherents and professional practitioners there. There are in all probability more practicing astrologers in India alone than in all of the rest of the world!

One of the points in which Indian astrology differs from the western version is the use of the zodiac: The Indian zodiac is sidereal! When, according to a Western astrologer the Sun is for instance located in Aries, his Indian colleagues place it in Pisces (see figure 3.6). And, mind you, the attributes which are ascribed to the signs with the same names in both systems are not fundamentally different. A tropical Aries has roughly the same characteristics as a sidereal Aries; the existing differences can be explained by the almost independent development of the two variants of astrology after the fall of the Roman Empire. A sidereal Pisces has far more traits in common with the tropical Pisces than with the tropical Aries.

Of course, that creates problems. Western astrologers use the tropical zodiac and claim to obtain excellent results with it. This can only be because, in their opinion, the (tropical) signs exert a clear "influence." Indian astrologers, on the contrary, use the sidereal zodiac and claim just as emphatically that this gives total satisfaction, in their eyes a proof that the (sidereal) signs are correct.

Since these two divisions of the ecliptic differ from one another by almost a full sign, then logically speaking, only a limited number of ways exist to explain this:

- One of the two systems is correct and the other is in error. But then why do the users of the "wrong" system obtain such good results? Do they collectively lie when they claim this?
- Both systems are correct—a point of view that is hard to defend. In that case one has to assume that it does not really matter which signs one uses or which characteristics are attributed to them. The importance of the signs in the horoscope is in that case very slight.
- Both systems are wrong and then we may refer the fancied characteristics of the zodiac to the museum. How much value can then be attached to the claims of the astrologers that their system "works"?

Whichever way one turns, the consequences that the precession had for astrology are not of a nature to reinforce our trust in it. (See also Intermezzo I.)

The little world of astrologers is more or less divided over this problem. Both systems have their fierce proponents and opponents who will not concede even an inch to each other. The discussions are heated, but that is the extent of it. Anyone who would think that this problem would be important enough to ask for a large-scale astrological research project does not know the astrological community very well: Much ado about nothing is the rule rather than the exception.

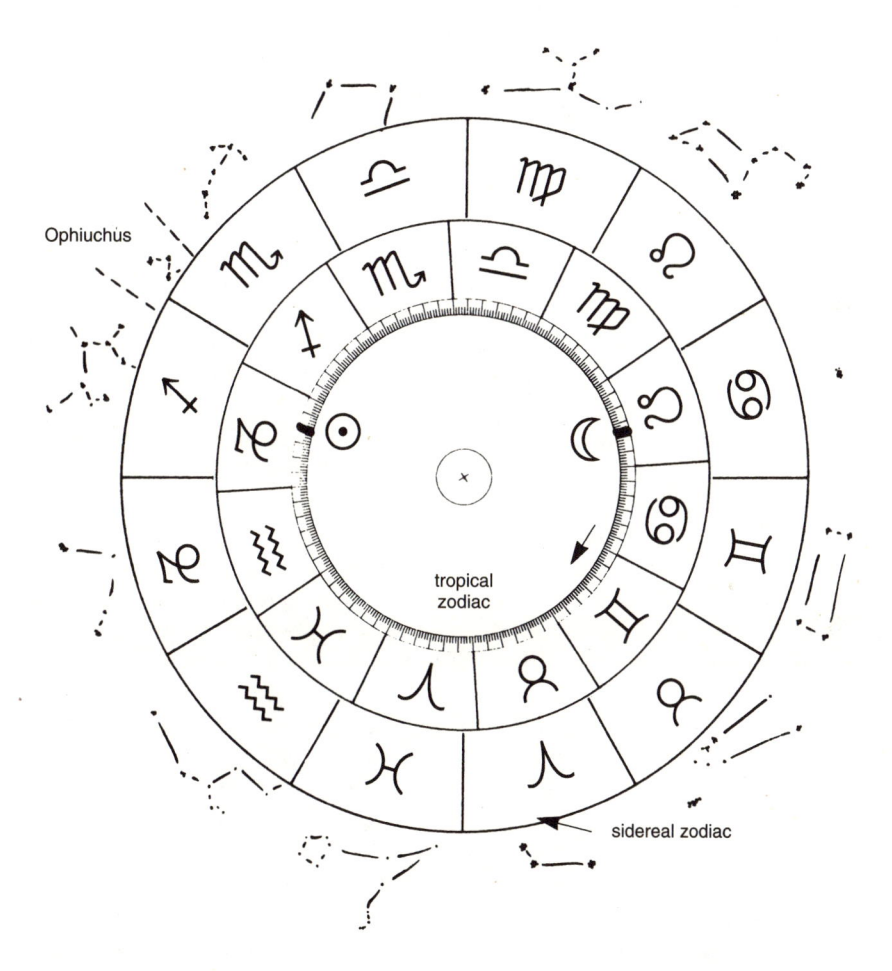

Figure 3.6. The difference between the tropical and the sidereal zodiac and the equivalent constellations.

64 Making Sense of Astrology

The internal quarrels do not remain limited to the kind of zodiac that is to be used, but even go on about the question *how many* signs there actually are.

Traditionally astrologers stick to twelve signs, in the tropical as well as in the sidereal zodiac. However, in the course of time astronomers made some changes to the boundaries of the constellations. As a result the Sun these days moves not through twelve constellations during one year but through thirteen. The thirteenth constellation is Ophiuchus, the Serpent Bearer. That constellation spans a rather considerable piece of the sky, taking up approximately 20 degrees of the ecliptic (the adjacent constellation, Scorpius [the Scorpion], takes up only 7°). Some astrologers, who are of the opinion that a zodiac should have a certain relation with the stars, therefore use thirteen signs. A few among them go even further: American astrologer S. Schmidt proposes fourteen signs, Frenchman Gérard Messadié fifteen. Messadié even points to the possibility of extending the zodiac to twenty-four signs!

All these proposals have one thing in common: They are unable to convince the large majority of astrologers, although according to their inventors they are considerably more successful than the traditional division. We therefore see the same thing happening as with the discussion between the tropical and the sidereal zodiac: Different systems are proposed which all claim to perform equally well. However the only result they have is to make us doubt the effectiveness of every zodiac.

Another source of disagreement is the correct relationship between the zodiac and the seasons. Some astrologers (Frenchman André Barbault is one of the best known) defend the thesis that the zodiac has always been tropical and that it therefore represents a symbolic expression of the seasons. Changes in the seasons would then find their expression in changes of the signs. According to that opinion the sign Aries has the qualities of energy and activity because when the Sun is in that sign spring begins and nature radiates energy and life. Capricorn would then be a "barren" sign, because winter starts when the Sun is in that sign. We already pointed out that there exists an undeniable relationship between some signs and seasonal activities, but this does not extend to *all* signs. The theory of Barbault, however, denies explicitly that the stars ever had anything to do with the signs.

This theory can be attacked for two reasons, the first of which we have already discussed extensively: The zodiac was originally sidereal. If it had always been connected to the seasons, why then was the vernal equinox placed at 8° Aries? Second, the proposed relation between the characteristics of the signs and the seasons is only valid for the *northern hemisphere!* This analogy is based on a civilization on the northern half of our planet. There a connection was indeed determined between the motions of the Sun among the stars and the seasons in these regions and these were projected on the sky. After that step was taken, astrology presumed that the characteristics which were derived from the seasons were valid for all of Earth.

But in the southern hemisphere the seasons run half a year ahead (or behind) of those in the northern hemisphere. When spring starts in Europe or North America (Sun in Aries), autumn begins in Australia. If the reasoning of Barbault and his supporters were to be followed consistently, then a different zodiac should be used in the southern hemisphere, one in which the characteristics have been shifted six signs with respect to its northern complement. Aries should then be located on the spot of the present Libra or in the southern hemisphere Libra should acquire the characteristics of the northern Aries. The same should happen with the other signs.

Do Australian or Argentinian astrologers use such a zodiac? No! They simply copy the methods and characteristics of their northern colleagues. And—as is to be expected—they do not obtain any worse or better results.

How things have to be done on the equator—where ideas such as spring and summer have no meaning—is completely unclear. But as a matter of fact, even on the same hemisphere the seasons differ greatly according the climatic zones. Astrology was developed in regions with a temperate climate. The effect of the seasons in Mesopotamia, for instance, is not the same as in Lapland or Labrador. This is another one of those things that astrology does not take into account.

Scientific Research on the Signs

Historical reviews and disagreement among astrologers are indeed interesting as background information, but they should never prevail over the facts. The important question to be asked in this context is: Can the astrological effects of the signs of the zodiac be verified? The preceding gives reasons enough for us to consider the chance of that to be very minimal, but even so, we shouldn't lose track of the value of experimental data.

One of the reasons for the success of science is the permanent exchange between the development of theories and the comparison of them with experimental data. The elaboration of a theory suggests certain experiments and may result in a different explanation of earlier experimental results, while the experiments, in turn, provide data which have to be explained by the theory. Sometimes it may be possible to ignore data that do not fit into the theory for some time, but in the long run one is forced to face them. Science is an activity that in due time is self-correcting and without doubt the foundation of its success has to be found it this fact.

In a certain sense science is the extension of common sense to areas that do not belong to our daily experience. In general (but to our regret not always) one may assume that people learn from their mistakes: The results of an act are related to the reasons why the act was performed and, if the result is not in accordance with the expectations, then one changes the ideas on

66 Making Sense of Astrology

which the decision was based. In that way "experiences" are collected, which normally speaking would lead to better ideas about the ways of the world.

By expanding experience to areas that are less obvious, such as the movement of the planets or the fundamental building blocks of matter, and by applying the "theory-test" rule systematically, a kind of knowledge is reached which is more complete and more reliable than common experience: This is *scientific knowledge*. This more extensive ordering and search for connections has made scientific theories more abstract and complicated. It turns out that mathematics can be applied in many areas and very many scientific conceptions are miles away from our daily experience. It isn't obvious anymore for an outsider that science in its essence is based on common sense.

One of the scientific instruments that inspire the strongest mistrust in the layperson is *statistics*. We all know the quip: There are lies, damned lies, and statistics. The distrust of this branch of applied mathematics can perhaps partly be explained by the caution with which its results have to be interpreted, and in order to be able to do this it is necessary to obtain some insight in the specific nature and the philosophy of statistics. Statistics is occupied mostly with *uncertainties* and its results are expressed as *chances* or probabilities. Unfortunately, reasoning with chances and uncertainties seems to be rather difficult for most people. As we will have to use statistics often in what follows, we ask the reader for some patience, attention, and effort to follow the method used.

Now, back to the zodiac. The question we asked was, Is it possible to demonstrate astrological effects of the signs of the zodiac? The statistical method is the only one that can provide a scientifically reliable answer to this question. The reasoning behind that method is in principle very simple: The data which one wants to test are divided in different groups, and then the groups are compared either with each other or with certain control groups. An example can clear things up a lot.

Suppose that we want to test a possible effect of the Sun in the signs of the zodiac. For instance we want to know if one or more signs are connected with having red hair. We can start with a large number of red-haired people and divide them into twelve groups according to the sign in which the Sun was located at birth. If the sun-sign effect exists then there should be one or more groups with a larger number of red-haired people than the rest. This is because the effect we are looking for, if it exists, *will be systematically collected in the same groups*. If the phenomenon is, however, connected with some other factor, for instance the position of the planet Mars, then this effect will be *evenly spread over all groups*. In the latter case the effect is averaged out so that the influence it has on each group is equally large and will therefore not be observed.

Let us work out this example further: Assume that the Sun in Aries has the tendency to give the children who are born then red hair, while other signs do not have that effect. It is clear, then, that all these red-haired persons will be found in the group "Aries as sun-sign." If Mars in Aries would show the same effect, then roughly one-twelfth of the persons who could thank Mars for their red hair would be found in the group "Aries as sun-sign," one-twelfth in the group "Taurus as sun-sign," etc. The effect of Mars cannot be discovered that way because the wrong division had been selected.

In this way the influence of an astrological factor can be examined. Everything depends on the suitable choice of the division of the data. By the way, the incidence of red hair has nothing to do with astrology, but everything with the parents. The example is imaginary but "neutral." We may just as well study characteristics like high intelligence, homosexuality, or criminal behavior. A condition that has to be met is that there is a *clear criterion* for the attribution of the characteristic (in the case of red hair this is no problem).

The application of statistics to astrology may appear obvious (and is done more and more), but most astrologers still appear to think differently about it. According to them it is *not* correct to apply statistics to astrology, because in that case one tries to isolate a certain factor (signs, planets, houses, or combinations thereof) from a whole (the horoscope) and that is considered unacceptable. To look at only one factor distorts the whole and must therefore lead to the wrong decisions. That is why, according to them, statistics is not a valid tool.

If they were right, then any attempt at a reliable test of astrology is impossible in advance. Maybe this is the intention of their argument. Of course, it is a fact that the astrological interpretation of an *individual* horoscope is determined by all the factors present, but, as was made clear above, by working with *large numbers* and selecting a suitable division of the material, the effects of the other factors will be spread evenly. As a result these factors counteract and neutralize each other. *Only the searched-for effect* can express itself. If we may presume that the total description of the subject of the horoscope is built from the correct parts, couldn't the correctness of each of these parts be demonstrated?

What does statistics yield for the zodiac? In the last one hundred years quite a few statistics have been drawn up to search for a zodiacal influence. In most cases the position of the Sun was selected, because that is very easy to determine (one only needs to know someone's day of birth). Moreover most astrologers are in agreement that this is a very important factor in the horoscope, in contrast to, for instance, the position of Neptune in the signs. As a matter of fact, many books were written about the sun-signs all by themselves, such as *Sun Signs*, the bestseller by American astrologer Linda Goodman, which has been translated into many foreign languages.

Nothing positive has ever come out of this, to the general displeasure of the astrologers. The majority of the studies did not show any effect and the few that did were not able to be replicated. We will discuss two examples as an illustration. (See also Intermezzo II.)

68 Making Sense of Astrology

Table 3.2: Politics and the Sign of Capricorn

Sign	Number	Corrected
Aries	**432**	458
Taurus	471	485
Gemini	471	470
Cancer	486	469
Leo	504	476
Virgo	497	466
Libra	**523**	**497**
Scorpio	488	474
Sagittarius	453	**454**
Capricorn	462	479
Aquarius	445	473
Pisces	460	491
Total	5,692	5,692
Average	474	474

(Data according to J. D. McGervey)

The Sun and Politics

One of the traits that is attributed to the sign of Capricorn is a talent for politics. That is why it is to be expected that among people who have Capricorn as sun-sign political interests occur more often than among people with the Sun in another sign. Personal interests certainly exert an important influence on the profession that someone chooses. A person with an interest in politics will have a stronger tendency to seriously become engaged in politics. It is therefore fair to presume that among politicians more people will be found with Capricorn as sun-sign than normally may be expected.

J. D. McGervey tested this proposition for 5,692 American politicians (table 3.2; figure 3.7). The sign of Capricorn appears not to be particularly noticeable for a surplus population. On the contrary, the average value per group amounts to 474 births, while under Capricorn only 462 politicians are found. The astrological hypothesis is certainly not confirmed. It is worth the effort to look at the numbers and graphs more carefully.

The first striking fact is that the deviations from the average are not all that large. The two extremes, Aries and Libra, differ respectively by 9° and 10° from the average; for all the other signs the deviation is much less. The question can be asked whether the two extremes are exceptional, in other words, if the assumption can be made that Libra exerts a "political" influence

The Zodiac 69

and Aries, on the contrary, diminishes it. The possibility of answering such questions is exactly the strength of the statistical method. However, to answer this question it is necessary to have an idea of what we may normally expect to find for these two signs.

In figure 3.7 we notice that five consecutive signs (Cancer through Scorpio) lie *above* the average and seven consecutive signs (Sagittarius through Gemini) fall *below* that average. This is rather unusual; a more irregular division would be expected.

The explanation for this course is that births (in general, not only for politicians) are by their nature not evenly spread over the year. There is a wavelike variation in the distribution: The figure shows clearly that more children are born in summer and fewer in winter. This wave has nothing to do with astrology: It differs from country to country, from region to region in the same country, and it shifts through the years. If a group of randomly selected Americans had been chosen, that wave would have been noticeable also.

In order to determine if the Libra effect is really an effect of the sign, that wave has to be eliminated. This is done in table 3.2 (in the "corrected" column) and in figure 3.8. There clearly is no extreme value anymore; Libra deviates less than 5 percent from the average and Sagittarius, instead of Aries, now presents the lowest value. The corrected value for Capricorn is just a little bit above average, a value that is far from remarkable.

Looking at these results, only one valid conclusion can be made: There is no indication that the presence of the Sun in the sign of Capricorn (or in any other sign) has anything to do with a talent for politics.

Signs and Science

Armed with this knowledge we can take a look at the next example. McGervey also collected data about the births of 14,644 scientists. According to astrology scientific aptitude is a typical characteristic of a Virgo. The data can be tested in the same way as explained above for politicians (See table 3.3; figure 3.9).

Again it is remarkable that the differences are not all that large. Virgo rises 6 percent above the average while Gemini remains 5.5 percent below the average. In spite of the small differences, Virgo still stands out (if that word can be used) as the sign in which the largest number is included. Is this an—albeit weak—confirmation of astrology?

As in the previous case, a yearly cycle is noticeable. This has to be eliminated first, which was done in table 3.3 ("corrected" column) and figure 3.10. The picture has become totally different: The largest deviation from the average has decreased to less than 4 percent (Gemini) and there are no extremes above the average anymore: Aquarius, Capricorn, Virgo, and

70   Making Sense of Astrology

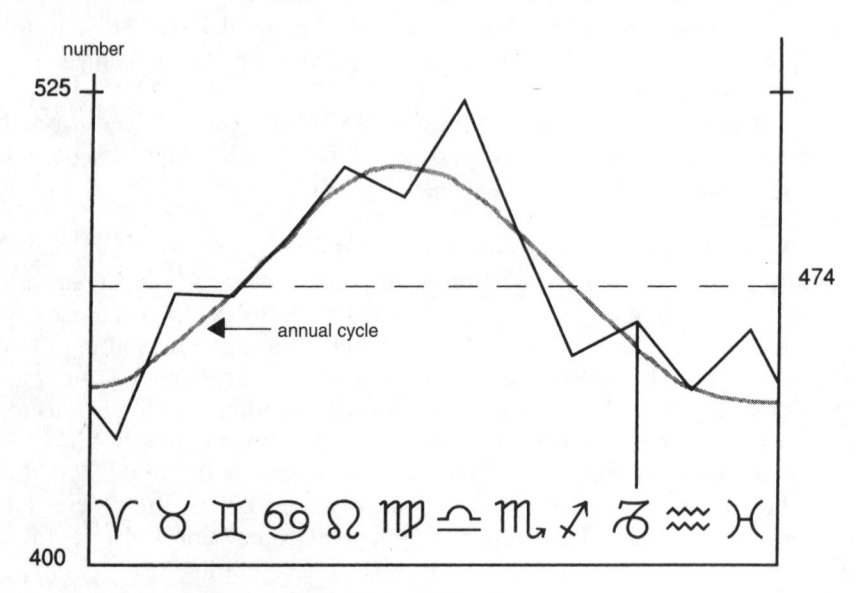

Figure 3.7. Politicians and the Sign of Capricorn.

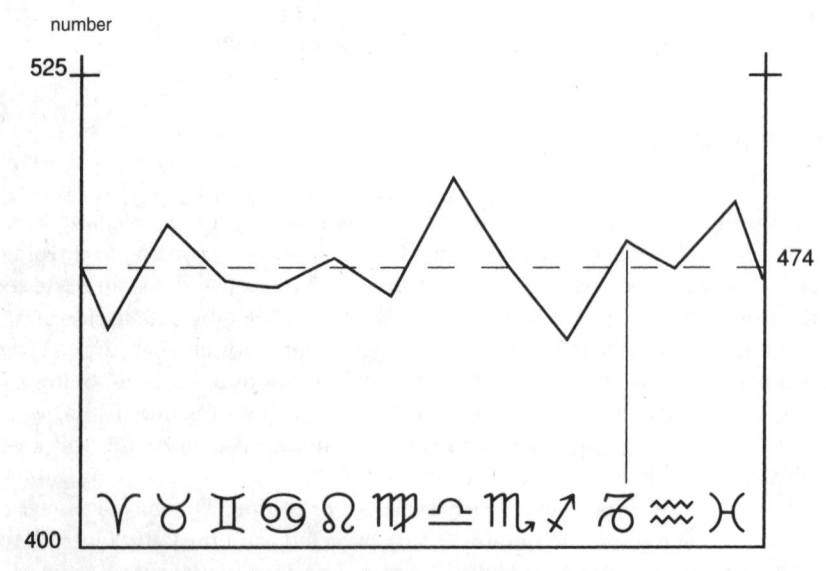

Figure 3.8. Politicians and the Sign of Capricorn (corrected).

The Zodiac 71

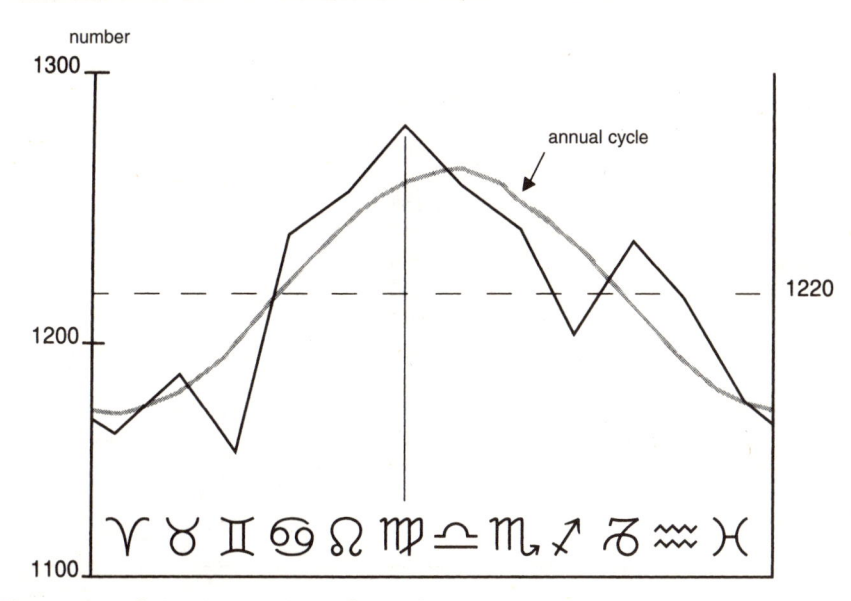

Figure 3.9. Scientists and the Sign of Virgo.

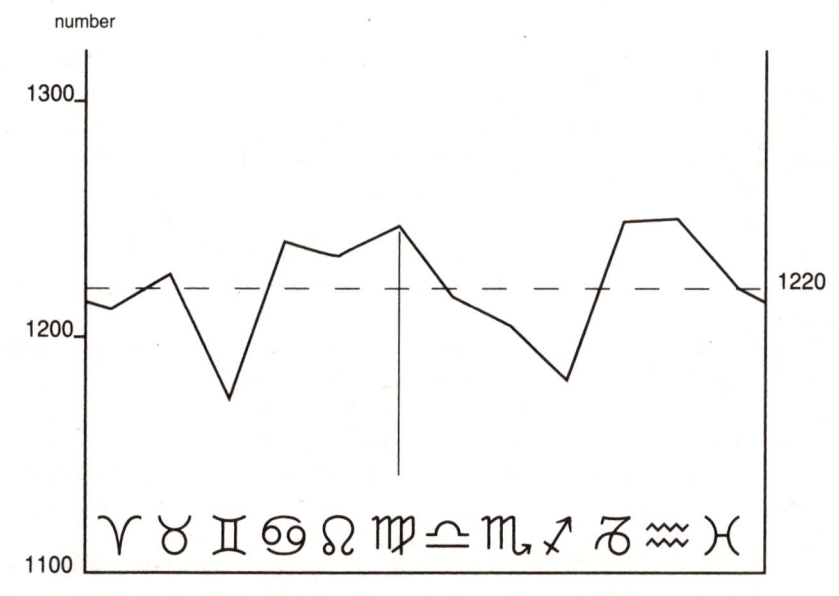

Figure 3.10. Scientists and the Sign of Virgo (corrected).

Table 3.3: Scientists and the Sign of Virgo

Sign	Number	Corrected
Aries	1,160	1,212
Taurus	1,185	1,227
Gemini	**1,153**	**1,174**
Cancer	1,245	1,240
Leo	1,263	1,233
Virgo	**1,293**	1,245
Libra	1,267	1,215
Scorpio	1,246	1,204
Sagittarius	1,202	1,181
Capricorn	1,241	1,246
Aquarius	1,217	**1,247**
Pisces	1,173	1,220
Total	14,644	14,644
Average	1,220	1,220

Cancer are almost equal to each other. Here too, there is no reason to conclude that there is a "scientific" effect due to the Sun in Virgo.

As an aside, we may remark that astrologers classify Gemini as one of the "scientific" signs, of which Virgo is the strongest. Theoretically this sign should have been well represented.

These examples make it clear that much care is required to interpret statistics. The fact that a certain group (in our case a sign) occurs more often than others does not necessarily mean that it is significant. Chance does play a role in the collection of the material to test, so that certain groups will be better represented than others. If you throw a die 600 times, do you then expect that each side will occur *exactly* 100 times? Only when one side is strongly over-represented (for instance occurs 140 times) is it permissible to ask questions. And if in addition one or more unexpected effects (such as the natural variation of the number of births through the year) contaminate the data, then the correct conclusion can be all but obvious. For those who are not yet satisfied, another example is given in Intermezzo II.

These two limited studies do not stand by themselves. G. Dean and A. Mather, for instance, conclude their extensive literature search (through 1976) on this problem with the following statement: "Numerous statistical and psychological studies show that signs as traditionally applied appear to have negligible validity."[1]

In addition, Michel Gauquelin, a French researcher whose work will be discussed later, could, after very extensive studies, show only negative results. He compared a number of psychological characteristics which described two thousand persons with the presence of the Sun, Moon, and Ascendant in the signs which astrologically symbolize these characteristics. Questions were asked such as "Are the Sun, the Moon, or the Ascendant more often found in the sign of Aries for 'boisterous' people than for others?" The results were negative over the whole line: In many cases the astrological tradition even produced the worst results!

Conclusion

The historical uncertainties, the quarrels among the astrologers, and the lack of positive results of the statistical studies make it more than doubtful that there is "something real" to the signs. There are many systems in use that contradict each other, the most important of which are the tropical and the sidereal zodiac. In principle these numerous problems could be solved by large-scale statistical studies. Practice shows, however, that with time astrological problems increase rather than decrease.

Furthermore, if scientific studies are unable to show any zodiacal influence, it is extremely improbable that the characteristics of the signs are derived from observations. This is confirmed by the historical data: The characteristics were derived in antiquity by analogies with the constellations, the names of which are much older than astrology itself. Among other things it therefore is difficult to assume that, in times when statistical methods were as yet unknown, systematic observations were performed which showed an "effect" that now, with much better scientific techniques, escapes us.

On the basis of these facts our conclusion is clear: The zodiac is an astronomical fossil that only ever lived or lives in the minds of the adherents of astrology.

Note

1. G. Dean and A. Mather, *Recent Advances in Natal Astrology* (Cowes, England: Recent Advances, 1977), p. 75.

[Editor's note: Throughout this book only direct quotes will be cited at the end of chapters. General references, such as that on page 72 to Michel Gauquelin, will be listed in the bibliography at the end of the book.]

Intermezzo I

THE AGE OF AQUARIUS

In astrological publications references to the so-called Age of Aquarius crop up regularly. According to astrology the beginning of this era will call for a period of peace and brotherhood, a utopia for which humanity has been waiting for centuries.

Where does that expectation for a New Age come from? For an answer to this we have to return to chapter 3, where it was explained how the tropical zodiac—fixed by the vernal equinox—shifts with respect to the sidereal zodiac, which is fixed by the stars. While 2,000 years ago the vernal equinox was to be found at the beginning of the sidereal sign Aries, it has, by now, arrived at the beginning of Pisces. And the shifting continues; in a period of about 26,000 years it will run through a complete zodiac. That movement, to be sure, runs in the opposite direction from the way the Sun moves through the signs: The Sun runs from Pisces to Aries, while the vernal equinox moves from Aries to Pisces. Therefore the vernal equinox will, in the future, after moving through the beginning of the sidereal Pisces, enter the end of the sidereal Aquarius.

The period during which the vernal equinox remains in a certain sidereal sign is indicated by the astrologers by the name of that sign. In this way we are now in the Age of Pisces, 2,000 years ago the Age of Aries was near its end, and before long the Age of Aquarius commences.

In certain astrological circles the movement of the vernal equinox led to the development of a sort of "astrological vision of history." The adherents of this vision assume that this movement of the zodiac is reflected in great periods of world history, each period showing characteristics of the sidereal sign in which the vernal equinox is found.

During the last two thousand years we were in the Age of Pisces, and

Intermezzo I: The Age of Aquarius

according to the astrologers that is expressed among other things by christianity, which, particularly in the first centuries of its existence was often symbolized by a fish! Admit it, the argument is irrefutable.

The period before that (from about 2000 B.C.E. to the beginning of the common era) was the Age of Aries, as witnessed (according to the astrologers) by the representation of the Egyptian god Amon by the head of a ram. An earlier era yet, that of Taurus (from about 4000 to 2000 B.C.E.) is then connected with Moses and the golden calf, or the worship of the Apis-bull in Egypt! Should we really see more in this than a rather childish attempt at placing a phenomenon that is unpleasant for the astrologers, the precession, in a (for them) favorable light?

To show how easily such connections are made, an Improved Astrological History can be composed.

For this exercise not the vernal, but the autumnal equinox, which lies straight across from it on the zodiac, is connected to history. According to this new and original interpretation* of the movements of humanity we are now in the Age of Virgo. Virgo is a "scientific" sign and look, hasn't science made unbelievable progress in these last two thousand years? Or take the period before that, that of Libra, which symbolizes harmony, aesthetics, and art. Weren't the two thousand years before our common era a time of great artistic flourishing? Just think of the Greek ideal of beauty and of Egyptian art. For the period before that similarities are also easily found. Between 4000 and 2000 B.C.E., the Era of Scorpio, the first systematic efforts were made to collect knowledge (Babylonia and Egypt), which suits Scorpio as a "scientific" sign perfectly. Among this we can also count the very beginning of medicine—medicine falls astrologically under Scorpio through the poison in the sting. And before that yet, from 6000 through 4000 B.C.E., man evolved from hunter (The Age of Sagittarius, the Archer) to farmer. Besides that the nature of religion (Sagittarius = religion/philosophy) changed to the fertility cults which would flourish fully in the next era. And with a little bit of good will it should be possible to explain even earlier periods just as accurately: the period from 12,000 to 8000 B.C.E., the Ages of Aquarius and Pisces without a doubt should be connected with the end of the last Ice Age, therefore lots of rain, and so on.

And what does our Improved Astrological History say about the future? According to the above system we are soon entering the Age of Leo. And to be sure, the omens are there already. Astrologically Leo stands for power and conquest. Isn't humanity standing on the threshold of the conquest of space? Of the intellectual conquest of new knowledge?

---

*Maybe not. After the improved Astrological History was invented by the authors of this book, but before its publication, we learned that some astrologers also are speaking now of the Age of Pisces and Virgo. We do not think we gave anything away, and, moreover, we did not plan to apply for patents . . .

We do not have to explain to our readers how gratuitous and superficial the Improved Astrological History is. But this thought exercise is no better or worse than any other division in "Ages." It is not difficult to adjust history to preconceived vague notions, especially if we limit ourselves to "our" history (the Western one) and leave other cultures outside our considerations.

The Age of Aquarius, then, is standing at our door. But when does it start exactly? When does the vernal equinox enter this sidereal sign? This is closely related to the borders of the sidereal signs and these borders are not exactly determined.

As was mentioned in chapter 2, constellations are formed by a characteristic pattern of the brighter stars. Between these recognizable—although imaginary—patterns there are areas without any bright stars. The borders which are found on modern starcharts are those which were proposed in 1927 by Delporte. The astronomers (not the astrologers, who do not occupy themselves with constellations) agreed to accept these as "official."

The sidereal signs agree approximately with the constellations of the same name, but have to be exactly 30 degrees long, whereas constellations differ greatly in size. Because of this the correct position of the sidereal zodiac with respect to the stars is not precisely determined, and no objective way to do this exists.

There are two methods which can be applied to decide where the sidereal zodiac begins: The place of starting point (sidereal Aries) can be fixed between the stars, or the starting point can be defined as the difference in length from the vernal equinox (the tropical zodiac). The second method usually is preferred. The Indian astrologers, who, as was mentioned, use the sidereal zodiac, even have a technical name for the difference in angle: the *ayanamsha*. If the ayanamsha amounts to 30° the vernal equinox has arrived in sidereal Aquarius and the Age of Aquarius begins.

Astrologers hold very different opinions about the value of the ayanamsha. Depending on their points of view about the relation between the sidereal zodiac and the vernal equinox we either have been living in the Age of Aquarius for a while already or we have to wait for it for several generations yet.

A few examples provide a small taste of this controversy:

- According to the Indian astrologer Raman the ayanamsha amounts nowadays to approximately 22°. Therefore the vernal equinox has to cover 8° yet to reach the sidereal sign of Aquarius. At a speed of 1.4° per century we still have a good five centuries to go yet.
- The anthroposophists (the followers of Rudolf Steiner) place the vernal equinox point at 29° Pisces. The New Age will begin within the almost negligible period of sixty years.
- The astrologer Johndro assumes a value of 31.5°, which means that we have been living in the age of astrological brotherhood for more than a century already. Haven't you noticed yet?

- For the hippies 1968 was in all likelihood "the dawning of the age of Aquarius."
- And then there are astrologers such as Herman De Vos who find all that talk about the Age of Aquarius nonsense.

Intermezzo II

☉ ♅ ☽ ☊ ☋ ♂ ⚹ ✳ □ △ ⚻ ⚼

THE EYSENCK CASE

The problems that emerge in working out statistics are evidently not limited to the interpretation of the final results. They start sometimes at the very beginning, when data is collected. A fine example of that reached the press about twenty years ago. At least, the—wrong—initial conclusions drawn from this research were widely acclaimed. But printing the correction was usually overlooked.

In 1977, British professor of psychology Hans Eysenck decided to test two astrological rules, the more important of which will be discussed here. In chapter 3 we mentioned that the zodiac can be divided in groups of signs. One of the possibilities uses two groups of six signs each. The first group of six, Aries, Gemini, Leo, Libra, Sagittarius, and Aquarius, the astrologers call "positive" signs. These signs are characterized by *extroversion*, meaning that people for whom these signs have an important place in their horoscope make contacts easily, are active, and have other such qualities. The six signs that remain, the "negative" signs, are then *introverted*, more inner-directed.

Eysenck had a very practical reason for wanting to test this division exactly: He had invented a psychological test by means of which it was possible to determine how introverted or extroverted somebody is. His test was therefore eminently suitable for checking to see if any truth was hiding in the astrological division.

The point of departure of the test was the sun-sign: The determination of it is simple and the Sun, to be sure, plays a prominent role in the horoscope. Earlier we explained that a possible astrological effect had to be expressed in the statistics. This was obviously also the opinion of Jeff Mayo, an astrologer who cooperated in this test.

The psychological test developed by Eysenck, the so-called Eysenck Personality Inventory (EPI), consists of a questionnaire to be completed by the test subject. To perform the test it was necessary to have "live material," i.e., human subjects, so the customers of the astrologer Mayo were addressed. People who ordered a horoscope first received an EPI with the request to complete and return it. Only after receipt of the form would they obtain the ordered horoscope.

On the basis of the answers the introversion/extroversion score of each person was determined, after which the average score for all persons with the same sun-sign was calculated. The results are presented in figure II.1.

The figure shows a striking agreement between the average scores of the signs and the expectations according to astrological theory. The positive signs indeed scored more points than the negative ones; they were thus more extroverted than the average.

As could be expected, this test was cited by astrologers as a clear confirmation of their theses. A newspaper, the *Gazet van Antwerpen,* even cited it in a rather long article headlined "Innovative Research into Cosmic Factors and Personality."

The scientific world, however, was not as convinced as the astrologers and journalists. The results were viewed rather suspiciously because such an outcome was not at all expected. Research into sun-signs had, to be sure, produced negative results most of the time. It was decided not to pass a final judgment too prematurely and to wait and see what replications of the experiment would show.

Such a replication was performed by the German researchers Kurt Pawlik and Lothar Buse from the University of Hamburg, but the "effect" was not evident in their results. Now the existence of the extroversion/introversion effect was again in doubt. But why then had Eysenck and Mayo obtained those positive results? In principle it could have been a freakish result. Just to be sure, the problem was delved into further.

During their research Pawlik and Buse had noticed a remarkable phenomenon. In their questionnaire not only the personality traits of the subjects had been gauged, but also their prior knowledge of astrology. If only the data of those familiar with astrology were used, then the expected astrological effect clearly turned up. The effect was thus obviously connected with the prior astrological knowledge of the subject.

Could the results of Eysenck and Mayo be explained this way? Initially Eysenck strongly doubted this. In his questionnaire the astrological knowledge of Mayo's customers also had been gauged. According to some people, however, the question asked was much too specialized: Eysenck asked whether the subject knew how a horoscope was cast—something which presumes a rather thorough knowledge of the astrological technique. A superficial knowledge of their own sun-sign turned out to be sufficient to explain the effect found in the subjects. If one then takes into account that *all* of

80   Making Sense of Astrology

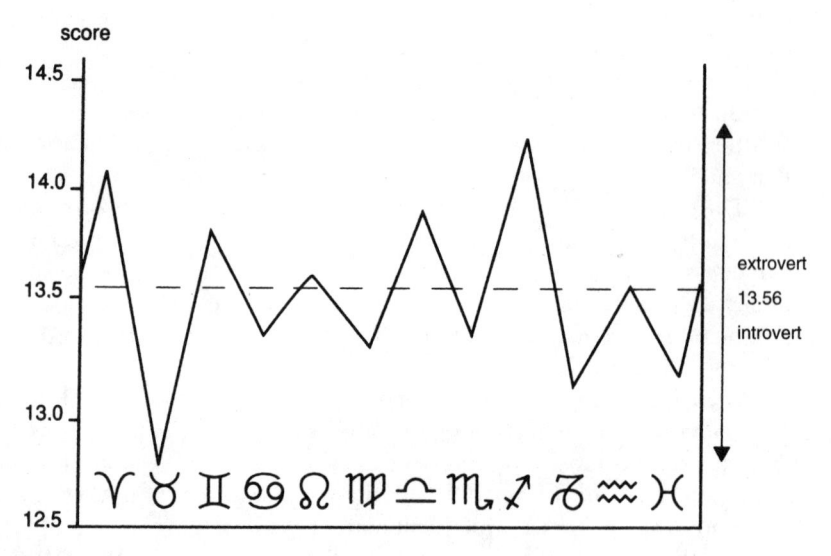

Figure II.1. Eysenck's results.

(from J. Mayo, O. White, and H. J. Eysenck, "An Empirical Study of the Relation between Astrological Factors and Personality," *Journal of Social Psychology* 105 [1978]: 229–36, table 1.)

Eysenck's subjects had ordered a horoscope from the professional astrologer Mayo, it was clear that they were convinced of the value of astrology in advance and that they probably knew the most important characteristics of their sun-sign. Having read a popular booklet entitled something like "Your Starsign Is" appears to be sufficient. *Unconsciously one tends to interpret one's own character in the light of the characteristics read:* The traits that match are emphasized; those that do not are forgotten. It is this interpretation that is expressed in the answers that are given to psychological tests such as the EPI. And that phenomenon played a trick on Eysenck.

To check if that explanation was indeed the correct one, Eysenck and his new partner Nias (Mayo had perhaps seen what was coming and had quit) repeated the experiment, but now with the required care. They chose subjects who were not aware of astrology: children too young to know much about astrology and members of the Salvation Army, who do not want to have anything to do with astrology for religious reasons. And this time the results did not turn up anything special: The effects could no longer be detected.

It is clear now what kind of error was made in this test: the astrological foreknowledge of the subjects skewed the statistical results. Knowledge of astrology does not change a person's character, but quite obviously it can alter the image that someone has of his own character. Even an authority in the field of psychological testing like Eysenck had not expected such a thing.

And the newspaper we mentioned earlier? It remained silent. Its readers would have to discover elsewhere that the "innovative study" had been refuted.

4

THE ASTRONOMICAL PLANETS

The next astrological element that will be subjected to a critical investigation is the effect of the planets. An astrology without planets is unthinkable; it is only the varying play of planetary movement that stamps a horoscope as unique. That is also why the Chinese system, in which someone's fate and condition are connected with the day of birth, cannot be considered an astrology. The personal element that has to validate the statements for that particular person is absent. Moreover, there is no reference in this system to the stars or the planets: It is literally an "astrology without astra."

But before we take a look at the astrological meaning of the planets, it is interesting to tell something more about how these celestial bodies appear to us in the sky and to give a short survey of what science has to say about them.

Astronomy divides the celestial bodies which constitute the solar system in different groups: the Sun, the center of our solar system; the planets, rather large celestial bodies which move in an orbit around the Sun and of which Earth is one; *satellites* which move around planets; and finally the smaller celestial bodies, such as *comets* and *asteroids* (also called minor planets), which also orbit the Sun.

From Earth only a few of these celestial bodies are visible with the naked eye: the Sun, our Moon, and five planets. Sporadically and for a short time a comet can be added to this list (remember Hale-Bopp in 1997).

When astrologers use the term "planet," they mean not only the celestial bodies that the astronomers refer to, but also the Sun and the Moon. Their use of that term is clearly a relic from older days, when people thought that just about everything turned around Earth.

Movement in the Sky

The regular movement of the Sun and the slightly less regular progress of the Moon between the stars were covered in chapter 2. As an approximation, their orbits can be pictured as great circles between the stars. For the planets, however, this is different.

Seen from Earth the planets are not much more than bright points of light which move among the stars. Our observation site, Earth, is, however, also a planet which just like the others moves in an orbit around the Sun. As a result of this, each planet appears to have a double movement: Its own movement around the Sun and a second movement, which results from our constantly changing point of view. The result of this combination is that the path we see the planet describe between the stars is very irregular. An example of this will explain a lot.

If, for instance, we observe the movement of Mars over a long time, we see that the planet at first for a few months moves in the same direction among the stars as the Sun and the Moon. Slowly but surely the velocity of the planet decreases; after a certain time the planet even stops its movement among the stars and for a few days just stands still. The astronomers call this the *first stationary point*. But this is not the end of it. After that the planet starts to move *in the reverse direction*. At the same time the planet has become much brighter; while Mars was at first only an unnoticeable orange-red "star" among many other stars, it now has a striking reddish appearance. This period of greatest brightness is called *opposition*. The reverse (*retrograde*) movement lasts only a few weeks; after that the planet slows down among the stars, stops (*the second stationary point*) and, while its brightness slowly begins to weaken, it resumes its former movement in the "normal" direction. (This is called the *opposition loop*. See figure 4.1.)

All the planets, from Mercury to Pluto, present such irregular behavior. In the case of Jupiter, Saturn, Uranus, Neptune, and Pluto the described opposition loop is much smaller than that of Mars, due to their larger distances from Earth.

The explanation of this remarkable "wandering" among the stars is simple, once one takes a point of view from outside Earth (see figure 4.2). When the Earth and Mars are far removed from each other (figure 4.2, point A) Mars moves for the observer in the "normal" (direct) sense with respect to the celestial background. The movement of Mars between the stars is then amplified because Earth moves in the opposite direction. Some time later the positions of the two planets in their orbits have changed in such a way that the movement of Earth compensates for the change of place of Mars against the celestial background: Seen from Earth it appears that the planet is now standing still among the stars (figure 4.2, point B). From then on Earth

84   Making Sense of Astrology

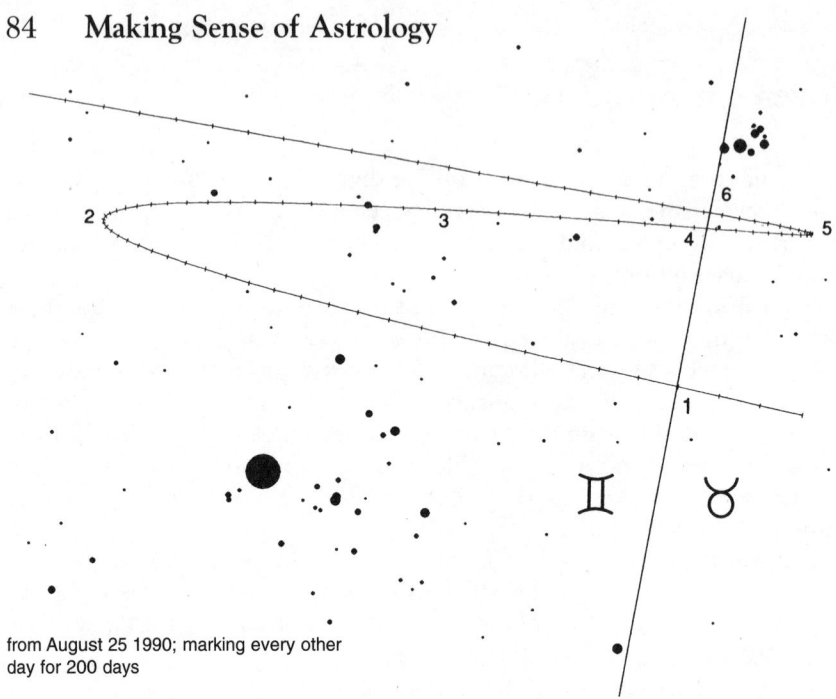

from August 25 1990; marking every other day for 200 days

Figure 4.1. The orbit of Mars in the sky (opposition November 1990).
1. transition ♉ → ♊ on August 31, 1990.
2. first stationary point on October 10, 1990.
3. opposition on November 27, 1990.
4. transition ♊ → ♉ on December 14, 1990.
5. second stationary point on January 1, 1991.
6. transition ♉ → ♊ on January 21, 1991.x

Figure 4.2. The opposition of Mars in 1990, "top view."

approaches Mars from the same side of the Sun, but since Earth moves faster in its orbit—the closer a planet is to the Sun, the greater its velocity—it catches up to Mars, so that it appears that Mars moves backward with respect to the stars (figure 4.2, point C). During this period the two planets reach their closest approach. Because the planet and the Sun are then standing opposite each other, this moment of closest approach was given the name of "opposition." It is also not surprising at all that Mars is then at its brightest and can be observed all night. This backward (retrograde) movement is only temporary; as Earth recedes from the planet the velocity of Mars among the stars decreases until the second stationary point is reached and the movement in the forward direction is resumed (figure 4.2, point D).

Because the orbits of the planets do not lie in exactly the same plane a second variation has to be added: one in latitude. This explains why the path of a planet among the stars is shaped like a loop.

For the other outer planets (planets which orbit farther from the Sun than Earth does) the explanation of their opposition loop is identical, only the distances are larger, and therefore the loops themselves are smaller. In addition the changes in brightness of these planets in the sky are much less.

The cause of the remarkable movement is now clear to us, but that is only because we know that Earth also orbits the Sun. For our ancestors this must have been a very strange phenomenon, one for which surely only the gods could be responsible.

For the inner planets (planets which orbit nearer to the Sun than Earth) the situation is different because in this case the loops are unnoticeable. These planets are always found in the neighborhood of the Sun and are therefore visible only at twilight, when there are only a few stars in the sky. Thus, an observer determines the position of Mercury and Venus with respect to the horizon rather than with respect to the stars. But even that position is quite capricious: The slopes of their orbits cause irregularities of their movements with respect to the horizon (see figures 4.3a and b).

The irregular character of the movements of the planets was one of the greatest obstacles to the development of early astronomy. The seemingly arbitrary movements of the planets in the sky made the opinion that they were directly influenced by the gods very acceptable, leading to the ease with which they were considered determiners of fate: Perhaps the unpredictability on Earth was a reflection of celestial arbitrariness? Add to that the clear relation between the movement of the Sun and the changes of the seasons, together with the undeniable influence of the Moon on the tides, and nobody will be surprised that the determining factors for just about everything in the sublunar world (literally that which is below the Moon) was sought in the play of the continual changes of the planets. An ideal soil for the rise and acceptance of astrology.

Astronomy since that time has not stood still. The Babylonians already

86   Making Sense of Astrology

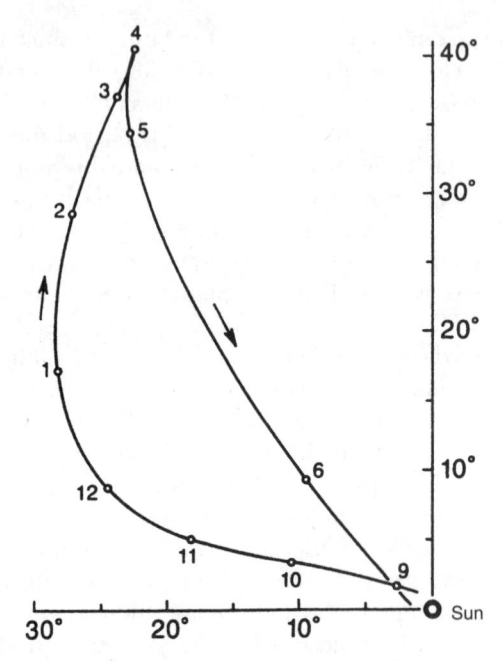

Figure 4.3a. The position of Venus with respect to the horizon and the Sun at sunset at the latitude of Brussels (51° N, longitude 4° E). The points 9,10, and so on through 6 indicate the location of Venus for September 1, 1995; October 1, 1995; and so on through June 1, 1996. (The higher Venus stands, the longer and more clearly it is visible.)

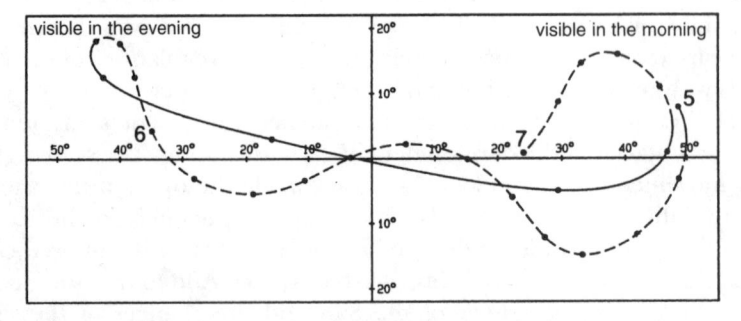

Figure 4.3b. The position of Venus with respect to the Sun, as seen from Earth. The zero point in the center indicates the position of the Sun. The points 5, 6, and 7 indicate the begining of 1995, 1996, and 1997, the other points indicate the beginning of each month. If Venus stands to the right of the Sun, then the planet rises before the Sun and is visible in the morning (and vice versa).

knew that some phenomena that were connected to the visibility of the planets showed a certain regularity in the long run. The Greeks worked out that idea of celestial regularity further and developed complicated geometrical models to picture and calculate the movements of the planets. In the most refined models the planets moved in circles, which in their turn moved on other circles. By combining circles in all sizes and in all velocities, just about any movement could be pictured. And from that the future positions of the planets could be calculated with a relatively good accuracy (which then in turn was useful for astrology). That system was developed most extensively by Alexandrian astronomer Ptolemy (Claudius Ptolemaios, about C.E. 150) who for fourteen centuries would remain the undisputed authority in the area of astronomy.

According to the classical Greek worldview, which became known in the West through the work of Aristotle, the spherical Earth was the center of the cosmos. There decay governed, it was the realm of the imperfect, there death and destruction took place. Around Earth there were a number of celestial spheres, each of which housed a planet.

The first sphere, or if you prefer, the first spherical layer around Earth, housed the Moon and its orbit. There the realm of decay—the sublunar area—ended and that of perfection and eternity began. Because the Moon was located on the border between both worlds, it showed, next to the perfection of planetary movement, some traces of imperfection: The blemishes on its surface were the proof of it.

Around the sphere of the Moon were the spheres of the planets Mercury and Venus. Their movements were coupled to those of the Sun, which moved in the next (fourth) sphere. That is why these two planets were always in the neighborhood of the Sun. Beyond the Sun were the planets Mars, Jupiter, and Saturn on the fifth, the sixth, and the seventh spherical layers, respectively. Beyond that was the eighth sphere with the fixed stars (the stars, therefore, were relatively close to Earth). Finally there was also a ninth—the absolute sphere which was added to explain the precession—and a tenth sphere, the Empyrean, which was the First Cause of all movements and which later was identified by the Christians as God.

According to our perception, it was a very small, almost cosy universe, with strict fatherly supervision from above.

When, at the end of the Middle Ages the determination of the positions of the planets improved, it became clear that the positions agreed less and less with what the calculations according to the theory of Ptolemy predicted.

Polish canon Nicolaus Copernicus (1473–1543) therefore proposed a new theory of the planetary system. According to his model, all planets, including Earth, circled the Sun (only the Moon still moved around Earth).

By letting Earth itself move also, the movements of the other planets could be greatly simplified. The final result, however, was still far from perfect. Copernicus's approach to the orbits of the planets was still the same as that of the Greek astronomers: a combination of circular movements.

German astronomer Johannes Kepler (1571–1630) discovered that most of the remaining problems could be solved by assuming that the planets did *not* move in circles but in *ellipses* around the Sun, but the great breakthrough came with the work of English mathematician and physicist Isaac Newton (1643–1725), who formulated laws of physics and applied them to the movement of the planets. Movements could be explained in a very precise way by the action of one single fundamental force of nature: gravity. Now one not only knew what shape the planetary orbits had, but also *why* this was so. From then on the movements of the planets could be described with a precision of which the Greeks had only dared to dream.

The Planets Close-Up

For the people of antiquity the nature of the celestial bodies was very unclear. They were often associated with emanations or dwelling-places of the gods. The Greeks were, as far as we know, the first to try to explain the nature of the celestial bodies physically. The Greek philosopher Anaxagoras of Clazomenae even contended that the Sun was a red-hot clump of rock, a blasphemous statement for which he was persecuted. It was only a philosophical speculation, of course, as all proof for it was lacking.

A beginning of real insight into this problem arrived only with the invention of the telescope. From then on it was clear that the Moon and the Sun were spherical celestial bodies on the surface of which details could be observed. The Sun was not a perfect body: The telescope showed sunspots on it. And on the surface of the Moon all kinds of landscapes could be seen. The planets no longer appeared in the shape of a point; Mars became an orange-red disc with white polar caps and grey-green smudges while Jupiter was shown to be a somewhat flattened sphere with colored bands of clouds. Saturn on the other hand had a strange shape; it took quite some time before it was clear that this planet was surrounded by a ring. Mercury and Venus, however, remained as mysterious as before: Both showed phases like the Moon (a confirmation that they moved around the Sun) but through the telescope no details could be discerned.

Beginning in the eighteenth century a number of new planets were discovered, and their orbits could be calculated without any problem. The orbit of Neptune was even predicted *before* that planet was discovered! But it remained difficult to get to know anything about the nature of these planets.

It was the development of spaceflight that increased our knowledge of the planets tremendously. Except for Pluto, all large planets have by now been visited by one or more space probes. Robots have landed on Venus and Mars, and men have walked on the Moon and returned lunar soil samples to Earth.

What do we know at present about the celestial bodies which populate our solar system? A short survey should be sufficient.

The Sun

According to cosmic standards the Sun is a star of average size which provides the rest of the solar system with energy (radiation). Like most stars, the Sun consists mostly of hydrogen, the lightest chemical element, which for that matter, constitutes the largest part of matter in the universe. This hydrogen is converted into helium in the center of our star through nuclear fusion. This conversion delivers an enormous amount of energy, which explains the high temperature of the Sun: 6,000°C at the surface, but 15,000,000°C in the center. That energy finally leaves the Sun as radiation, only a part of which is visible to us.

Only a very small quantity of that radiation reaches the surface of Earth, but it is nevertheless the source of all life here; it provides the energy that the vegetable kingdom needs in order to grow and the vegetable kingdom then becomes food for the animal kingdom.

The Moon

The Moon, the other celestial body on which some detail can be observed with the naked eye, is a bleak and above all things dry world of rocks. On its surface traces are still visible of its early, billions-of-years-old history. What strikes one even through a small telescope are the countless craters on the surface which are present in all sizes, including gigantic basins hundreds of kilometers wide that are often inundated by lava. These craters were formed by a bombardment of the surface by smaller celestial bodies, a process which was very important during the early history of the solar system.

The Moon is literally a dead world; not only because absolutely no life is present there, but also because during the last few hundred million years nothing of importance has happened on it.

The Planets

Now the planets. Closest to the Sun is the planet Mercury. This planet is not much larger than the Moon and it shows a lot of similarity with our satellite: vast solidified lava surfaces interspersed with large and small craters.

A little bit farther from the Sun, between Mercury and Earth, orbits

Venus, a planet of about the same size as Earth. In contrast to what her name would let one presume (Venus is the Roman goddess of love) the landscapes on this planet form an all but lovely environment to reside in. The name "Hell" would have been a better choice, as due to an extreme greenhouse effect the temperature at the surface rises to about 500°C. The reason for this is to be sought in the composition of the atmosphere, which is about ninety times denser than ours and consists almost exclusively of carbon dioxide, a well-known greenhouse gas.

The first planet with an orbit outside Earth's is Mars. Mars is a lot smaller than Earth. Because its soil contains many iron oxides—think of rust—it has a reddish color, and therefore is also called the Red Planet. It is the planet in our solar system which most resembles ours: A Martian year is a little bit shorter than two Earth years; there are seasons; the planet has its own, although very rarefied, atmosphere; and there is water, although this is almost completely in the form of ice. The surface looks a little bit like the Moon, with many impact craters. Besides that there are a number of striking geological structures, such as volcanoes as high as 25 kilometers and canyons as much as 4,000 kilometers long, 6 kilometers deep, and 700 kilometers wide. The presence of what appear to be dry riverbeds lets us suspect that the climate on Mars was much milder in a far distant past.

In contrast to the previous planets, Mars has two little moons, Phobos and Deimos, probably former members of the asteroid belt that have been captured by the gravity of Mars. Phobos in particular looks more like a beaten up potato than a spherical body.

Besides the nine "true" planets we also know of a couple of thousand minor planets or asteroids. Every year new ones are discovered. The largest, Ceres (which, in 1801, was the first asteroid discovered by means of a telescope), has a diameter of less than 1,000 kilometers. Asteroids are probably remnants of the kind of celestial bodies from which the other planets originated. The disturbing gravitational influence of Jupiter, however, has prevented them from sticking together to form a larger, planetlike body. Most of these minor planets are found between the orbits of Mars and Jupiter, but there are also some with very irregular orbits. Once in a while one approaches our Earth closely (within a few million kilometers). Long ago there must have been an occasional collision between our planet and such a piece of rock and it is not at all impossible that such a thing would happen again in the future.

The giant among the planets is Jupiter. The astronomical namesake of the Roman supreme god is a sphere with a diameter eleven times as large as that of Earth. The planet is surrounded by a dense atmosphere in which extensive bands of clouds with complicated weather patterns are visible.

Jupiter consists mainly of hydrogen. On Earth hydrogen is a gas, but because of the gigantic pressure on Jupiter this element is found primarily in liquid form (and at greater depths probably even as a liquid metal!).

Jupiter and its surrounding satellites form a small-scale planetary system: four large and a dozen small moons orbit the main planet. The largest satellite is even larger than our Moon. These large and small moons are worth being studied all by themselves. On the moon Io, for instance, active volcanoes are found. The next moon, Europa, is one gigantic layer of ice cut by hundreds of chasms and crevices; there are indications that under the ice an ocean may be present. Ganymede, the third and largest moon, shows remarkable, capricious bands on the surface together with impact craters. On Callisto, the farthest of the four, almost nothing but craters are to be seen. The surfaces of Ganymede and Callisto as well as Europa consist mainly of ice. The other satellites of Jupiter are nothing but irregular pieces of rock.

A somewhat smaller brother of Jupiter is Saturn, the well-known ringed planet. This planet looks in many respects like Jupiter; it consists mainly of hydrogen, it also has a turbulent atmosphere with colored bands of clouds and it also is found to be the center of an extensive system of satellites. However, the most remarkable feature is the presence of the rings around the planet. Saturn is not the only planet to have rings (Jupiter, Uranus, and Neptune have them, too), but it is the only planet with rings that are so extensive, complex, and bright. The complete system of rings is only a few tens of meters thick and consists mostly of pieces of ice which are not larger than a few meters: a very thin disc indeed.

At least eighteen moons have been discovered in orbit around Saturn. The largest, Titan, is larger than our Moon and is surrounded by a dense atmosphere. The surface is possibly covered by an ocean of liquid methane or ethane (the temperature is $-180°C$).

Still farther removed from the Sun than these two kings of our solar system we meet the two smaller gaseous giants, Uranus and Neptune. Uranus turns out to be a smaller copy of Jupiter, with an atmosphere of barely discernible bands of clouds, a few rings, and numerous little moons (fifteen of them are known, all smaller than our Moon). The most noticeable characteristic of this planet is that it lies "on its side": the axis around which the planet rotates lies almost flat in the surface of its orbit. That is exceptional; the axes of the other planets are more or less perpendicular to the surface of the orbit.

Neptune seems to be a twin of Uranus, but without the remarkable orientation of the axis. The bands of clouds, however, are much clearer, and due to the presence of methane in the atmosphere the planet has a very deep blue color. It is no exaggeration to state that Neptune is the real "blue planet" of our solar system. Eight satellites have been discovered around this planet, only one of which (Triton) is rather large.

Finally we have Pluto, a rather small planet with a remarkable orbit. Part of it falls within the orbit of Neptune, so that Pluto at some times is closer to the Sun than Neptune. We know very little about Pluto. To be sure, Pluto has a relatively large moon, Charon, the diameter of which is barely four times smaller than that of Pluto, and which is located exceptionally close to the planet. The Pluto-Charon system is therefore also called a "double planet."

It is not at all impossible that there are other planets beyond Pluto, but we know nothing about that. Apart from this the solar system certainly does not end at Pluto. Just a bit farther a belt of small bodies (comets) known as the "Kuiper Belt" has been discovered. Still farther the comets come from a kind of "cloud" around the Sun that is hundreds of times farther away than the farthest known planet.

This short (and very incomplete) survey is only meant to give you some idea of one of the most fascinating areas of modern astronomy: planetology or the study of the planets. After this simplified scientific explanation we will move again to the higher astrological spheres.

5

THE ASTROLOGICAL PLANETS

In the previous chapter an astronomical picture was sketched of the planets, of their movements in the sky and their physical nature. According to the astrologers this picture is certainly not wrong—after all, it is very difficult to quarrel with it—but very incomplete. In their opinion the planets are not "merely" gaseous spheres and pieces of ice or rock but also factors which play an important role in life on Earth. Their positions occupy an essential place in the horoscope. The combination of their "influences" with those of the signs and the houses determines the specific and very private nature of the interpretation of the horoscope.

The Characteristics of the Astrological Planets

As with the signs, the characteristics of the planets were fixed during the early development of astrology. Its modern form, which is found in the astrological handbooks, is nothing more than a psychologically adapted version of ancient ideas. A short survey of the astrological characteristics of the planets can be found in table 5.1.

To each planet astrologers assign an influence on different areas of life. The Sun, for instance, symbolizes *biological* characteristics that are described by words like "(organic) energy," "vitality," and so on. In the horoscope certain organs or bodily functions were supposed to be under the influence of the Sun: the heart, the circulatory system, and the eyes. Besides that the Sun was supposed to exert a psychological influence: It stands for a lust after power, ambition, a choleric (short-tempered) temperament. These rather

Table 5.1
The Astrological Characteristics of the Planets

SUN ☉   **Force**
Life force, self-esteem, power and ambition, authority (the father)
Heart, circulation, eyes

MOON ☾   **Subconscious**
Fertility, metabolism, subconscious, consciousness, emotions (the mother)
Stomach, belly, uterus

MERCURY ☿   **Communication**
Intellect, ability to adapt
Nervous system, brain, speech organs

VENUS ♀   **Harmony**
Emotions, eroticism, artistic ability, relationships
World of art
Organs of smell and touch

MARS ♂   **Energy**
Energy, desire, choleric temperament, courage, force
Military and technical world
Muscular system, blood, genitals

JUPITER ♃   **Expansion**
Philosophical and religious thought, nomadic nature
Financial and judicial world
Liver, lungs

SATURN ♄   **Concentration**
Concentration, melancholic temperament
Earth, soil, lonely places
Bones, skin

URANUS ♅   **Crisis**
Intuition, independence
Engineering, revolution, occultism (astrology!)

NEPTUNE ♆   **Inspiration**
Sensitivity, inspiration, confusion, exaggeration
Chaos, psychology

PLUTO ♇   **Turning point**
Turning points, crisis, death

personal characteristics can then be extended to the family and even to society as a whole. In that case, the Sun is connected with authority, the exercise of power, and leadership functions: the head of the family, the father, the king, the government.

The analogy (here again) that connects the different areas is clear enough. Mercury, for instance, rules the nervous system and, in analogy with this, that rule is extended to the nervous system of a country: the postal system, telephone, radio, highways, railroads, and similar systems. In this way astrologers can easily assimilate new technologies (such as the Internet) into their system.

In antiquity, when only the Sun, the Moon, and five planets were known, these celestial bodies were connected with the signs. In order to divide seven heavenly bodies over twelve signs the Greek astronomers started with a simple rule. The Sun belonged in the sign of Leo—the Sun is in Leo during the worst summer heat—and alongside came the Moon in the sign of Cancer. After that ten signs were left which could be assigned to five planets. The assignment started with the signs of Gemini and Virgo, which are next to Cancer and Leo, and after that ran according to the order of the planets in the solar system. In this way Virgo and Gemini were assigned to Mercury; Taurus and Libra to Venus; Aries and Scorpio to Mars; Pisces and Sagittarius to Jupiter; and finally the last two signs, Capricorn and Aquarius, to Saturn (see figure 5.1). In the astrological terminology it is said that these planets are the "rulers" of these signs. Therefore the phrase "Venus as the ruler of Taurus."

A planet which is in its own sign is supposed to show a stronger influence; its activity would then show itself in a favorable sense. For instance, according to this rule Mercury in Gemini is exceptionally favorable for the development of a keen intellect. On the other hand if a planet is in the *opposite* sign, for instance Mercury in Sagittarius, then the unfavorable characteristics will be emphasized.

In order to give these resemblances a "natural" touch, the astrologers emphasize those characteristics that show a lot of similarity. Mercury rules understanding, intelligence, and is the symbol of communication; Gemini also has characteristics connected with communication, so these two are astrologically compatible. On the other hand, in the case of Mercury and Virgo the intellect and the scientific character of the two are emphasized. In the same way the Sun is the ruler of Leo because both have the characteristics of domination, the Moon in Cancer is favorable because both are ruled by sensitivity, the philosophical characteristics of Sagittarius are connected to those of Jupiter, and so on.

In judging the value of such similarities one should keep in mind that in the course of the centuries an exchange of characteristics between planets and signs took place. For instance a taste for art and luxury belongs to Taurus nowadays, because Venus is the "ruler" of Taurus. That transfer explains the similarity between planets and signs and is not a "natural" given.

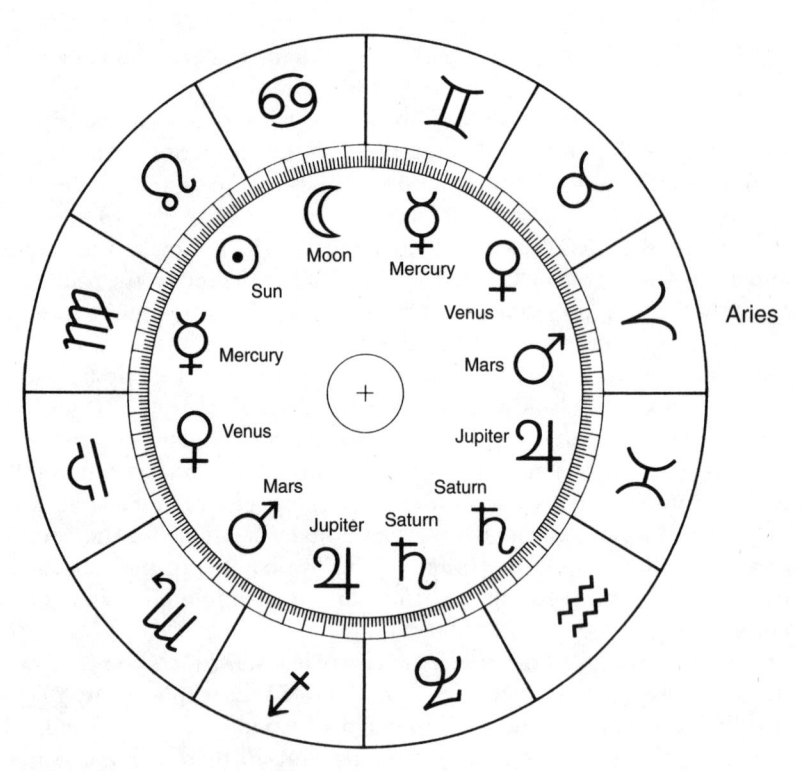

Figure 5.1. The signs and their "rulers."

The reasoning which connects the planets with certain signs goes even further in practice. When interpreting the horoscope not only should attention be paid to the sign in which a planet is located, but also to the planet which is the "ruler" of that sign. In that way both planets influence the effect of each other. If Venus is in Aries, the sign ruled by Mars, then that means that there also exists a special relation between both planets.

How does the case stand now with respect to the three planets that were discovered later? After their discovery several attempts were made to fit them into the system. However, opinions about the assignments differ quite a bit. In most cases he Greek system is simply extended, that is, the order Saturn–Capricorn, Uranus–Aquarius, Neptune–Pisces, and Pluto–Aries is assumed. However, in this case Saturn, Jupiter, and Mars still remain rulers of Aquarius, Pisces, and Aries, respectively, so that these signs then obtain two rulers. Some astrologers, however, move into the reverse direction to Pluto, so that Pluto becomes the ruler of Scorpio. Here we are already right smack in the center of confusion, and we haven't even started our criticism.

Now, what does an astrologer do with the planets in practice? For the construction of the horoscope she needs the place, day, and hour of birth. With the help of the last two pieces of information the positions of the planets in the zodiac at that moment are looked up in an astrological almanac (our ephemeris*), after which these are noted in the horoscope (see Intermezzo III, where we cast the horoscope of our imaginary friend A. S. Trologer).

The most difficult part of the work that can show up here is the interpolation between two values of the table. In the astrological yearbooks the positions of the planets are stated for each day or, for the outer planets, for every three or five days, usually at midnight universal time ("Greenwich time"). However, if the "customer" was born at 5 A.M., the intermediate value that is valid for that time of birth has to be calculated. That is of course as simple as can be: One only has to know how to add, subtract, multiply, and divide. Now that more and more astrologers use computers, even that does not have to be known. Yet some astrologers dare to create the impression that the composition of a horoscope requires very complicated calculations, as though they themselves had to calculate the tables of the planets! Apart from that, the determination of the places of the planets in the horoscope is the only act in astrology which has something to do with the "cosmos." In order to do this not a single astrologer has to look at the planets themselves (and as a result many of them never have done so).

---

*An *ephemeris* is a prediction of the positions of the planets, phases of the moon, tides, and the like on the basis of astronomical calculations. The composition of ephemerides is a purely astronomical matter. However, there exist special ephemerides for astrologers, because they need the positions of the planets with respect to the zodiac, which astronomers use only very rarely. Instead of tables, special computer programs are now used for this.

Planets in Trouble

In contrast with the signs, the planets are not purely mathematically calculated points in a horoscope, but celestial bodies which really do move in the firmament. Even the greatest skeptic agrees with the astrologers about that. That does not mean that the characteristics and the influences ascribed to the planets are accepted. There are solid grounds to express doubts about that.

The astrological planets obtained their characteristics, just like the signs, in Greco-Roman times. It is therefore not at all surprising that a number of arguments that were posed with respect to the signs are also valid for the planets. After all, the history of both were influenced by the same factors.

The most obvious question that one can ask an astrologer is, of course, "How did the planets obtain their characteristics?" Why does Mercury rule over commerce and Venus over love? Why is Mars aggressive and military and is Jupiter the patron of the judicial system? After all, shouldn't there be a reason for the attribution of exactly those characteristics to exactly that planet?

Most of the time no satisfactory answer is given to these questions. Astrologers juggle with terms like "tradition," "experience" and the like, but those are only words that hide (unintended?) ignorance. And by looking into this a little further it soon becomes clear why.

The solution of the problem has to be sought in the *names* of the planets. These names are the names of well-known Roman gods—and that is clear to everybody who knows anything about classical antiquity. These gods (and each of them had been put on par with a god of the Greek pantheon) possessed their own attributes and ruled certain domains of social life.

And what is striking about that? That the attributes of the planets agree with the characteristics and attributes of the Greco-Roman gods!* An exact comparison makes this clear right away. Take Mercury, for example. The Roman Mercury (the Greek Hermes) was the god of commerce (and the thieves; that teaches us something about the status of commerce in antiquity), and so the planet Mercury rules commerce in astrology. The same with Venus (the Greek Aphrodite), the goddess of love. You don't have to look very far in order to derive the astrological characteristics of Venus as a planet from that. And then there was Saturn, a god who was not well liked in the view of the ancients. According to Greek mythology, Kronos (the Greek counterpart of Saturn) ate his children and because of that the astrologers considered Saturn an unfavorable planet from which not much good could be expected. Because of a confusion with *chronos* (time) Saturn also became the symbol of

---

*Some characteristics became so well known that they became part of everyday language: "jovial" (Jupiter), "martial" (Mars), "Venereal" (Venus). Both astrology as well as knowledge of the ancient world of the gods must have played a role in this process.

the irrevocably forward-moving time and, connected with that, of death. This in turn was the occasion for the presentation of the planetary god as "Father Time" or the man with the scythe who inexorably cuts the thread of life. Not exactly a pleasant gentleman.

As was the case with the signs, one could presume here also that the analogy worked the other way round, that the characteristics of the planets were known (in whatever way possible) and that the astronomers/astrologers leaned on that in order to ascribe characteristics to the gods of the same name. It was "known," so to speak, that the planet Mars was aggressive and a god was found who symbolized that: a god of war. This reasoning (which astrologers most of the time do not propose explicitly, but for which the suggestion is often present) is easy to refute: The Greek gods and their attributes are older than the introduction of astrology in Greece (for Rome that is true even to a much larger extent) and therefore much older than the characteristics that were attributed to the different planets.

How that connection between planets and gods was brought about is worth a short digression. Astrology experienced its very early beginning in Mesopotamia (this is discussed in more detail in chapter 9). There a tradition existed that connected certain gods with certain celestial bodies. Sin was the god of the Moon, Shamash the Sun god, Ishtar resided in the planet Venus, etc. When astrology was "invented" these celestial gods were incorporated into the system. When early astrology spread to the Hellenistic world these gods were replaced by gods who were very similar. In antiquity it was not unusual to consider foreign gods as local variations of one's own gods (which made religious wars superfluous beforehand). When the Greeks heard about the Babylonian goddess Ishtar, who was, among other things, the goddess of love, they recognized in her right away their own goddess of love, Aphrodite. According to this process the Greeks "translated" the Babylonian planetary gods into their own mythology.

But there was a snag: The Greeks did their best to find deities that agreed as much as possible with the foreign variants, but that never succeeded completely. The Babylonian gods also ruled areas of life or had characteristics which did *not* belong to the domain of the equivalent Greek gods. For instance, Ishtar was not only the goddess of love, but also of war. The Greeks thought here of Aphrodite, but she was only the goddess of love, not of war. For that the Greeks had Ares (Mars). His Babylonian counterpart, Nergal, in contrast, ruled over the plague and death, but not over war. As a result a partial exchange of characteristics of the planetary gods took place.

When astrology spread over the Roman Empire and the planets obtained their Latin names (which they still have; the names are therefore Latin translations of Greek translations of Babylonian originals which may have had Sumerian origins), they were contaminated with a number of characteristics that were typical of the Roman gods. Saturn, for instance, the Greek Kronos, was a Roman god of agriculture. Therefore the astrological Saturn rules the soil, the land, and agriculture (hence the scythe of Father Time). The Babylonian Saturn, Ninurta, was more involved with the weather (storms, hurricanes) and war (together with Ishtar).

What is becoming evident from this? It is no coincidence that the astrological planets and the Greco-Roman gods have analogous characteristics. The characteristics of the astrological planets were simply derived from the gods who were much older than astrology. Here too, the analogy with religion and mythology determined the results. As was the case with the signs, the planets changed their characteristics when they were adopted into another culture. This does not create much trust in the reality of the planetary influences.

It can be said with confidence that the old gods are not dead: They still exert their influences on humanity, disguised as astrological planets.

The application of the above-mentioned principle to determine the characteristics of the planets did not remain limited to a distant past. In 1781 German-British astronomer William Herschel discovered the planet we now call Uranus.* Later on it appeared that Uranus's movement did not agree with what was to be expected according to theory. That could be explained by assuming that there was yet another, unknown, planet that distorted the orbit of Uranus. On the basis of calculations this planet was discovered in 1846, fairly close to the predicted position; it received the name of Neptune. After further distortions in the orbit of Uranus were found, the same procedure was followed and in 1930 the planet Pluto was discovered.†

The names of the three outer planets were given by astronomers.‡ The astrologers had nothing to do with it, but were quick to research them "astrologically," to attribute characteristics to them and to adopt them into their system. That's why they are now found in the horoscope.

And, dear reader, which characteristics do you think the astrologers attributed to these three planets? Right, the characteristics and dispositions which agree exactly with the Greco-Roman gods of the same names! Uranus (Greek Ouranos) in mythology had to settle a rebellion by the Titans against his authority. Therefore the astrological characteristics are independence and revolution. Neptune (the Greek Poseidon) was the god of the sea and in

---

*That name did not come out of the blue. Herschel called his discovery the "Georgian planet," after his king, George III of Britain. German astronomer Johann Elert Bode found that name not universal enough. In order to follow the ancient tradition he proposed the name "Uranus," which was rapidly accepted. Only the British astronomers continued speaking of the "Georgian planet" for decades.

†Ironically, it was later determined that the deviations of the observations with theory on which the search for "planet X" was based had nothing to do with Pluto!

‡The name "Pluto" was chosen because the first two letters are the initials of the American astronomer Percival Lowell, who first looked for the unknown planet. In the symbol for Pluto we find the "PL" again.

antiquity water was connected to sensitivity (think of the relation Pisces–water–sensitivity). Thus the astrological Neptune rules sensitivity, inspiration, psychology, and so on. The god Pluto (or Hades) was the ruler of the underworld, so that death and everything that is connected with it belong to the domain of his astrological counterpart.

With all these examples the analogy, the childlike comparison of and playing games with names is very obvious. Who can still take the statements of the astrologers seriously that these characteristics arose from experience or observation? The planetary characteristics are reflections, "astrologized" versions of the old gods. Not only are the old gods still with us, but in the last few centuries three of them were revived!

Astrological Disagreement (Part II)

The three outer planets of the solar system, Uranus, Neptune, and Pluto, are not visible from Earth without instruments (under very favorable conditions Uranus can be seen with the naked eye as an exceptionally weak star, but is usually too dim to be noticed). Only after the invention of the telescope did people become aware of them. Classical astrology therefore worked with only five planets (besides the Sun and the Moon).

After the discovery of Uranus, Neptune, and Pluto, however, these newcomers were assimilated into the Western astrological system. We purposely write "Western astrological system"; Indian astrologers (those of the sidereal zodiac) never accepted these three "new" planets. Out of tradition they still work with five planets. That means that in their system three existing planets are very consciously *ignored*. But in actual practice that does not seem to lead to worse results. If the planets are such indispensable and important factors in the horoscope, how can this be explained? That question can, for that matter, be extended to the past of astrology: The astrologers worked for more than 2,000 years without these outer planets. Did they never notice that their system was incomplete? That important factors were missing in their analysis? Obviously not.

The truth is it doesn't matter at all: For centuries astrologers have had the impression that their system was satisfactory. According to ancient tradition wrong results were (and are) ascribed to the incompetence of the practitioner, never to the errors in the system, let alone in its basic ideas.

If in earlier times people were satisfied without using the additional planets, why then do Western astrologers use the new trio? Something is not quite right. Either these planets are superfluous (then why should one use them?) or they are necessary (then why was the earlier astrology then so "good" without these planets and why is the Indian astrology successful still?).

We can even go further: If Uranus, Neptune, and Pluto are astrologically ineffective (who are we after all not to believe the Indian astrologers?), who says that Saturn has any influence? If three planets are negligible, why then not four or five or more? Why draw the line at Saturn?

The whole matter again points to the absence of any objective observations in astrology. If characteristics were based on experience, have the ancient or the Indian astrologers never observed or experienced the "action" of the three additional planets? Did Western astrologers then really observe them at all? There is nothing indicating that this has been the case.

A similar problem arises with respect to the asteroids. As was mentioned earlier, there are many tiny planets. A few thousand are known. It is difficult to estimate their total number, but it certainly amounts to more than 50,000. Most of them are no larger than a few hundred meters. Only thirty of them have a diameter of more than 200 kilometers. The one that was first discovered, Ceres, the largest, has a diameter which is about three times smaller than that of the Moon.

The asteroids do not belong to classical astrology—only on New Year's Day of 1801 was Ceres discovered. But it should not surprise anybody that a number of modern astrologers take some of these celestial bodies, particularly Ceres, Juno, Pallas, and Vesta—the four that were discovered first—into account.

Again we have a disagreement here: Some astrologers make use of the asteroids, others do not, and that difference apparently does not seem to have any serious consequences. All the arguments that were made with respect to Uranus, Neptune, and Pluto are just as valid in this case.

It becomes a little bit predictable, but here too it is obvious that the astrologers derived the characteristics of the four asteroids from their names, which were awarded in the nineteenth century. Astrologer H. C. Meier connects Vesta, the Roman goddess of the hearth, with hearth and home. Zipporah Dobyns associates Juno with close relationships and marriage; Juno was the Roman guardian goddess of women and childbirth. Pallas was allotted group activities and politics, and by "sheer coincidence" Pallas Athena happened to be the guardian goddess of the city of Athens, the cradle of democracy. If this kind of analogy is taken in earnest, one can wonder which characteristics astrologers would give to the asteroids 1685 Toro ("combative tendencies toward animals" or just "bullfights"?), 1981 Midas and 904 Rockefellia ("businessman who changes all he touches into gold," financial success), 2101 Tantalus and 1866 Sisyphus (toil and trouble), 1227 Geranium (love of horticulture), 558 Carmen (likes opera), 1814 Bach and 1815 Beethoven (musical talent)? Or 916 America and 886 Washingtonia? Not to speak of 1772 Gagarin ("wants to climb ever higher"), 1958 Chandrasekhar and 2709 Sagan (names of astronomers: "often see stars"), 3352 McAuliffe (the poor teacher who perished in the explosion of the space shuttle *Challenger*: "misfortune in space

Table 5.2: Characteristics of Gods and Planets

Name	Babylonian God	Greco-Roman God	Astrological Meaning
Mercury	NABU: God of wisdom, commerce, and scholars who handles the stylus of the tablets of Destiny.	HERMES/MERCURY: god of commerce and impostors, herald of the gods, patron of music, literature, and sports	Psychological: intellect, mind. Social: commerce, science, literature, communication.
Venus	ISHTAR: as the morning star the goddess of war and conflict; as the evening star goddess of love, luxury, and fertility.	APHRODITE: goddess of love, beauty, and fertility. VENUS was also the goddess of abundance.	Psychological: taste for art, eroticism, love. Social: luxury, abundance, passion.
Mars	NERGAL: god of the underworld, the plague, death; the great cause of disaster.	ARES/MARS: god of war, battle, murder, discord; brawler.	Psychological: energy, desire, choleric type. Social: military, war, technical professions, medicine.
Jupiter	MARDUK: the supreme god, ruler over the other gods and the world; omniscient.	ZEUS/JUPITER: supreme god, defender of justice and order.	Psychological: philosophy, religion, love of travel. Social: judicial system, finance.
Saturn	NINURTA: god of hurricanes, war, and the hunt, of family and household.	KRONOS: ousted supreme god who ate his own children. SATURN: god of agriculture.	Psychological: profoundness, seriousness, melancholy. Social: conservatism, earth, soil.

flights")? And what about 1109 Tata, 1127 Mimi, 501 Urhixidur, 1286 Banachiewicsa, 1903 Adzhimushkaj, and 1888 Zu Chong-Zhi? Just try to fit these celestial objects (and they all exist!)* in the horoscope. Or do we strongly underestimate the creative powers of the astrologers?

---

*Every discovered asteroid for which an orbit is calculated obtains an official name and number from an international astronomical commission. Because the number of known asteroids has become so large (more than 5,000), almost all thinkable names are admitted. Some asteroids are even named after children, lady friends, or pets of astronomers (e.g., Spock). Comic-strip figures are also immortalized.

An additional problem is the *number* of asteroids that the astrologer has to take into account. If four asteroids are valid, why then not 10 or 200 or 1,000? There is a gradual change in size from Ceres (900 kilometers) to the smallest asteroids (less than 1 kilometer). Why is Juno used, but none of the *eleven* asteroids that are larger than Juno's 250 kilometers? Juno was discovered earlier because of its greater brightness, but is that a reason to neglect the latecomers?

Most of the astrologers do not take the position of the asteroids in the horoscope into account. But, why not? After all, there is no essential difference between the minor and major planets. Most of the asteroids come closer to Earth than Jupiter, some even much closer than any celestial body with the exception of the Moon. And some asteroids are significantly brighter than Neptune or Pluto. Why not take them into account? Of course, the horoscope will then become a little more complicated, but for the sake of precision . . .

The previous arguments were in regard to the use or non-use of *existing* celestial bodies. The discovery of the three outer planets in the last two centuries, however, caused another curious astrological phenomenon: the *hypothetical* planets.

What happened? The discovery of Uranus made it clear that there were more planets than the traditional seven (five planets plus Sun and Moon). Because of that people asked themselves if other undetected planets could possibly exist. And when Neptune was found in 1846, this was considered a confirmation of this supposition. However, from then on astrologers became even more audacious. They did not limit themselves to waiting patiently until the astronomers discovered a new planet, but they started to predict these themselves . . . with astrological methods, not with the methods of celestial mechanics. Some of them went even further: They developed astrological systems in which the not-yet-discovered (hypothetical) planets had already been included, with characteristics and all! They certainly were running ahead of the future.

There are two astrological schools of any importance which use such hypothetical planets. The Dutch school of Theo Ram uses three hypothetical planets, with the names Persephone, Hermes, and Demeter. The characteristics have been worked out in detail; even tables of their positions have been published! This school also has the irritating habit of awarding different names and symbols from those in classical astrology to the existing planets, which only increases the confusion. The Hamburg school of Witte (more popularly known as *Uranian Astrology*) accepts the existence of no fewer than eight hypothetical planets. They bear the names of Cupido, Hades, Zeus, Kronos, Apollo, Admetos, Vulcanus, and Poseidon. They all have characteristics (derived from mythology of course) and ephemerides. Notice that some names are the Greek equivalent of the Latin names of existing planets: Zeus is the Greek Jupiter, Hades is another name for Pluto, Kronos is the Greek

Saturn, Apollo the Greek sun god, and Poseidon the Greek Neptune. The characteristics of these hypothetical planets look very much, indeed, like those of the analogous existing planets.

Both schools show a number of common characteristics. We quote the critical study of Dean and Mather:

> Each [school] was led by a man considered by his students to be a genius, each established its results from a study of events over many years of work and built them into a complex metaphysical system, each failed to meet the most elementary standards of objective investigation, and each was convinced it was right.[1]

The most striking difference between the schools lies in the positions of the hypothetical planets: They do not agree with each other! The two systems claim to be based on experience and observations but reach contradictory conclusions. This clearly shows that the methods used to "find" these planets were unsound. For the school of Witte (Uranian Astrology) something else showed up: The eight hypothetical planets had all been predicted before 1930, the year in which the astronomers discovered the (existing) planet Pluto. *Not a single position* of a hypothetical planet of Witte was found in the neighborhood of Pluto, but yet Pluto was later included in their system. We hit on a paradox: Either the method of Witte is correct (but why then was Pluto not discovered by it?) or Pluto does not have any astrological significance (but why then was it included in the system after all?).

Besides Ram and Witte there are also other astrologers who work with one or more hypothetical planets. Altogether there are at least twenty-five hypothetical planets for which the astrologers have published a position. One can then declare with a rather large certainty that, if a new planet is ever discovered, a hypothetical planet will be "found" somewhere in the neighborhood. Astrologers then can claim triumphantly that they had predicted this one long ago. They will probably be silent about the other twenty-four.

Thus, confusion and contradiction abound. In order to be complete we have to add here that the confusion is also true for the connection of the planets with the signs. Traditionally, the planet Mars is the ruler of the sign Aries, but there are, as mentioned earlier, also astrologers who place Pluto here. There exist other variants of the systems of astrological rulers (the schools of Ram and Witte each use such a variant) but there are also astrologers who—on the basis of years of research, they claim—reject the whole idea of rulers as worthless.

Astronomical Criticism

Not only can the internal muddle among astrologers be criticized, but a number of problems can be pointed out from "outside" astrology as well.

The first objection proceeds from what was explained in the previous pages: If astrology works that well, why did it ignore the three outer planets until they were discovered by astronomers?

A second astronomical difficulty is the complete absence of any concept of *distance*. In astrology the distances from the planets to Earth are not taken into account, but only the angles in a horoscope (see chapter 7). Now, whether a planet is close to Earth or is far removed from it is of no importance at all according to the astrologers. Mars in the sign of Sagittarius at a distance of 365 million kilometers (as was the case in December 1993) has the same meaning in the horoscope as Mars at 68 million kilometers in the same sign (as in July 2001). Now it is well known that just about all known phenomena decrease in strength as the object upon which they act is farther removed: This is valid for gravity, electrical attraction and repulsion, and the brightness of a light source. Do we now have to concede that the assumed influences of the planets escape this general rule?

The distances to Earth vary most strongly for Mars and the inner planets, Mercury and Venus. The distance of Mercury to Earth varies from 92 million kilometers to 209 million kilometers, Venus between 42 million and 258 million kilometers, and Mars from 56 million to 380 million kilometers—and astrologers do not take this into account at all.

Historically this is easy to explain: Astrology arose in an environment in which it was thought that the planets revolved around Earth and that during one revolution their distances did not change much. The only important changes that could be determined were the changes in angular distances. Even after the development of a more correct conception of the solar system these changing distances were never included in astrology. Do we now, at the end of the twentieth century, still have to attach more than some historical value to a vision that runs centuries behind the times?

Scientific Research

Are there—as with the signs—also scientific (statistical) studies about a possible astrological influence of the planets?

The question is not so simple because astrologers never busied themselves properly speaking with the planets as such, but always with their positions in the horoscope. For them the planets are something like the hands of a clock. A planet is always located in a sign and—as will be explained in the next chapter—in a house. Each astrological influence is due to the effects of the planets in the signs and the houses, combined with any angles between the planets themselves (the aspects). That is why there are not many studies that treat the planets by themselves. In this area there is only one serious piece of research worth mentioning, the work of Michel Gauquelin, which will be discussed in chapter 6.

Besides that, the question can be asked more generally in how the Sun, the Moon, and the planets exert influences on us. The existence of these influences does not mean, however, that astrology has anything to do with it. In Intermezzo IX we pay more attention to these possible cosmic influences and in Intermezzo X we will look more specifically at the supposed influences of the Moon on humanity.

Note

1. G. Dean and A. Mather, *Recent Advances in Natal Astrology* (Cowes, England: Recent Advances, 1977), p. 244.

Intermezzo III

☉ ♆ ☽ ♌ ☊ ♂ ♃ ✶ □ △ ⚹ ☍

THE PLANETS IN THE HOROSCOPE OF A. S. TROLOGER

In order to illustrate the calculation of a horoscope we will describe the different steps of this process in a number of short pieces with the help of an example. We will not discuss the interpretation of the horoscope—whoever would like to do this can refer to the classical astrological manuals.

We will calculate the horoscope of someone born in Brussels, Belgium, on January 10, 1950, at exactly 8.00 A.M.*

To begin with, the positions of the planets for the moment of birth are determined. We presume that tables will be used for this. From above-mentioned data a modern computer program calculates a complete horoscope right away. However, for many people, the computer is a black box into which one puts the data, but with which one loses control over what is properly happening during the calculation. A small error somewhere in the program can lead to totally absurd results without the user being any the wiser. Not that this would have such catastrophic consequences for astrology...

The first step is the determination of the time of birth according to the time which is used in the tables with the planetary positions (the ephemerides). Generally *universal time (UT)*, the local time at Greenwich, England (the conventional position of 0° latitude), is used. This time differs one hour from the clock time that was used in Belgium in 1950—in the case of daylight savings time there would have been an additional difference of one hour. The time of birth for which the planetary positions have to be calculated is thus 8h00 − 1h = 7h00 UT.

---

*This horoscope as written is also valid for another place on 51°N, but the only major North American city with that latitude is Alberta, Canada, and in all cases the Ascendant will not be totally the same.

Intermezzo III: The Planets in the Horoscope of A. S. Trologer 109

Now the table. In it the planetary positions are given for midnight in Greenwich. As an example we take the Sun and the Moon. In an ephemeris for 1950, we find the following values, each at 0h00 UT:

Position of the Sun on	Jan. 10: 19.19° Capricorn
	Jan. 11: 20.21° Capricorn
Position of the Moon on	Jan. 10: 0.50° Libra
	Jan. 11: 14.48° Libra

In astrological planetary tables the positions of the planets are given with respect to the ecliptic. The two numbers by which this position is determined are the *ecliptical longitude*, the number of degrees in the zodiac where the planet is found, starting from the vernal equinox, and the *ecliptical latitude*, the "height" of the celestial body above or below the ecliptic (figure III.1).

Another system, one which is almost always used by the astronomers, exists. In this system, the circle of reference is not the ecliptic but the celestial equator. The longitude in that case is called the *right ascension* and the latitude the *declination*. The positions in both coordinate systems can be easily converted from one into the other, taking the precession into account, of course.

In astrology ecliptical coordinates are almost exclusively used. Because the ecliptical latitude of a planet is usually small—only Pluto can move rather far off the ecliptic—the astrologers often ignore it. Therefore only the longitude will be used in this example.

In the table the positions at midnight are given. In order to know the positions at 7h00 UT we simply have to interpolate:

For the Sun we then find:

position at 7h00 UT = position at midnight + (7/24) × the movement during 24 hours
 = 19.19° Capricorn + 0.2917 × (20.21° − 19.19°)
 = 19.19° Capricorn + 0.29°
 = 19.48° Capricorn

In the same way we find for the Moon:

position at 7h00 UT = position at midnight + (7/24) × the movement during 24 hours
 = 0.50° Libra + 0.2917 × (14.48° − 0.50°)
 = 0.50° Libra + 4.08°
 = 4.58° Libra

In the same way the positions of the other planets can be calculated. Thus, the following list is obtained:

110   Making Sense of Astrology

ecliptical longitude = 71°
= 60° + 11°
= 11° ♊

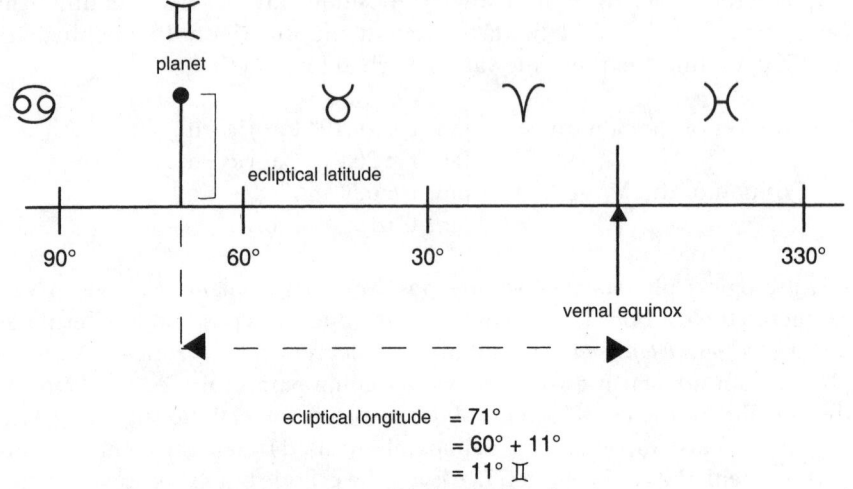

Figure III.1. The ecliptical longitude and latitude of a planet.

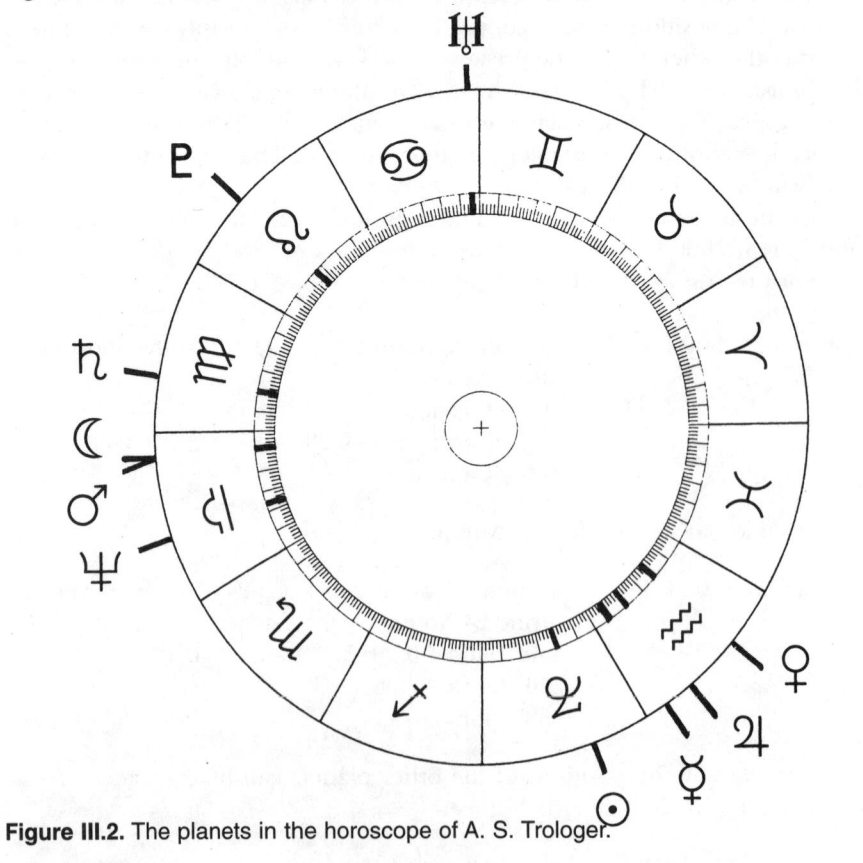

Figure III.2. The planets in the horoscope of A. S. Trologer.

Intermezzo III: The Planets in the Horoscope of A. S. Trologer

Sun	19.5° Capricorn
Moon	4.6° Libra
Mercury	3.9° Aquarius
Venus	18.8° Aquarius
Mars	5.4° Libra
Jupiter	8.6° Aquarius
Saturn	19.3° Virgo
Uranus	2.3° Cancer
Neptune	17.3° Libra
Pluto	17.6° Leo

In drawing up a figure of the horoscope most astrologers use forms with preprinted schematic pictures of the zodiac divided in twelve parts. However, the symbols of the signs have not yet been written in these twelve partitions. One of the edges of the circle of the zodiac is usually divided in degrees. This is done to increase the accuracy when the form is being completed.

The symbols of the signs are now written into the partitions and after that the planets are put into their respective positions (see figure III.2). In this way the first step in casting a horoscope has been executed.

6

THE HOUSES

The two astrological factors which were discussed in the previous chapters had a *cosmic* character. The signs are a division of (a part of) the firmament and the planets are astrological elements that are found outside Earth. If astrology used only these cosmic data then a horoscope drawn up with the aid of these should be valid for *all* people born around that time at any place in the world. Because of the slow movement of the zodiac not much would be found in such a horoscope that was very specific. The unique character of it, which the astrologers like to stress so much, would be absent. In the most optimistic case only one horoscope per hour would have to be drawn up.

In order to make astrology more personal, a *local* element, the *house division,* was introduced in addition to the cosmic elements. As with the signs, this is also a division of the sky in twelve parts (usually). However, this time the starting point is not a point on the moving celestial dome, such as the vernal equinox, but a local reference point, the *horizon.* Starting from here the part of the ecliptic that is above the horizon and the part that is below the horizon are each divided in houses. By the addition of this new factor the complexity of the horoscope increases tremendously, of course. The house division, combined with the movement of the zodiac around Earth and the movements of the planets within it, makes it necessary now to treat not only the positions of the planets in the signs but also their places in the houses and the relation between signs and houses.

The Division of the Houses

What precisely are the astrological houses? As explained above, they are *a division of the ecliptic with the horizon of the observer as the point of reference.* For a natal (birth) horoscope this is the horizon as observed at the place of birth.

The horizon divides the celestial dome and the zodiac in two parts: a visible half *above* the horizon and an invisible half below the horizon. Because of the daily movement of Earth around its axis, the signs of the zodiac rise one by one above the eastern horizon. Just like the Sun, each sign rises daily in the east, eventually reaches its highest point, sets, and then disappears under the western horizon. That movement is, of course, continued below the horizon: The sign revolves underneath Earth, reaches its lowest point, and then rises again on the eastern horizon. Because Earth is a sphere, it goes without saying that the position of the zodiac with respect to the horizon differs at any moment from place to place.

According to the astrologers four signs in each horoscope play an exceptional role: the sign that *rises* at the eastern horizon, the sign that *sets* opposite at the western horizon, the sign that stands *south* in the sky, and the opposite sign that is located (under the horizon) in the the *north* (figure 6.1).* In order to determine the houses the astrologer starts at the eastern horizon. The rising sign is called the *Ascendant (Asc)*; it plays a very important role in the interpretation of the horoscope. Opposite the Ascendant at the western horizon stands the *Descendant (Desc)*, the setting sign, that, according to them, is far less important. Right in between them, in the south, is the sign "in the middle of the heavens": the *Midheaven* or *Medium Caeli (MC)*, a sign that they consider only slightly less important in the horoscope than the Ascendant. The counterpart of the MC under the horizon is the *Imum Caeli (IC)* or the "lowest part of the heavens." These four together (Asc, MC, Desc, IC) form the basic corners of the horoscope and divide it in four sectors (figure 6.2).

These four pieces are now each trisected, creating twelve sectors called *houses.* They are numbered counterclockwise, starting from the Ascendant and indicated by Roman numerals.

Of course, Earth does not stand still; viewed from any one place the zodiac makes one complete turn per day. The rise of a sign lasts two hours on the average (approximately twenty-four hours for twelve signs) so that births in the same place, but with a difference of a few hours, show a completely different horoscope. Astrologers do not even have to wait that long: A difference of a few minutes can alter the horoscope, for instance when one person is born with the

---

*At least in our (northern) hemisphere. On the southern half of Earth's sphere it is just the other way around: There the highest point of the sky is in the north and the lowest (invisible) one in the south. In the following explanation "north" and "south" have to be exchanged if it concerns a horoscope in the southern hemisphere.

114   Making Sense of Astrology

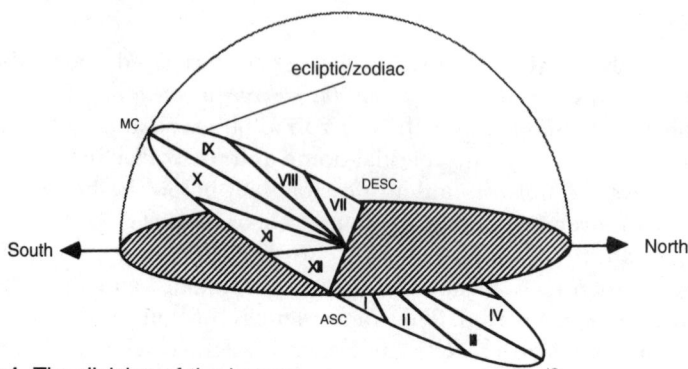

Figure 6.1. The division of the houses.

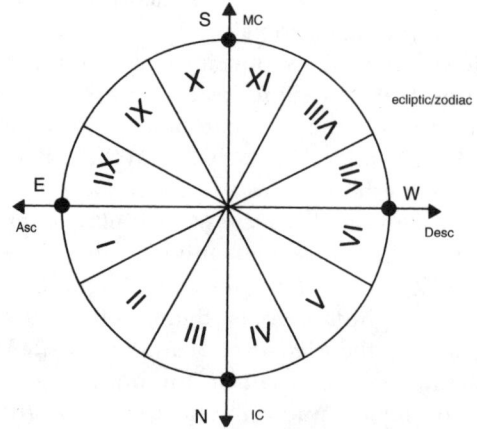

Figure 6.2. Orientation of the four cardinal points and the numbering of the houses.

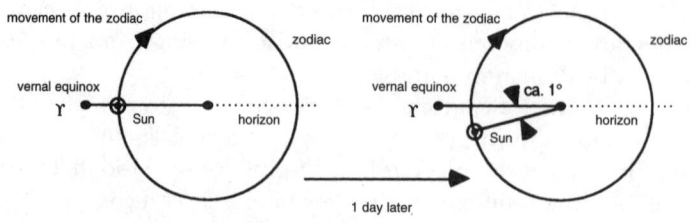

Figure 6.3. The (apparent) movement of the zodiac.

The Houses

sign of the Ascendant almost completely above the horizon, while at the next birth the beginning of the next sign starts to appear above the horizon.

How does the astrologer fit the new elements into the horoscope? As mentioned before, he has the date and time of birth at his disposal. From that the *sidereal time* is derived. This is a time-keeping system that is used by astronomers and which, in contrast to our normal time-keeping system, is not based on the movement of the Sun but on the movement of the vernal equinox. As mentioned in chapter 2, the vernal equinox has a daily movement that is somewhat faster than the Sun. Therefore a sidereal day is slightly shorter than a solar day; the difference amounts to about four minutes per day. The sidereal day is divided into twenty-four sidereal hours, so that a sidereal hour is slightly shorter than a normal hour. And just as the normal solar time gives an indication about the place of the Sun in the sky—at 12:00 o'clock noon the Sun is located due south—the sidereal time indicates the position of the vernal equinox. At 00:00h sidereal time the vernal equinox is in the south.

Solar time differs from place to place, and so does the sidereal time. When the Sun shines in Europe it is night in Japan, and when the vernal equinox stands high in the American sky, that is not the case in Australia. Because the sidereal time indicates the position of the vernal equinox with respect to the horizon, and the vernal equinox is by definition the start of the (tropical) zodiac, it follows right away that the sidereal time fixes the position of the zodiac with respect to the horizon. In actual practice sidereal time is expressed as the number of (sidereal) hours that have passed by since the last time the vernal equinox reached its highest point in the south (the *culmination*). Just as "it is four o'clock in the afternoon" means that four (solar) hours earlier it was noon, 3:00h sidereal time means that three sidereal hours ago (a little bit less than three normal hours) the vernal equinox—the beginning of the sign Aries—reached its highest point. From these data the position of the other signs can be derived.

The sidereal time and the normal solar time change with respect to each other in the course of one year. This will be explained by means of an example.

Let us follow the movement of the Sun through the first day of spring. On that day the Sun is located at the vernal equinox in the zodiac. At sunrise on that day the Sun and the vernal equinox rise at the horizon at the same time. One day later, however, the Sun has arrived at a point a little bit farther in the sky (approximately 1/365 of a circle, which, rounded off, is 1°). There now is a 1° difference between the position of the Sun and the vernal equinox (see figure 6.3). Therefore the vernal equinox rises the next day a little bit earlier than the Sun (about four minutes). As the days pass by the difference increases until it amounts to twenty-four (solar) hours. The Sun is then again at the vernal equinox: the beginning of spring of the following year.

In practice the calculation of the houses is reduced to determining the sidereal time for the moment and place of birth. This is done in a number of simple steps:

- With the aid of the date of birth the sidereal time for that day is determined *at midnight* (00:00h) or *at noon* (12:00h) at Greenwich.* This is the number of sidereal hours that went by at Greenwich since the last transit of the vernal equinox through the south. This value can either be calculated or looked up in tables.
- After that the sidereal time (still for Greenwich) is calculated for the time of birth itself.
- Finally the result is corrected for the *place of birth* (just think of the difference in time between America and Europe).

When the sidereal time is known the noncomputerized astrologer looks up the corresponding house divisions in a table of houses.† Because the part of the ecliptic that appears above the horizon also depends on the geographical latitude (refer to figure 2.4a, page 32) the latitude of the place of birth has to be taken into account. Which degree of the zodiac the start of each house agrees with, given a certain sidereal time, can be found in the tables.

For the mathematically inclined, an example of such a calculation is given in Intermezzo V.

The Astrological Meaning of the Houses

The houses play a more than important role in astrology, they enable the astrologer to project the characteristics of the planet onto a certain *sphere of life* of the subject of the horoscope.

The other elements (zodiac and planets) were cosmic and therefore of a somewhat general nature. From the places of the planets in the signs a rough draft can be made of someone's attitudes—according to the astrologers. In order to make this draft more personal, to give a better description of the person involved, the houses are considered in the interpretation. The characteristics, indicated by a planet in a sign, are transferred to the spheres of human life which are indicated by the house in which the planet is located.

As an example we can take a horoscope in which the planet Mercury is in the tenth house in the sign of Aries. Mercury, the planet of the intellect, in Aries, the tempestuous sign, indicates a sharp and militant mind. In which sphere of life will this be expressed in this particular case? The presence of Mercury in the tenth house, which determines profession and social position,

---

*The famous observatory at Greenwich, England, is the starting point for the location of places on Earth. Therefore the calculations are started at this point.

†"Traditional" astrology consists especially of searching in tables (looking at the sky is not done at all). Error-free copying used to be a very appreciated astrological skill. Too bad that the rise of the personal computer has put an end to this.

Table 6.1
The Meanings of the Astrological Houses

Number of the House	Some Characteristics
I	Personality, body type, the person, the ego
II	Financial means, possessions, economics, wages
III	Next of kin, brothers, sisters, neighbors
IV	Parents, the home, ancestors, real estate, agriculture
V	One's own children, education, love life
VI	Wage labor, (military) service, health
VII	The other, social relations, marriage, politics, partners, enemies
VIII	Death, burial and things connected with it, legacies, occultism (astrology!), and mysticism
IX	Spiritual life, religions, philosophy, long travels
X	Social status, profession, honor, fame
XI	Friends, social life
XII	Confinement, illness, seclusion, loneliness, secrets, crime

gives us some indications about this: It can be used to improve one's social status. In this way each planet in a house has a meaning. A survey of the meanings of the houses is to be found in table 6.1.

There is a more or less clear connection between the houses and the signs. House II, for instance, is oriented toward economics, like the sign of Taurus. House IX is directed toward spirituality, like the sign of Sagittarius. The eleventh house stands for, among other things, friendship, which is also a characteristic of the eleventh sign: Aquarius. The agreement between the other houses and the signs is perhaps less clear, but can still be distinguished after some searching. The relationship between the houses and the signs is very straightforward: The first house agrees with the sign of Aries, the second house with Taurus, and so on. The principle of the houses is partly copied from the signs, which, by the way, also explains why there are twelve houses.

The twelvefold character of the system of houses enables one, just as with the signs, to make divisions in groups of three and four. In this ways three groups of four houses are distinguished: the *cardinal houses* (I, IV, VII, X), the *succedent houses* (II, V, VIII, XI) and the *cadent houses* (III, VI, IX, XII). The houses in a group are presumed to have common characteristics.

Further, there exists a distinction between the houses under the horizon (I through VI) and those above the horizon (VII through XII). The last six represent social life, the first six symbolize private life. The more planets there are in the houses above the horizon, the more the subject of the horoscope would get outside the house and draw attention to himself (symbolic, isn't it?). A horoscope that contains any planets under the horizon then points toward a stay-at-home.

Houses: The Great Astrological Apple of Discord, or, Astrological Disagreement (Part III)

In previous chapters it was shown that a difference of opinion exists among astrologers about the uses of signs and planets. Within one definite astrological system, however, there is very little disagreement. Western astrologers use the tropical zodiac and work with the ten known astrological planets. Only a few dissident schools have different ideas.

With the houses, however, this is drastically different. If there is one astrological element that fires the emotions and heats up the passions the most during discussions among astrologers, it certainly is the house division. An astrological congress in Toronto in 1974, which was completely devoted to this problem, degenerated into a shouting match.

Some astrologers completely reject the use of the houses. This applies mostly to the adherents of the so-called cosmobiology, who followed the teachings of German astrologers Reinhold and Elsbeth Ebertin* (although some adherents of that school later tended toward the use of houses again). Kepler, the famous astrologer/astronomer, also rejected the houses because he thought that their application was based on superstition.

The overwhelming majority of astrologers, however, apply a certain house system. The great disagreement among them concerns the way in which the houses have to be calculated, or better said, in which way the local heavens are to be divided. This is an important astrological problem.

Now follows a brief survey of the most important systems, just to show how great the confusion is:

- The *"equal house"* system, especially used by astrologers in Great Britain, India, and, slightly less, the United States of America. It is the simplest division of the sky. Just start at the Ascendant and take exactly 30° for each house. The result for the horoscope of our friend A. S. Trologer is shown in figure 6.4a. In this system the mid-heaven (MC) is always 90° ahead of the Ascendant. No further calculations are needed to make the drawing: once the Ascendant is drawn, the rest follows automatically.
- The houses according to *Placidus* (named after Placidus de Titus, Italian Franciscan friar and astrologer, 1603–1668), which is used especially in Europe and the United States. It is very remarkable that the

---

*Elsbeth Ebertin, Reinhold's mother, claimed to have predicted Hitler's future.

The Houses

popularity of this system is due only to the easy availability of tables! A much-used handy table from the end of the last century (about 1880, when astrology experienced a revival) was drawn up according to Placidus, therefore its success. (For those interested, more explanation is provided in Intermezzo IV.) Figure 6.4b applies this system. Notice the difference from the equal house system.
- The system of *Campanus* (named for an Italian astrologer who died in 1296). Some astrologers consider this division the only correct one. As is shown in figure 6.4c, this gives yet other values for the houses.
- The division according to *Regiomontanus* (a German astronomer/astrologer, 1436–1476) also has its fervent adherents in the small world of astrology. The principles are exposed in Intermezzo VI, the corresponding representation is figure 6.4d.
- The system according to *Koch*, a German variant which originated in this century (figure 6.4e).
- the *topocentric* division. This one does not differ much from Placidus and experiences an increasing popularity among astrologers lately (figure 6.4f).

These are the five most-used house divisions. In the course of history there have been many more divisions that once knew great success or that were applied by just a small number of adherents, as may be made clear by the following list:

- Houses based on a division of the ecliptic:
  * the M-houses
  * the system according to Porphyry
  * the "Natural Graduation"
  * the equal house system
- Houses based on a division of the celestial equator:
  * the meridian system
  * the system according to Morin de Villefranche
  * the system according to Regiomontanus
- Houses based of the division of the Prime Vertical:
  * the system according to Campanus
- Houses based on the division of the horizon:
  * the system according to Zariel
  * the zenith system
- Houses based on the division of the semiarcs:
  * the system according to Alcabitius
  * the system according to Placidus
  * the system according to Koch
  * the topocentric system

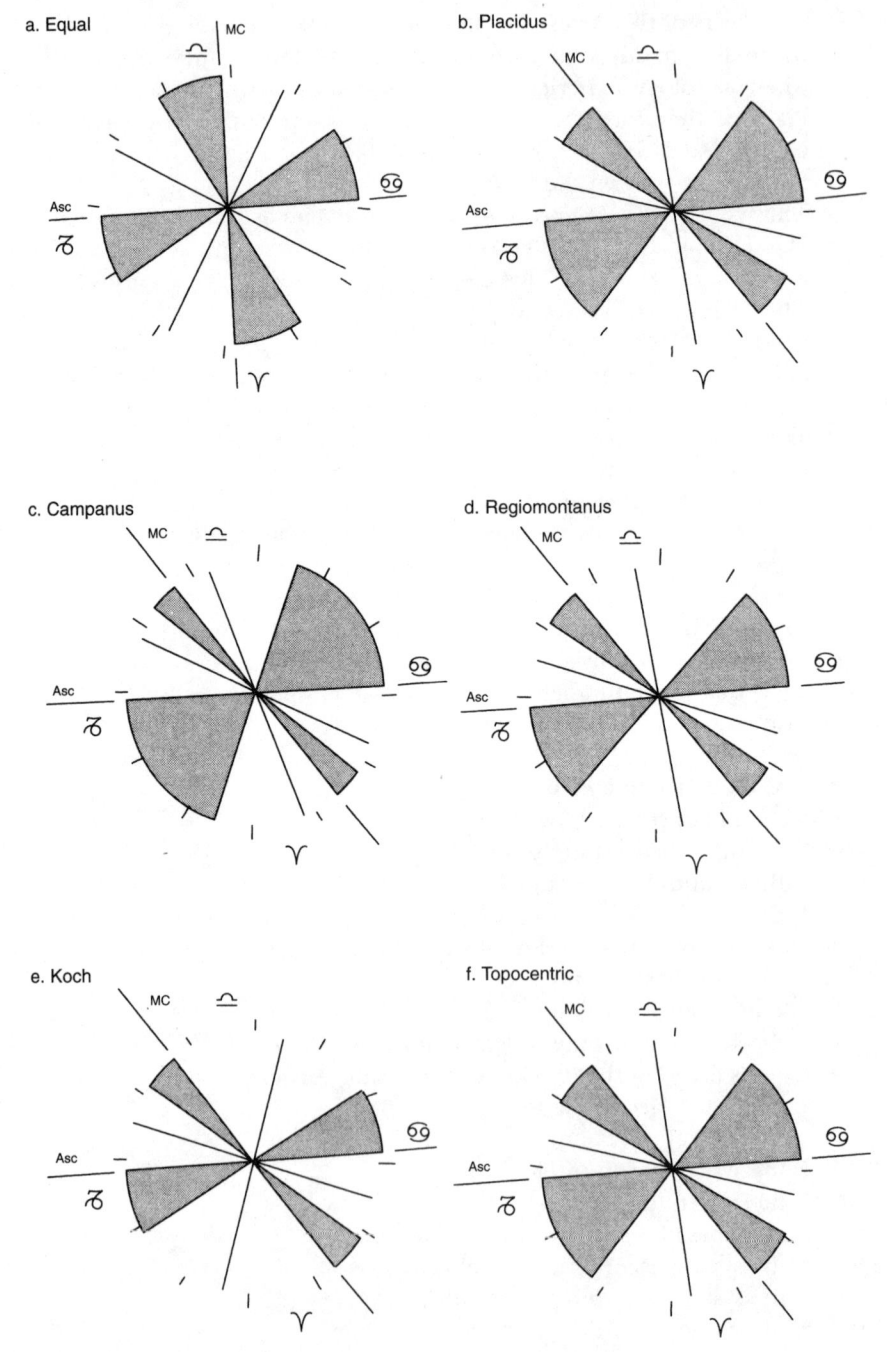

Figure 6.4. Some divisions of the houses.

The Houses 121

We hope that this listing is sufficient (it is claimed that in the course of the centuries more than fifty different systems have been proposed!) to give the reader an idea of the seriousness of the problem.

However, that's not all of it. Besides these systems, which all use twelve houses, divisions have been proposed with eight, ten, twenty-four, and even forty-eight houses! Most of the systems use twelve houses and count these counterclockwise, beginning at the Ascendant, but there are also systems that take another starting point (the MC for instance) or that count the other way around. The number of possible divisions certainly becomes exceptionally large in this light.

This review clearly shows the total confusion and disagreement in the astrological camp. And, exactly as with the signs and the planets we have to notice here again that not a single house system was introduced on the basis of experience or observation. In order to avoid repetition, we will not cite that argument again.

Houses: Astronomical Nonsense

It may seem superfluous, after this review of the confusion in the astrological kitchen itself, to come with outside criticism. However, there are a few small problems which have not come up for discussion yet and with which most of the systems have to wrestle. In order to make this clear, we will look at the houses from the astronomical point of view.

The Size of the Houses

The astrological meaning of the houses, as was mentioned earlier, has to be found in the projection of other astrological factors (the planets) on spheres of activities of humanity. It is reasonable to assume that the size of a house in a horoscope mirrors the importance of that sphere of life, because the chance of finding a planet there is dependent on the size of the house—which can vary considerably from system to system, from place to place, and from time to time.

The Differences According to the System

By definition the different house divisions yield different sizes of houses. One particular division, the equal house system, is not troubled by this handicap: All the houses are of equal size (30°). As soon as the Ascendant is known the rest can be determined without any problems. In the equal house system the Mid-

122   Making Sense of Astrology

heaven (MC) is always located 90° from the Ascendant, a place that agrees with the highest point of the ecliptic above the horizon at that moment.

The other systems, however, do not define the Midheaven as the bisection of the ecliptic above the horizon, but as the intersection of the ecliptic with the *central meridian*. This is the arc which runs from the north over the zenith (the highest point in the sky) to the south. As a result the MC is the most *southerly* point of the ecliptic (which is not necessarily the highest point). The two—most of the time unequal—sectors obtained in this way, Asc–MC and MC–Desc, are then subdivided in their turn into three houses each. The symmetry of these systems then makes it possible to project the houses thus obtained on that part of the zodiac that is below the horizon. Houses that are opposite each other are therefore of equal sizes.

What does this yield in the horoscope? In table 6.2 the corresponding houses have been calculated for those six house systems that are most often used for a geographical latitude of 52° north and a sidereal time of 12 noon. It is clear that the houses can differ considerably in size in one and the same system (compare, for instance Placidus XII with II) as well as between divisions (for instance, House XII in the equal house system and Placidus). Notice too, that the MC according to the equal house system differs almost 30° (a full sign) with the others.

If one may assume that the distribution of the planets over the zodiac is more or less even, then on the average more planets will be found in a house if its size is larger and that house will be more important in the interpretation of the horoscope. According to this reasoning, the Koch Houses II and IX should be three times as important (60.3° each) than Houses XI and V (each 20.8°), but according to Campanus this is not the case. (There it is, 25.8° versus 18.2°.) There are also large differences with respect to the part of the zodiac which they include: Just compare Houses II and III according to Koch with those according Campanus (see figure 6.5).

These differences of course must have their consequences for the interpretations of the horoscope, but astrologers obviously are not aware of that yet.

Differences from Place to Place

At the same sidereal time the sizes of the houses are also strongly dependent on the geographical latitude of the place for which they have to be calculated. This is shown for the division according to Regiomontanus in table 6.3 and figure 6.6. The figure clearly shows that with increasing latitude the houses deviate more and more from each other, not only with respect to their sizes but also with respect to their places in the zodiac. And yet, in the equal house system all houses are of equal size!

Do we really have to believe that the importance of certain spheres of life

Table 6.2
Comparison of Some House Systems

Latitude: 52° N, Sidereal time: 12 noon

The Starting Points of the Houses
(given as degrees in the ecliptic, 0 = 0° Aries, 30 = 0° Taurus and so on)

Division according to:

House	Equal	Placidus	Regiom.	Camp.	Koch	Topoc.
X(MC)	153.0	180.0	180.0	180.0	180.0	180.0
XI	183.0	207.5	205.5	197.9	201.0	207.2
XII	213.0	227.2	223.9	216.1	221.8	227.3
I(Asc)	243.0	243.0	243.0	243.0	243.0	243.0
II	273.0	277.1	271.2	289.3	266.7	277.8
III	303.0	321.2	317.2	334.2	299.7	321.3

The Sizes of the Houses in Degrees

Division according to:

House	Equal	Placidus	Regiom.	Camp.	Koch	Topoc.
X/IV	30	27.4	25.5	17.9	21.0	27.4
XI/V	30	19.8	18.4	18.2	20.8	19.9
XII/VI	30	15.8	19.1	26.9	21.2	15.7
I/VII	30	34.1	28.2	46.3	23.7	34.8
II/VIII	30	44.1	46.0	44.9	33.0	43.5
III/IX	30	38.8	42.8	25.8	60.3	38.7

differ so much when one is born at another latitude? In extreme cases (see the division at 89°, close to the North Pole) it is even possible that many houses together take up only a small part of the horoscope.

Differences in the Course of the Day

Seen from Earth the celestial dome rotates once around its axis during the course of one (sidereal) day. The ecliptic turns together with the celestial dome, as was discussed in chapter 2. Therefore the places of the houses in the zodiac change, just like their sizes. That evolution as a function of time was calculated for a place at 52° N and the results of these calculations are shown in table 6.4 and figure 6.7.

124   Making Sense of Astrology

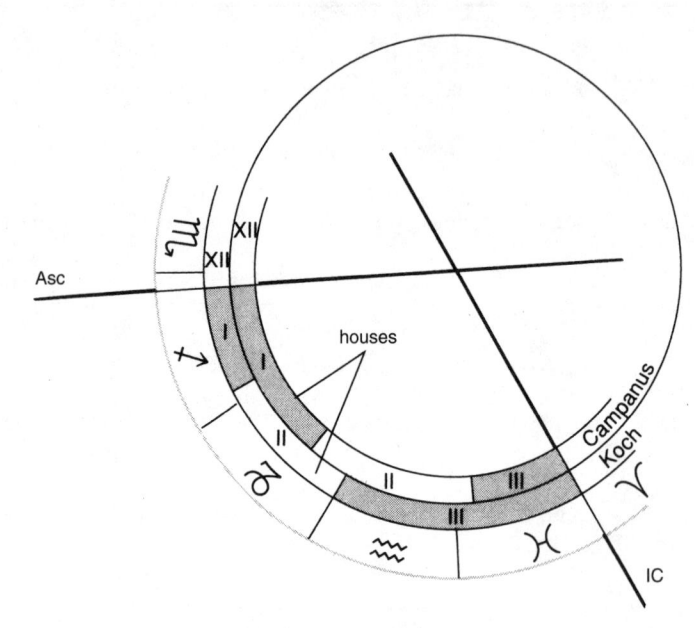

Figure 6.5. The differences in size between the houses in the systems of Koch and Campanus.

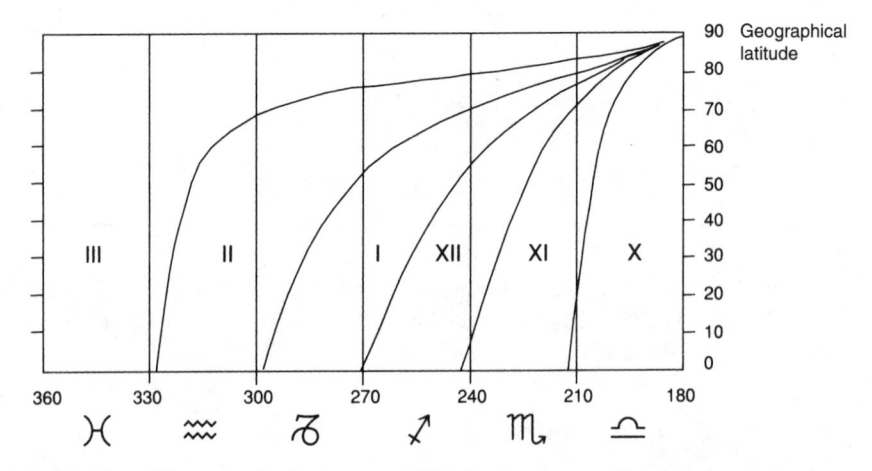

Figure 6.6. The differences in the system of Regiomontanus with varying geographical latitudes.

Table 6.3
Differences within the Same House System According to Geographical Latitude

Sidereal time: 12h   Division according to Regiomontanus
Values = Position for the beginning of each house in the zodiac

House	Geographical latitude (degrees North)					
	0	30	60	70	80	89
X (MC)	180.0	180.0	180.0	180.0	180.0	180.0
XI	212.2	208.8	203.7	200.4	194.6	182.3
XII	242.1	232.8	219.4	211.6	199.7	182.5
I (Asc)	270.0	257.1	235.4	222.5	203.9	182.5
II	297.9	286.7	260.9	240.6	210.1	182.6
III	327.8	323.7	312.0	296.4	236.3	182.7
IV	360.0	360.0	360.0	360.0	360.0	360.0

Size of the house (degrees)

| III/IX | 32.2 | 36.3 | 48.0 | 63.6 | 123.7 | 177.3 |

The Polar Problem

The idea of a division of the zodiac in houses arose in the Greco-Roman world (in the Mediterranean area), where the zodiac stands high in the sky. There was therefore no objection to developing a house division in which the Midheaven was determined as the intersection of the zodiac with the central meridian. In this region the resulting differences in the sizes of the houses are only minor. However, what in those times was considered to be logical and obvious produces serious problems when one moves out to more northerly (or southerly) regions.

We should not lose track of the fact that each system of houses is based on the Ascendant and the Descendant, the intersections of the ecliptic (zodiac) with the local horizon. Above and on the polar circles the ecliptic is much nearer to the horizon than in more temperate zones. Phenomena such as midsummer's night and the long arctic nights are a direct result of this. In astrology this leads to all kinds of strange and even absurd situations (for more detail see Intermezzo VI). Not only do the horoscopes for the arctic regions show extremely odd house divisions, but in some cases the definitions just do not work at all:

- On the Arctic and the Antarctic Circles the ecliptic coincides with the horizon at a certain time of the day. *Ascendant and Descendant then are everywhere—or nowhere—and houses cannot be defined.*

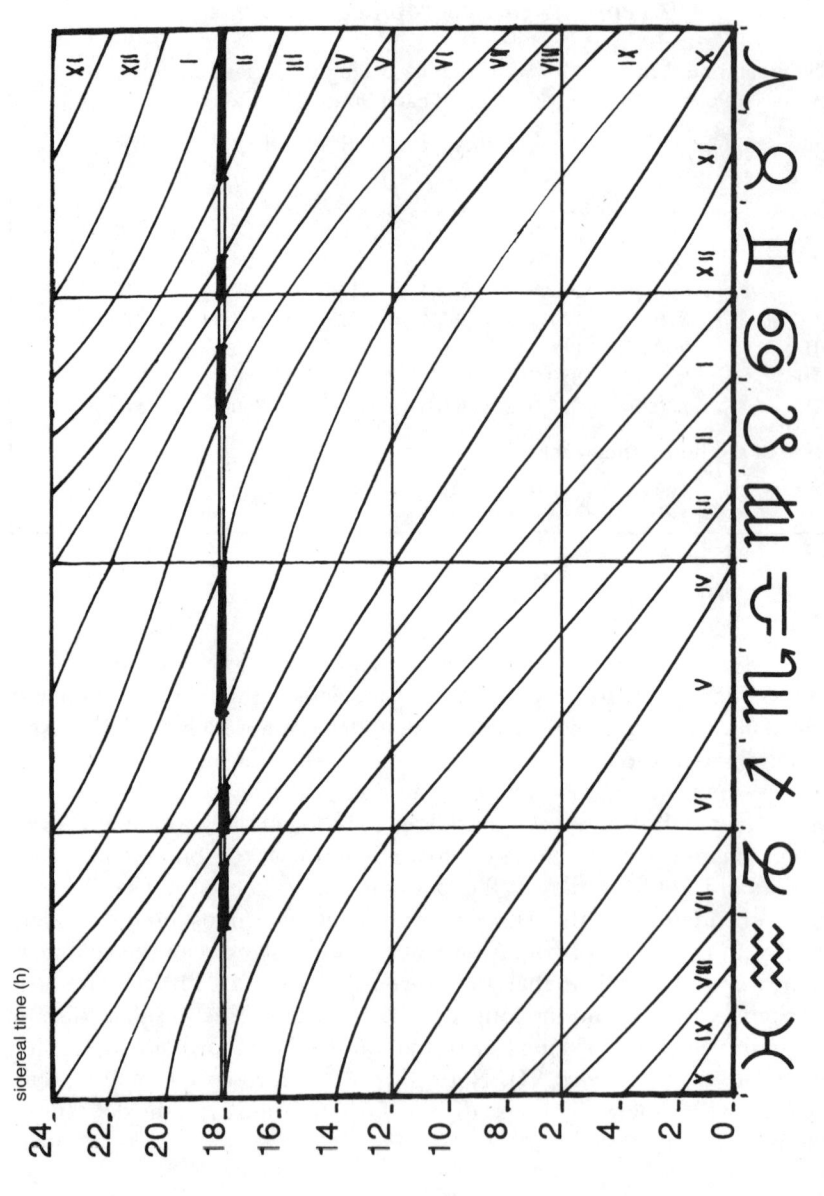

Figure 6.7. The houses as a function of sidereal time. A section according to sidereal time (see example at 18h) determines the size of the houses.

Table 6.4
Position of the Houses as a Function of Time

Latitude: 52° N — Division according to Regiomontanus

Sidereal Time		X	XI	XII	I	II	III
0h	0.0	42.8	88.8	117.0	136.1	154.5
2h	32.2	76.7	113.8	138.2	158.0	180.0
4h	62.1	104.3	136.1	159.0	180.0	205.5
6h	90.0	129.5	158.0	180.0	202.0	230.5
8h	117.9	154.5	180.0	201.0	223.9	255.7
10h	147.8	180.0	202.0	221.8	246.2	283.3
12h	180.0	205.5	223.9	243.9	271.2	317.2
14h	212.2	230.5	246.2	266.7	305.3	0.0
16h	242.1	255.7	271.2	299.7	0.0	42.8
18h	270.0	283.3	305.3	0.0	54.7	76.7
20h	297.9	317.2	0.0	60.3	88.8	104.3
22h	327.8	0.0	54.7	93.3	113.8	129.5

- Even when the ecliptic does not exactly coincide with the horizon, the situation becomes critical if these circles almost coincide. The smallest inaccuracy in the time of birth can lead to huge differences in the house division.
- Above the Arctic Circle there is a problem in determining the Midheaven. If Midheaven is defined as the southernmost point of the zodiac, then it is *under* the horizon part of the time. If, on the contrary, it is defined as the highest point of the zodiac, then it is to be sought at that time in the *north*.
- At places inside the (Ant)Arctic Circle a part of the zodiac never rises above the horizon. *Certain signs can never be Ascendant there.*
- At those same places there is a problem with the Ascendant. Where one normally expects the Ascendant—at the eastern horizon—the signs at a certain moment start to *set* instead of to rise. The Ascendant (if defined as the point at which the zodiac rises) "jumps," so to speak, to the other side of the heavens. The signs do rise there, but *in the reverse order.*
- On the North and South Poles not only do half of all the signs remain permanently below the horizon, but *not a single sign ever rises*. The height of the signs above the horizon does not change, so Ascendants and Descendants are out of the question. And by the Poles' very nature, there is no east or west.

- Finally (see also Intermezzo IV) some systems, such as that of Placidus, *cannot be used at all* inside the polar circles.

It should be clear that these kinds of anomalies are a result of the way in which the astrological system was thought out. In cultures in which astrology developed, nobody took the situation in the arctic regions into account.

Even today astrology hardly pays any attention to the polar or arctic problem. Should it not therefore be presumed that there is something unusual, astrologically speaking, with persons born in the northernmost (or southernmost) regions? Do their characters show systematic deviations because of the absence of certain signs in the Ascendant or because of the presence of very uneven houses?

According to some astrologers such considerations are only nit-picking (according to the principle "if you cannot solve a problem, deny that it is of any importance"). One astrologer even remarked in this connection: "Really, there are also no strawberries growing on the North Pole." That is correct and a discussion about agricultural problems in that region is certainly rather senseless. But children are born in regions above the Arctic Circle. One glance at the globe shows that there are indeed cities in that region (like Barrow, Alaska; Narvik and Hammerfest, Norway; Murmansk and Norilsk, Russia). If the astrologers want to claim any completeness for their "art," then they cannot avoid these problems. Or did the remark of the astrologer only mean that astrology is not interested in those people?

However one looks at it, the whole idea behind the division in houses makes no sense because it is based on analogy. Just as the zodiac had been divided into twelve parts, the ancient astrologers also wanted the local sky to be divided up. And because astrology is mainly involved with the planets, each division of the local sky had to be related to the zodiac, because the planets could only be found in that region. As long as one stays out of the Arctic and Antarctic Circles, there are relatively few problems, but as soon as one comes near or passes them insurmountable difficulties arise. That is not, as some astrologers proclaim because "the house system is a work of man" (and therefore not perfect), but because certain astronomical data (the angle the ecliptic makes with the celestial equator) are in the way. And nothing can be changed about that.

Houses and Statistics

In order to calculate the houses in a horoscope the correct time of birth as well as the place of birth have to be known. That exact time of birth in particular is a great obstacle for statistical research into the reality of the houses.

Compared with the work performed for the signs, little has been done on the level of the houses. Fortunately there is one great exception on that rule: the work of the French psychologist Michel Gauquelin. In his youth he was strongly interested in astrology and he devoted an important part of his life to the statistical testing of all kinds of astrological assertions.

Thus, among persons of a certain "vocation" he examined whether the planets occurred more often in the houses that are traditionally connected with the nature of the "vocation." For instance the fifth house stands for creativity (look at the connection with the fifth sign, Leo), so that it can be expected that among artists this house is more strongly occupied by planets. Unfortunately for the astrologers, it was evident after an examination of the birth data of 906 painters and 410 sculptors that this was not the case. If chance only had been involved in the case of the painters, then each planet would have been found 76 times in the fifth house; the actual result was 75. Among the sculptors the expectation on the basis of chance was 34, the actual result 32. Among other groups the actual results also agreed with what was to be expected according to chance. Among 884 priests it was shown that neither House IX (religion, church; compare this with the "spiritual" ninth sign Sagittarius), nor House XII (seclusion, confinement, therefore monastic life) deviated significantly from the average. Among 903 authors House II (communication, compare with Gemini) was also not overrepresented. Nor was this the case for House XII (confinement, in this case literally) for 623 criminals and for the Houses VII (illness) or VI (service) for physicians.

The occupation of the houses by the planets evidently does not agree with whatever the astrological tradition prescribes. Still this does not prevent the astrologers from continuing to follow that highly praised tradition uncritically. This enticed Geoffrey Dean and Arthur Mather, authors of *Recent Advances in Natal Astrology*, to write the following account:

> These results [of Gauquelin] were first published over 20 years ago, and repeatedly since then, but the conflict with tradition has been largely ignored by astrologers. This illustrates the absence of an objective approach and is apt comment about the credibility of astrologers in general.[1]

So much for the research into the validity of the classical interpretation of the houses. We can only add that now, more than forty years after the first publication of the results of Gauquelin, nothing much has changed.

But there is more. In the discussions about the validity of astrology there is an argument that returns every time, an astrological showhorse for the defense of astrology in general and the houses in particular. And strangely enough it comes from the research of Michel Gauquelin, the same man who refuted the classical house interpretation.

Michel Gauquelin's Statistical Discoveries

Gauquelin's position in the debate about astrology gave him the epithet of "astrologer despite himself." Astrologers compared him mockingly with someone who claims that the works of Shakespeare are not written by Shakespeare, but in fact by someone else who was also called Shakespeare and who accidentally also lived at the same time and in the same place as Shakespeare! This judgment, however, is not quite correct.

Gauquelin claimed to have found a clear connection between certain planetary positions and the human personality. Now there are, of course, many astrologers who also claim something like that. Gauquelin's thesis, however, did not refer to the classical astrological characteristics, but to correlations which he discovered in accurate and extensive statistics. Even critics of astrology had to admit that the standards of his research methods were high and that it was therefore necessary to examine his claims seriously.

What did Gauquelin claim exactly? During the analysis of the "state of the heavens" (comparable to a horoscope) at the birth of a large number of successful people he found that the locations of the planets were not divided randomly. Some planets were found more often in a certain part of the sky (comparable with an astrological house) than expected; the planet for which this was the case seemed to be connected with the area in which these persons had reached prominence.

Thus Gauquelin analyzed the planetary positions at the birth of 2,088 sports champions. He found 452 champions for whom Mars was located in two sectors which roughly coincide with the astrological Houses XII and IX,* while only 358 were expected. The probability that this difference of 94 births was due to chance amounted to roughly 1 out of 5 million according to Gauquelin!

He found something similar for the position of Saturn at the birth of 3,647 famous scientists (table 6.5 and figure 6.8). Here too, the probability of such a deviation was very small: 1 out of 300,000.

From these and other statistics Michel Gauquelin thought that he could conclude that in tracing the distribution of the planetary positions at the births of persons who reached the absolute top in a certain profession a systematic deviation was found. The deviation is such that a certain planet—Mars for athletes, Saturn for scientists, the Moon for authors, Jupiter for the military, etc.—is more often found just above the horizon or just past the central meridian (the astrological Midheaven), or to translate this in astrological terms: in Houses XII and IX according to Placidus.

The probability that the deviations from the expected values—consid-

---

*Gauquelin works with sectors instead of houses. These sectors agree roughly with the houses according to Placidus. The difference is practically negligible.

Table 6.5: Saturn at the Birth of Famous Scientists

Sector	House(*)	Found	Expected	Difference	%(**)
1	XII	355	299	56	119
2	XI	292	299	7	98
3	X	286	299	13	96
4	IX	349	299	50	117
5	VIII	284	299	15	95
6	VII	282	299	17	94
7	VI	318	309	9	103
8	V	290	309	19	94
9	IV	289	309	20	94
10	III	311	309	2	101
11	II	267	309	42	86
12	I	324	309	15	105
	Total:	3,647	3,648(***)		

(*) number of the house according to Placidus which approximately agrees with the sector of Gauquelin
(**) expected value: 100%
(***) not 3,647 due to rounding

Sources: M. Gauquelin: *Cosmic Influences on Human Behavior*, p. 53; M. & F. Gauquelin: *Birth and Planetary Data Gathered since 1949*, Series C, Vol. 1 (Profession—Heredity) p. 86.

ering all twelve sectors—may be attributed only to chance amounts to approximately 1 out 750 (calculated by the statistical chi-square test).

The probability that the observed difference between sectors 1 and 4 as a group with respect to the rest is due purely to chance amounts to approximately 1 out of 450,000 (chi-square test).

The probability of sectors 1 and 4 together according to the "critical ratio" (binomial distribution as theoretical distribution) amounts to approximately 1 out of 300,000. It is always the distribution according to the "critical ratio" which is mentioned in the text.

Naturally, this extraordinary result caused astonishment. The astrologers cried victory (they "forgot" Gauquelin's other results, all of which turned out to be unfavorable for astrology). But elsewhere the results also attracted attention. Some philosophers saw in it the Achilles' heel of the traditional-scientific worldview, the possible beginning of a scientific revolution. There was even talk about a "Gauquelinian paradigm."

Critically oriented scientists found the claims rather suspicious. Was the approach of Gauquelin sound? Specialized groups tried to repeat his

132　Making Sense of Astrology

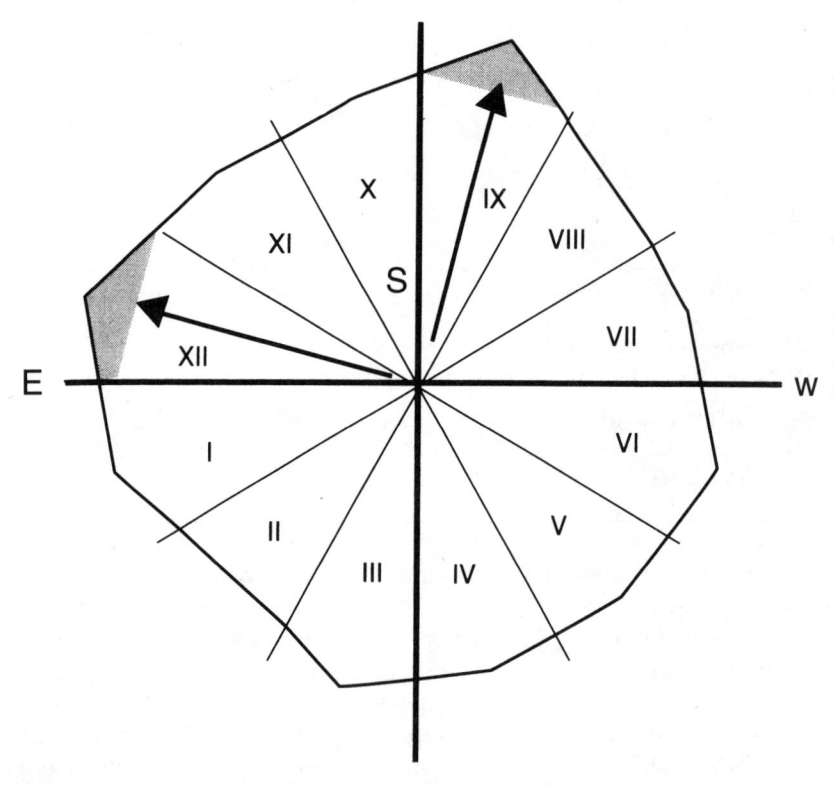

Figure 6.8. Michel Gauquelin: Saturn and 3,647 scientists. The arrows point to the observed deviations.

research. And they could count on the cooperation of Gauquelin. After all he seemed to desire nothing more than the scientific recognition of his work.

In the process of checking the work of Gauquelin the attention was focused on the "Mars Effect" for top athletes, because this was the most pronounced effect according to Gauquelin's results. (A more extensive report of this complicated but captivating controversy is described in Intermezzo VII.)

The first test was performed by the Belgian Comité Para,* together with Gauquelin. That test analyzed the position of Mars for 535 sports champions and found the same distribution as Gauquelin had discovered earlier. However, the Comité Para did not think that a Mars Effect had been shown. It was of the opinion that Gauquelin could not show that the distribution only occurred in a selected group of sportsmen. Maybe something like that appeared also in an arbitrary group of people who had been born in about the same places and at about the same times.

The American organization CSICOP† tried to answer that question. In a test of its own CSICOP compared the distribution between the sectors for Gauquelin's champions with a group of normal people with roughly the same places and dates of birth. Did the normal people also have Mars more often in sectors 1 and 4? That turned out not to be the case. The increased number in the two sectors were only to be found for top athletes.

However, CSICOP also performed a second experiment and the result this time was negative: No Mars Effect could be found. In this case they had worked exclusively with the data of American athletes. Gauquelin had used mainly Europeans in his statistics, and above that mostly Frenchmen. Gauquelin rejected the second experiment because he believed the American researchers were not strict enough in their selection of the champions.

According to Gauquelin the "planetary effect" is after all only found for the cream of the crop of a certain group: Only sports champions show the Mars Effect. It is absent for less famous athletes. (The same is true for the other correlations, such as for scientists and generals; only the best of the best appear to be subject to it.)

The question rises, which criterion has to be used for that "top," especially if different sports in different times have to be taken together? Is the top of bicycle-racing of 1910 comparable to that of 1960? Are the best players of basketball on the same level as the best in soccer? Are aviators or mountain-climbers also athletes? No wonder there were endless discussions between Gauquelin and those who wanted to duplicate his tests.

Another requirement of Gauquelin in order to find the "effect" was that the birth should have taken place completely naturally. Medical intervention

---

*Comité Belge pour l'Investigation Scientifique des Phénomènes Réputés Paranormaux (Belgian Committee for the Scientific Investigation of Reputed Paranormal Phenomena)
†Committee for the Scientific Investigation of Claims of the Paranormal

changes or moves the moment of birth and this made—according to Gauquelin—the proof of this effect disappear. In fact this means that the planetary correlations are completely absent for births after 1950, because from then on the number of medically induced births increases. For the youngest generation of champions no Mars Effect is found anymore. Of course that is particularly tiresome, because it makes independent tests of Gauquelin's theses more difficult year by year.

Finally the French organization *Comité Français pour l'Evaluation des Phénomènes Paranormaux* (CFEPP) organized a new test. This one was again limited to French champions, so that the results were more comparable with those of Gauquelin. In a sample of 1,066 athletes no Mars Effect was even in sight.

Of the four tests that were performed, the first two gave the same strange distributions as those of Gauquelin, while the next two did not. But for the first two tests, use was made of data which had mainly come from Gauquelin himself, while for the other tests the material was collected independently. Does this point to a bias of Gauquelin in selecting his sports champions?

This appears indeed to be the case. Afterward it came out that in the end Gauquelin did not include as "champions" about half of the athletes for whom he had collected data. Looking more carefully it appears that he did not use any clear-cut criteria. In his selection the presence of Mars in a key sector could have played a role, because the group of unused sportsmen does not show any Mars Effect at all.

Gauquelin himself proposed corrections in the composition of the sample for the CFEPP test. If these had been taken into account they would have promoted the Mars Effect systematically, in spite of the fact that the reasons Gauquelin put forward for the corrections were debatable.

Does that mean that Michel Gauquelin was an impostor? The fact that he allowed others to check his data seems to point to the honesty of his intentions. His enormous amount of work did not earn him any personal profit. He did indeed strive for recognition and in that he was not exactly modest. But even if he acted in good faith, he may still have unconsciously skewed his statistics. We can imagine that initially he did indeed discover something exceptional for a limited, extremely select group of champions (by accident, or due to an unclear demographical factor, for instance because a good number of the champions came from the same region). In order to confirm his results and to increase the significance he started to select more and more names. If the Mars Effect of the new group was disappointing, he may have thought that he had not taken the "best of the best" and adjusted his criteria until he obtained a selection that showed better results. Finally, by trial and error, he reached a group with an enormous significance, but on the basis of a selection that could no longer be called objective.

Such an "adjustment" of the data to confirm a discovery is certainly not unique in science. Now and then a researcher does things that are not allowed in order to make his results more convincing. This is not a disaster so long as sooner or later the results are confirmed by independent research. But for Gauquelin this was not the case.

Our conclusion? The Mars Effect has not been confirmed by independent tests based on independently collected data, and it looks as if Gauquelin, in collecting his data, helped his own effect along. Of the other "planetary effects," which were far less convincing, the same can be conjectured because they were discovered in the same way. Anyhow, for astrology all of this means very little. There are some good reasons why the "Gauquelin effect," even if it had existed, would never have proven that astrology holds.

In the first place the sectors in which the effects were found did not agree with the expected astrological houses. The preferred houses are numbers XII (sector 1) and IX (sector 4) and in astrology these houses are not exactly known to enhance one's social position. The twelfth house is preponderantly of a negative nature: confinement, retirement (the hell of the horoscope); the ninth house is more directed toward philosophical/religious occupations. These are the two houses in which the discovered relations would be expected the least of all. From an astrological point of view these relations should have had much stronger connections to the first (personality) and the tenth (social position) houses, but this is clearly not the case.

Maybe it sounds remarkable, but in not a single astrological handbook can it be found that famous sportsmen are born with Mars in House XII or IX, or that Jupiter in these houses promotes a military career. The simple fact that the only effect that just might have been a little bit real was not predicted by the astrologers makes the statement that Gauquelin showed that astrology was correct absurd. But in addition, the results of Gauquelin's researches date from the end of the 1950s and are commonly known in astrological circles. Many astrological books cite this "proof" triumphantly, but in not a single handbook has the meaning of the houses been adjusted to it. This is the best proof of the fossilized condition in which astrology finds itself.

But even if the effect had been real and all this had been included in the astrological theory, then it still would have served no purpose. The presumed relations could not have been useful for any practical purpose. For instance, look again at table 6.5. The first sector includes 19 percent more births than expected, the fourth sector 17 percent more. This averages to 18 percent, an important increase statistically speaking with respect to the numbers that are expected in these sectors. But in total there are 106 births more than expected in a total of 3,647; this is barely 2.9 percent. For the "Mars Effect" this is somewhat higher, namely 4.5 percent. This means that for the "Saturn Effect" more than 97 percent of the famous scientists were born as if only chance played a role; for only 3 percent of them could one have spoken of a real effect. The "Mars Effect"—if it had been confirmed—is also absent for 95 percent of the sports champions. The other 5 percent give a very clear statistical deviation (1 out of 5 million), but if in practice anything can be done with it is very doubtful.

Let us assume that we had wanted to apply the "Mars Effect" to the choice of profession of a young man who asked himself whether he could become a successful athlete. Even if it were certain that he had had a natural birth (according to Gauquelin a requirement for the effect), we would have been nowhere yet. There are namely two possibilities. His Mars is situated in one of the two "good" sectors—the case with 22 percent of the great sports champions but also with 17 percent of the common people. Or, his Mars is not located in a good sector, as for 78 percent of the champions and 83 percent of the "others." On such a basis nobody will take the risk of recommending to the young man to start a sports career.

The correlations could possibly have been considered as a proof of the astrological idea, namely that there is a statistical connection between planetary positions at birth and someone's social success (or certain characteristics necessary to reach this success). But for the reasons already mentioned this could hardly have been interpreted as a proof of the astrological system: The results were not predicted, are in contradiction with the astrological tradition, and are not included in that tradition. We can add to this that Gauquelin claimed an effect only for Mars, Jupiter, Saturn, and the Moon (Venus was a borderline case). He did not find anything for the other planets, just as his research in the other domains yielded nothing. But while quite a few astrologers wrongly consider that the Mars Effect or the Saturn Effect are a proof for astrology, they are as quiet as the grave about the negative results.

In connection with Gauquelin's work one sometimes points to his studies about "planetary heredity." In two studies, in 1961 and 1977, the data pointed to the existence of a correlation between the planetary positions at the births of the children and those of the parents. For instance, if one of the parents had Jupiter in sector 1, then a higher probability should exist that Jupiter would be found in the same sector for the child.

Checking these data with the computer, however, brought out a systematic error that artificially increased the size of the "effect." Disturbed by this, Gauquelin decided to repeat the test, collecting the data of 50,000 persons. For this group not a trace of astrological heredity was found. The reality of this idea can therefore be considered as very doubtful.

It is to Gauquelin's honor that he also published these—for him negative—results as a matter of fact. That happened in 1984, a quarter-century after he had triumphantly announced his discovery of the "planetary heredity." There are most likely very few examples of researchers who after that much effort willingly made themselves targets of criticism. Michel Gauquelin did not wait for the final judgment of his work, however; he committed suicide in 1991, more than forty years after he had started his research. There are rumors that he stated in his will that his collection of original data should be destroyed, but the truth of this could not be traced.

Astrological Consistency

A house system is considered essential by most astrologers because it offers the possibility of translating the figure of the horoscope into daily life, which, together with predictions, is evidently more important for most clients than the much praised character analysis and the gaining of insight into one's own personality. That, however, is no guarantee of its value. Concerning the zodiac and the planets it is still possible to reject the "dissident" opinions (at least for Western astrology) as marginal, but with respect to the houses this is impossible. The disagreement and the confusion are simply too large and widespread for that.

This situation is, for that matter, characteristic for all the "occult sciences": In the course of time the number of competing systems only increases. The problems pile up without ever being solved. This is only logical, because not a single objective method is used that can lead to a solution. And if a system or element disappears, it is not because it is experienced as wrong, but only because it fell into disuse.

Neither the disagreement in their own camp nor the lack of proof for the different systems prevented the astrologers from proclaiming Gauquelin's statistics as the ultimate proof of astrology. This approach is also typical for most of the adepts of the "occult sciences": A possible proof for a small part is immediately interpreted as a confirmation of the whole, and well-founded criticism is always disposed of as coming from ignorant and prejudiced critics.

Not only the results that turn out to be negative, but also the research methods that are used for proving the absence of the claim are rejected by the adherents as "not adapted to the problem." Most astrologers declare that applying statistics to astrology is not justified because it isolates one of the many facets which determine the complete horoscope. But (a well-defined part of) the work of Gauquelin, which is no more than an application of those abhorred and evil statistics, is welcomed. That these results, in addition, are contrary to astrological theory is then forgotten for the moment. It is not only the weather vanes that can adjust themselves to the prevailing winds.

Notes

1. G. Dean and A. Mather, *Recent Advances in Natal Astrology* (Cowes, England: Recent Advances, 1977).

Intermezzo IV

☿ ♆ ☉ ☊ ☋ ♂ ♀ ✶ □ △ ⚺ ☍

THE PRINCIPLES OF THE DIVISION OF THE HOUSES

All the house divisions are intended to divide the ecliptic. How exactly this is done depends on the properties considered to be essential for a good house system.

Three basic principles can be applied:

- direct division of the ecliptic;
- division of a circle in the sky other than the ecliptic, after which the points obtained are projected onto the ecliptic;
- division of the so-called semiarcs.

The Direct Division of the Ecliptic

This is the by far simplest method. Just start at the Ascendant and count 30° for each house (the equal house system). The Midheaven (MC) is always located at 90° from the Ascendant, in contrast to the other systems.

The Division of Another Circle

In the sky the following great circles—circles in which the observer stands at the center—can be discerned other than the ecliptic (see figure IV.1):

- the celestial equator;
- the central meridian, which runs from the north over the zenith to the south;
- the prime vertical, which runs from the east over the zenith to the west;
- the horizon.

Intermezzo IV: The Principles of the Division of the Houses 139

Except for the central meridian, which is not used in astrology, these circles are divided in twelve equal parts, always starting in the east. Thereafter the points so obtained are projected onto the ecliptic where they determine the starting points (the *cusps*) of the houses.

1. The division according to Campanus divides the prime vertical in twelve equal parts. The starting point is in the east, where equator, horizon, and prime vertical intersect. From this point the prime vertical is divided into pieces of 30° (see figure IV.2). These twelve points are then projected onto the ecliptic along great circles which start at the north point of the horizon. The intersections of these circles with the ecliptic determine the cusps of the houses.
2. The division according to Regiomontanus runs along the same lines: The difference from the previous system is that the celestial equator is divided instead of the prime vertical. The points obtained are projected from the northern horizon onto the ecliptic, just as for Campanus (see figure IV.3).
3. Other, less frequently applied, methods differ based on the circle that is divided or the poles from which the projections are drawn:

   - the meridian system divides the equator like Regiomontanus, but projects from the north celestial pole (in the neighborhood of which Polaris is located) instead of the north of the horizon;
   - according to Zariel (a pseudonym of a nineteenth-century English astrologer) the horizon is divided in twelve parts, after which the projection is done from the celestial pole;
   - the Zenith system starts in the same way as Zariel, but projects from the zenith.

These divisions have four common features:

- The Ascendant: All divisions start from the eastern horizon and, since they are symmetrical with respect to the central meridian, they also have in common
- the Descendant.
- The Midheaven (MC): The equator, horizon, and prime vertical go through the east-west axis, which automatically means that the points that are exactly halfway in between all lie on the central meridian. As the projection always takes place from a point that is also located on the central meridian (the arc north–northern celestial pole–zenith), an identical projection is obtained on the ecliptic. Because of the symmetry this is also true for
- the lowest part of the heavens, the Imum Caeli (IC).

140   Making Sense of Astrology

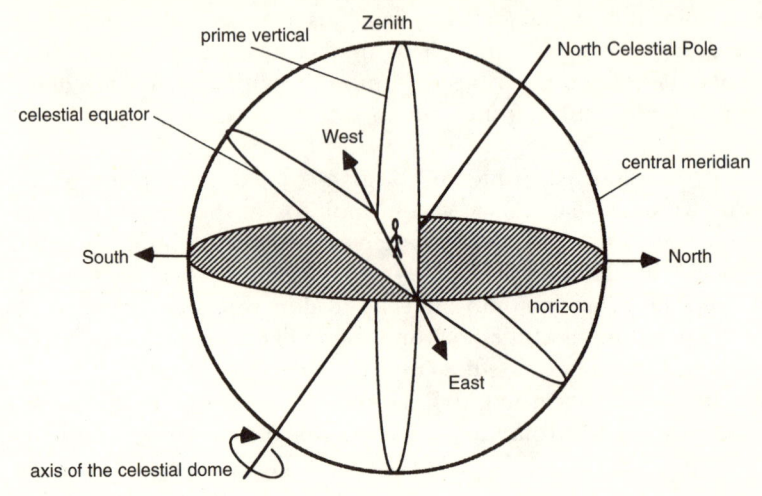

Figure IV.1. The Great Circles in the sky.

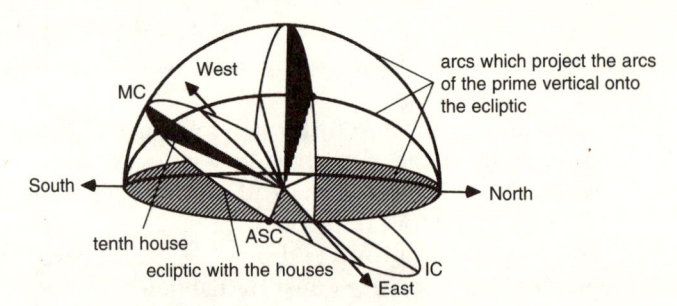

Figure IV.2. The division of the houses according to Campanus.

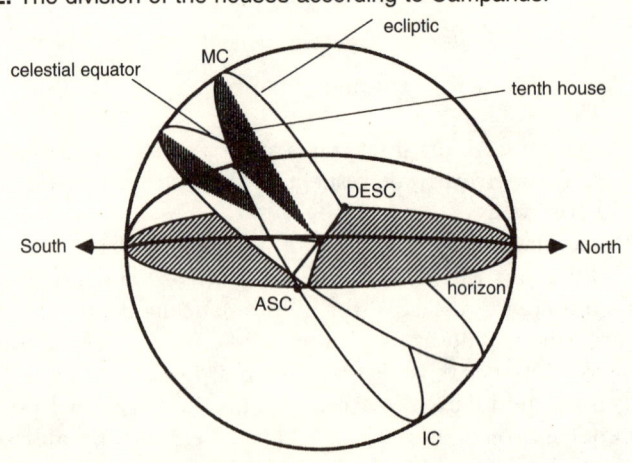

Figure IV.3. The division of the houses according to Regiomontanus.

Intermezzo IV: The Principles of the Division of the Houses

In addition there also exists a system proposed by the French astrologer Jean Baptiste Morin de Villefranche (1583–1656). In this system the equator is divided as for Regiomontanus, but the projection is done from the pole of the ecliptic. Therefore, this system yields different values for the MC and IC than Regiomontanus's, because the pole of the ecliptic is not always located on the central meridian.

The Division of the So-Called Semiarcs

A semiarc is a part of the arc along which a star travels during the day, and particularly that part that is located between the horizon and the central meridian. As figure IV.4 shows, that is only possible for stars and planets (or mathematical points on the celestial dome) that are sometimes above and sometimes below the horizon. For points that are always above the horizon, the so-called circumpolar points (circle 3), and points which are always below the horizon (circle 4) no semiarcs in this sense can be determined.

The four semiarcs that can be obtained can be used to determine houses. The choice of the semiarc gives rise to different systems.

1. For the—now only seldom used—system of Alcabitius (al-Kabisi, Spanish-Arabian astrologer of the tenth century) the semiarc that agrees with the Ascendant (that is, the semiarc of the point of intersection between the ecliptic and the horizon) is calculated. This semiarc is divided into three equal parts and the points so obtained are projected from the north celestial pole onto the ecliptic.
2. The much-used system of Placidus is more complex. In that case one tries to find exactly that point on the ecliptic that lies on the division of the semiarc. One can also draw the lines connecting the points that divide all semiarcs in three equal parts (see figure IV.5); the starting points of the houses according to Placidus are then the intersections of the ecliptic with these connecting lines. That requires rather tedious calculations, but since the rise of the microcomputers that is of course no problem anymore.
3. The division according to Koch starts from the semiarc which travels through the Midheaven. This semiarc is then divided into three pieces, after which the position of the Ascendant is calculated for the moment at which these divisions coincide with the horizon. These Ascendant positions (that is, points on the ecliptic) indicate the cusps of the houses.
4. The topocentric system. This house division dates from the 1960s and is considered by some astrologers as the ultimate solution of the house problem. However, it is not clear, as Dean and Mather remarked,

142 Making Sense of Astrology

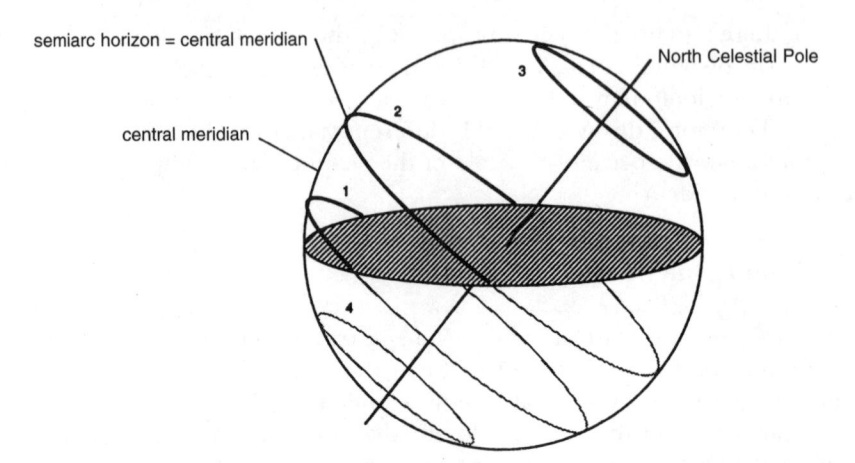

Figure IV.4. The division of the semiarcs.

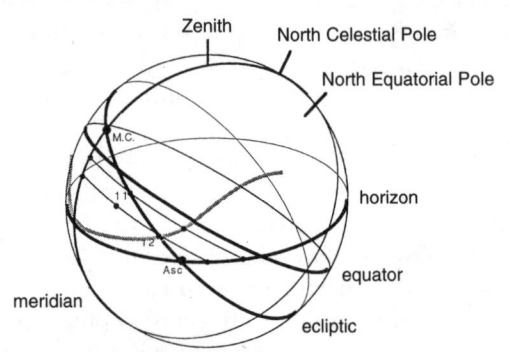

Figure IV.5. The division of the houses according to Placidus.

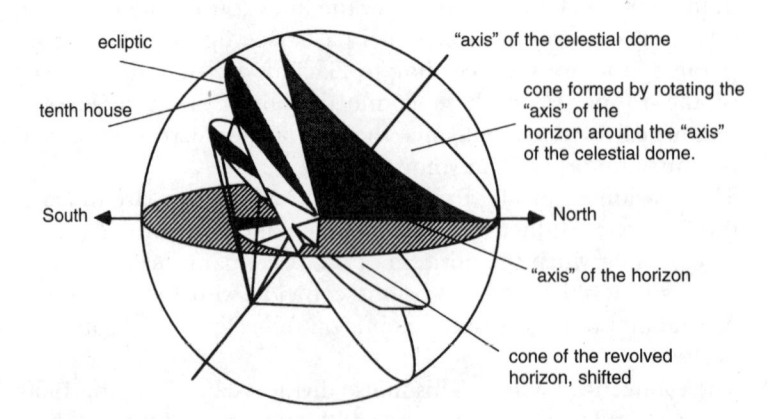

Figure IV.6. The topocentric division of the houses.

Intermezzo IV: The Principles of the Division of the Houses 143

whether the system is meaningful or simply an ingenious exercise in geometry. The system literally turns around the axis on which the celestial dome is seen to rotate from the place (*topos* means place) of observation. First the horizon is rotated around that axis, so that a cone is obtained (see figure IV.6). This cone is then divided into equal sectors: The intersections of these sectors with the ecliptic determine the houses.

The systems based on semiarcs have one shortcoming in common: None of them can be used at latitudes within the Arctic Circle. The connecting lines of, for instance, Placidus are too short to intersect the ecliptic everywhere so that not all houses can be fixed. The numerous adherents of this system clearly do not want a universal house system.

Perhaps in the meantime it has become clear that the geometrical ingenuity of the astrologers is directly proportional to the lack of proofs for the correctness of their inventions.

Intermezzo V

☿ ♆ ☽ ☊ ♅ ♂ ♇ ✶ □ ⚹ ☍

THE HOUSES IN THE HOROSCOPE OF A. S. TROLOGER

In Intermezzo III the birth data of our "test person" were given: born on January 10, 1950, at 8:00 A.M. in Brussels, Belgium. Based on this information the houses will be calculated.

Just as at the determination of the planetary positions, the time of birth has to be reduced to the equivalent universal time: we found that this amounted to 7h00 UT.

The next step is to determine the sidereal time for the moment of birth. The point of departure here is the sidereal time at Greenwich on January 10, 1950, at 0h00 UT. This is then corrected in two steps to the desired place and time of birth. From tables (or calculations) we find that the sidereal time in Greenwich at 0h00 UT on that day was equal to 7h15min47s.

The first correction is the transition from 0h00 UT to the real birth time of 7h00 UT. Here we have to take into account that one sidereal day of 24 hours is equal to 23 hours 56 minutes solar time: 1 solar hour therefore is equal to 24 hours/23 hours 56 min = 1.0028 sidereal hours. For the true time of birth the correction becomes 7h00 × 1.0028 = 7h01min10s. Therefore, on January 10, 1950, the sidereal time for Greenwich at 7h00 UT was 7h15min47s + 7h01min10s = 14h16min57s.

For the second correction, the difference in geographical longitude has to be taken into account. Brussels is 4.4° east of Greenwich. That is equivalent to 4.4 × 24/360 = 17min36s (360 degrees on the globe are equivalent to 24 sidereal hours).

Since Brussels is east of Greenwich, it is later there than in Greenwich; as a matter of fact the sun rises in Brussels about seventeen minutes earlier than in Greenwich. Therefore, this correction has to be added to the sidereal time

Intermezzo V: The Houses in the Horoscope of A. S. Trologer 145

already calculated: 14h16min57s + 17min36s = 14h34min33s. This is the sidereal time at the moment of birth.

Provided one has suitable tables or formulas handy, for the geographical latitude of 50.8° (Brussels is located at 50.8° north) at the above-mentioned sidereal time the following values for the houses (according to Placidus) can be found:

House X(MC):	11.1° Scorpio	IV(IC):	11.1° Taurus
XI:	1.7° Sagittarius	V:	1.7° Gemini
XII:	18.7° Sagittarius	VI:	18.7° Gemini
I(Asc):	6.2° Capricorn	VII(Desc):	6.2° Cancer
II:	25.3° Aquarius	VIII:	25.3° Leo
III:	11.4° Aries	IX:	11.4° Libra

(Because of the definition of the houses the positions in the right-hand column differ exactly six signs from those in the left-hand column; in actual practice we have to look up only six houses.)

These houses can now be drawn into the figure of the horoscope. (See figure V.1.)

In actual practice the calculation of the houses, not the determination of the planetary positions, is usually the first step in casting a horoscope. The reason is purely practical: It is preferable to draw the horoscope in such a way that the Ascendant–Descendant line is approximately horizontal. Whatever is located above that line stood above the horizon at the moment of birth, what lies under the line was then invisible. However, in order to be able to do this one first has to know which sign contains the Ascendant (which will be farthest to the left in the figure), and this is only known when the cusp of House I has been determined.

When the sign of the Ascendant is found, then the symbol for this sign is placed in one of the "boxes" of the zodiac on the horoscope form that is farthest to the left. The other signs are then filled out in the right order, after which the houses are drawn and the planets are added. Using this procedure the houses in different horoscopes will roughly be found in the same place in the figure, while the zodiac can have any orientation. The figure of the horoscope in that way represents a schematic view of the zodiac as seen from the place of birth looking toward the south.

However, there are also astrologers who work with fixed signs. For them Aries is always in the same place in the figure and the houses can be in any place whatsoever. This representation is confusing, however, because in this way in many cases figures are obtained in which all that is above the horizon is in the bottom half of the picture, or an Ascendant–Descendant line runs from top to bottom or vice versa.

A schematic that is even harder to read is that in which the boxes for the

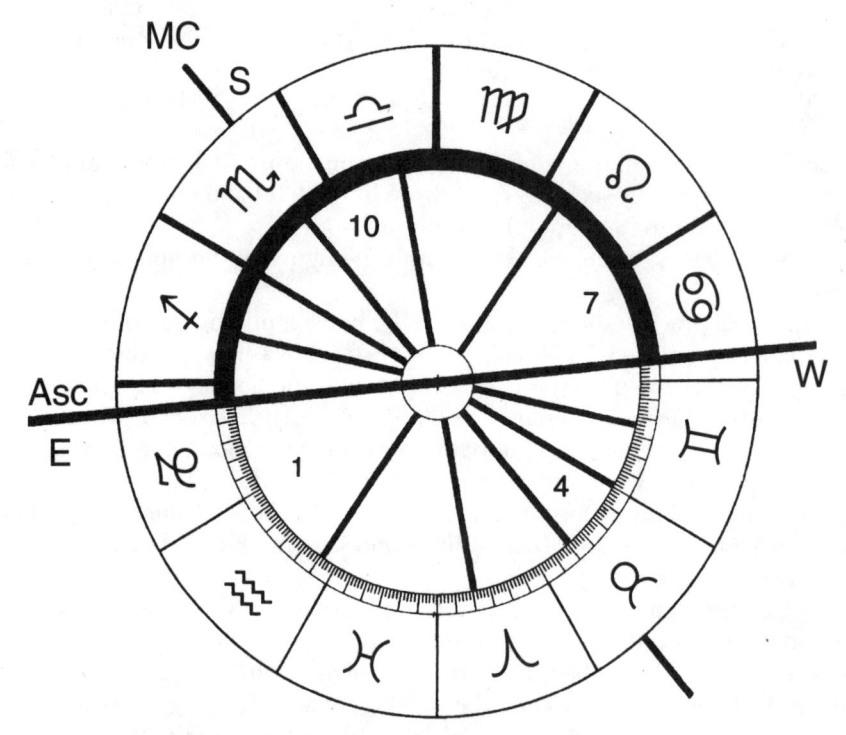

Figure V.1. The houses in the horoscope of A. S. Trologer.

Intermezzo V: The Houses in the Horoscope of A. S. Trologer

houses—all of them of equal size—are drawn in ahead of time, but where there is no place left for the sign. At the starting point of each house (the cusp) a note is made of the position of the cusp in the zodiac. The tiresome part of this is that the planets cannot be drawn in the zodiac. Their positions are simply noted in the box of the house in which they are located.

Intermezzo VI

☉ ♆ ☽ ☊ ☋ ☌ ⚺ ✳ □ △ ⚻ ☍

WEIRD HOUSE SITUATIONS IN ARCTIC HOROSCOPES

As has already been mentioned in chapter 6, as the latitude increases the differences in sizes between the houses becomes more and more noticeable. Some houses then can include only a few degrees, while others span more than one-fourth of the horoscope. (Refer to table 6.3, page 125.)

When the Arctic Circle is crossed the problems increase further. In order to make this clear we will follow the location of the ecliptic during the course of one day.

Let us assume that we are standing at about 50° north and that we are looking southward. We can then picture the celestial equator as a great circle, half of which is above and half of which is below the horizon, as depicted in figure 2.2 (page 26). The height at which the celestial equator is located above the horizon in the south depends on the geographical latitude of the observer: The closer we are to the geographical North Pole, the lower the celestial equator is located in the sky. On the (Earthly) equator it runs right through the zenith, but as we set out for regions farther and farther north, the celestial equator descends more and more toward the southern horizon. When we find ourselves on the North Pole, the celestial equator coincides with the horizon.

From a fixed place on Earth the position of the celestial equator is fixed in the sky. During the day it rotates, to be sure, but its height, the angle formed with the horizon, does not change.

However, astrology does not work with the celestial equator, but with the ecliptic, and the latter makes an angle of 23.5° with the celestial equator. (Refer to figure 2.3, page 30.) The ecliptic can be imagined as a great circle that is connected to the celestial equator at the vernal equinox, because of this, the ecliptic rotates along with the celestial equator. This rotation causes the *height* of the ecliptic in the sky to change during the course of a sidereal day.

Intermezzo VI: Weird House Situations in Arctic Horoscopes 149

At 0h sidereal time the vernal equinox is located due south (figure VI.1a). To the west of it the ecliptic is found *below* the celestial equator (the signs Pisces, Aquarius, and Capricorn); east of it, the ecliptic is *above* the celestial equator (the signs Aries, Taurus, and Gemini). The two intersections with the horizon, the Ascendant and the Descendant, are therefore not exactly in the east and the west: The Ascendant has shifted a little bit to the north, the Descendant somewhat to the south.

Now we let the celestial dome execute its daily movement from east to west. We see that in the south the ecliptic rises higher and higher until the apex is reached at 6h sidereal time (ST; figure VI.1b). At that time the ecliptic stands 23.5° above the celestial equator.

The celestial dome continues to rotate and we see now that the ecliptic descends in the south and at about 12h ST it will coincide there with the celestial equator (figure VI.1c). After that the part of the ecliptic that is located below the celestial equator goes through the south and reaches its lowest point at 18h ST. This point lies 23.5° *below* the equator (figure VI.1d). After this the ecliptic again ascends in the south until it coincides with the celestial equator at 0h ST.

During one day the ecliptic swings around the celestial equator, this is valid for *each* place on Earth (figure VI.2).

Expressed in numbers we obtain the following picture: at 50° north at 0h ST the ecliptic intersects the equator in the south. Its height amounts to 90° − 50° = 40°. At 6h ST the ecliptic reaches its highest point, 40° + 23.5° = 63.5° above the horizon. At 12h the height has decreased back to 40° again and at 18h ST the height is down to only 40° − 23.5° = 16.5°.

Now, what happens when we move northward? The celestial equator tilts more and more and in the south will be located closer and closer to the horizon. At 60° that height is only 90° − 60° = 30° and at 66.5° north, the Arctic Circle, only 90° − 66.5° = 23.5°. On this circle the angle the equator makes with the horizon has therefore the same value as the inclination of the ecliptic with respect to the equator. On the Arctic Circle we see the following happening during a sidereal day: at 0h ST the vernal equinox is in the south at a height of 23.5°. At 6h ST the ecliptic stands above the equator at a height of 23.5° + 23.5° = 47°. At 12h ST that height has shrunk back to 23.5°. And at 18h ST the ecliptic is located 23.5° *below* the equator, which itself stands at 23.5° *above* the horizon. This means that the ecliptic coincides with the horizon.

In short, *at the Arctic Circle once a day the ecliptic coincides with the horizon*. In that case there is no Ascendant or Descendant, neither a Midheaven nor an IC. And since these points determine the four cardinal points of the house systems, there are also no houses.

Of course, an astrologer can (and will) object that this is a purely theoretical case. This situation occurs only for an infinitely tiny moment, namely at *exactly* 18h00m00s. One second before or after this moment there are indeed

150 Making Sense of Astrology

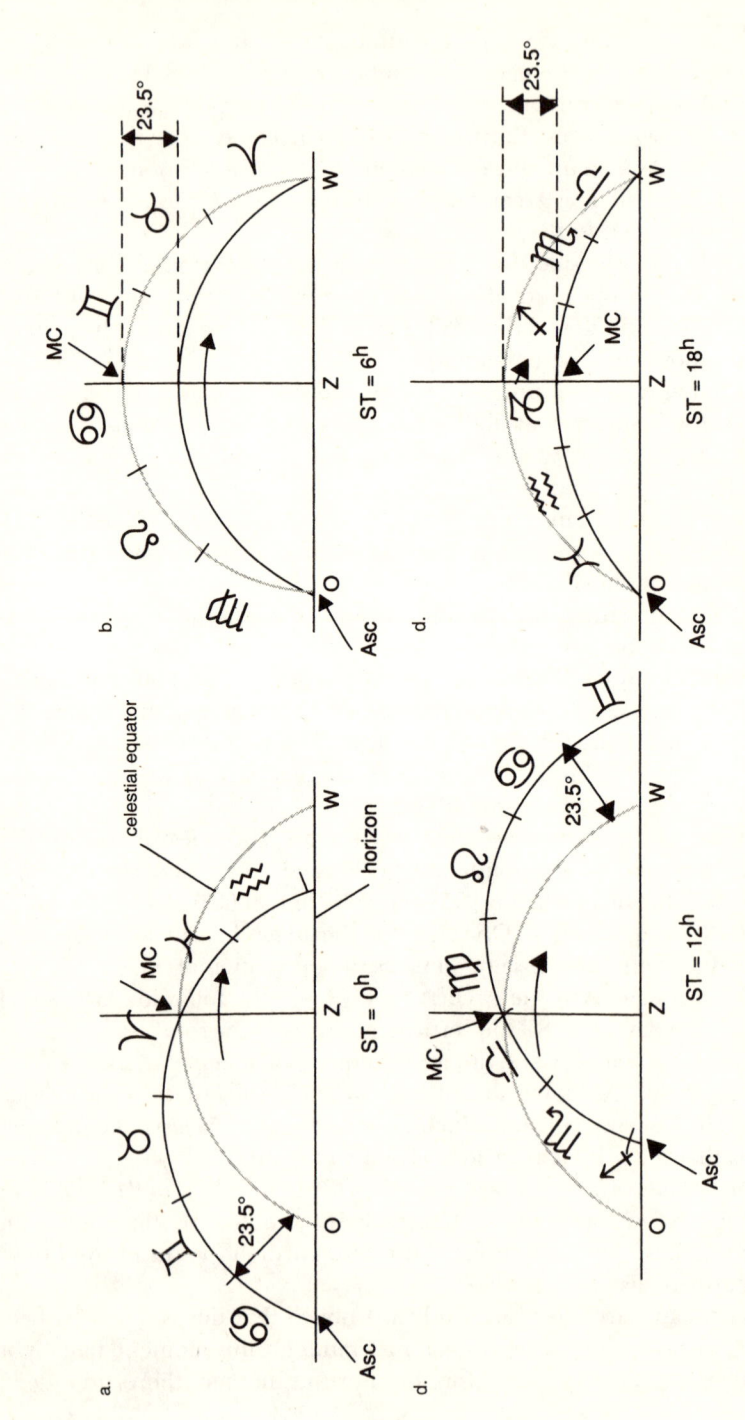

Figure VI.1. The movement of the ecliptic during a sidereal day from a fixed place on Earth.

Intermezzo VI: Weird House Situations in Arctic Horoscopes   151

Table VI.1: The Sizes of the Celestial Sectors at the Arctic Circle

Latitude 66.5° N
This table is valid for all the systems in which the MC is located on the central meridian (Regiomontanus, Campanus, Placidus, Koch, etc.). The sizes are expressed in degrees.

Sidereal Time (h)	Asc–MC	MC–Desc
0	132.5	47.5
2	115.6	64.4
4	101.6	78.4
6	90.0	90.0
8	78.4	101.6
10	64.4	115.6
12	47.5	132.5
14	29.9	150.1
15	21.7	158.3
16	14.1	165.9
17	6.9	173.1
17.5	3.4	176.6
18	—	—
19	173.1	6.9
20	165.9	14.1
22	150.1	29.9

houses. Strictly speaking this is correct, but it is better to ask the astrologer how large he thinks these houses might be. In table VI.1 the sizes of the sectors Asc–MC (the sum of Houses X, XI, and XII; note that the sector IC–Desc, the sum of Houses IV, V, and VI, is identical in size) and the sizes of the sectors MC–Desc for the Arctic Circle in the course of one day are shown. Notice how small the angle MC–Desc becomes from about 15h ST. At 17h ST, for instance, Asc and MC are only 7° apart. Three houses must fit into this space! That also means that for about three hours per day, all the children born at the Arctic Circle have in their horoscopes six houses that together span less than 20°. The remaining six houses have to fill up the other 340° (17/18 of the zodiac). The bizarre situation in which a horoscope contains a conjunction (two planets are close together in the zodiac; see chapter 7) that locates the planets respectively in the first and third house, or a square (two planets that are about 90° removed from each other) in the same house, can occur.

At 18h ST a sudden change takes place: at one minute before 18h ST Houses X, XI, XII, IV, V, and VI take up less than one-fourth of a degree, but two minutes later (at 18h01min) they fill up 359.75°! Is it then possible,

152 Making Sense of Astrology

taking into account the uncertainty in the exact time of birth for most people, to calculate a horoscope?

The absurdity has only just started. It will become worse when we cross the Arctic Circle and we are located, for instance, at 70° N. What will happen here between 0h and 24h ST?

At 0h ST the vernal equinox is located in the south and therefore located on the celestial equator. The latter is located at 90° − 70° = 20° above the horizon. At 6h ST this becomes 20° + 23.5° = 43.5°. At 12h ST the ecliptic coincides again with the equator; the height is again 20°. But at 18h ST the ecliptic stands 23.5° below the equator which itself stands only 20° above the horizon. This means 20° − 23.5° = −3.5° or 3.5° *below* the southern horizon! The visible part of the ecliptic, and therefore also of the zodiac, has to be found above the *northern* horizon! This swing is shown in figure VI.3 and table VI.2. As can be seen from figure VI.3, the house system changes its sequence at about 15.8h ST, so that between that moment and 20.2h ST the signs of the zodiac that are above the horizon can be found in the north. This sounds like an astrological curse.

Where can the Midheaven be located at 18h ST at 70° N? The answer depends on how Midheaven is defined. If it is presumed to be located in *the south* (like the values in the "South" column in table VI.2), then it is necessary to look for it *under* the horizon. What would a Greek astrologer have thought about that? If, on the other hand, the MC must per se be *above* the horizon, then it is located in *the north* (just add 180° to the numbers in the "South" column in table VI.2) . . . in exactly the opposite place in the heavens. Certainly a very serious astrological problem!

A similar remarkable behavior holds for the Ascendant. The name Ascendant is derived form the Latin *ascendere*, to rise. It is therefore the point of the zodiac that is rising above the horizon at the moment of birth. However, what do we see if we run through the values in the "East" column in table VI.2? ("East" indicates the place of the ecliptic which intersects with the eastern horizon.)

From 0h ST until about 15.8h ST the latitude of the eastern point of intersection increases. We see the signs Leo, Virgo, Libra, and Scorpio rise, in that order. This point is therefore clearly the Ascendant. But from the table it is also evident that the rise occurs more and more slowly until the end of Scorpio is reached. And then it happens: At 15.8h ST the sign of Scorpio starts to *set* instead of to rise. A setting Ascendant?! If by definition the Ascendant is the rising sign, then this has to mean that it is located diametrically opposite of Scorpio, therefore in the sign of Taurus. The Ascendant has suddenly jumped to the other side of the sky (as in figure VI.4). At 15.80h ST it is still located in Scorpio, but at 15.85h ST, a few minutes later, it stands suddenly in Taurus.

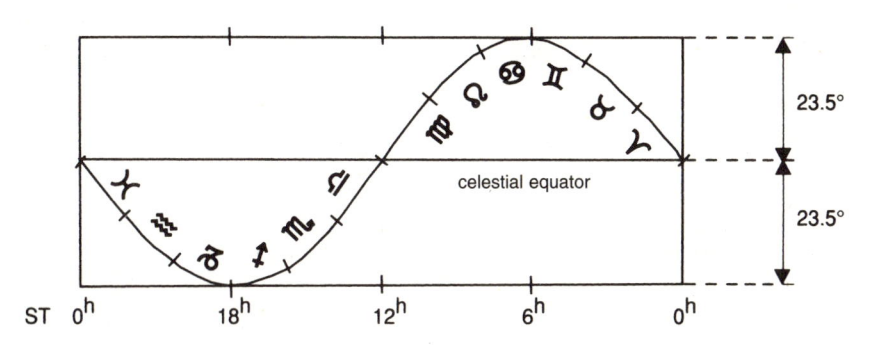

Intermezzo VI: Weird House Situations in Arctic Horoscopes 153

Figure VI.2. The fluctuations of the ecliptic and the zodiac around the celestial equator.

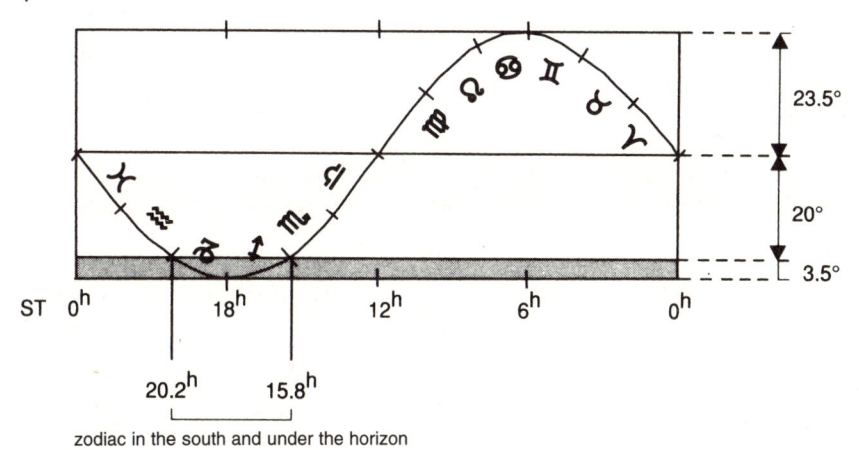

zodiac in the south and under the horizon

Figure VI.3. The position of the zodiac at 70° N: Sagittarius and Capricorn never come above the horizon.

Table VI.2: The Ecliptic at 70° N during One Sidereal Day

Values in degrees on the ecliptic. "East" equals the intersection of the ecliptic with the eastern horizon, "South" equals the intersection of the ecliptic with the southern meridian.

ST(h)	East	Sign	South	Sign	Size East–South
0	137.5	Leo	0.0	Aries	137.5
3	157.9	Virgo	47.5	Taurus	110.4
6	180.0	Libra	90.0	Cancer	90.0
9	202.1	Libra	132.5	Leo	69.9
12	222.5	Scorpio	180.0	Libra	42.5
14	233.8	Scorpio	212.2	Scorpio	21.6
14.5	236.0	Scorpio	219.9	Scorpio	16.1
15.0	237.8	Scorpio	227.5	Scorpio	10.4
15.5	239.03	Scorpio	234.85	Scorpio	4.18
15.6	239.16	Scorpio	236.31	Scorpio	2.85
15.7	239.24	Scorpio	237.77	Scorpio	1.47
15.75	239.26	Scorpio	238.49	Scorpio	0.77
15.80	239.27	Scorpio	239.21	Scorpio	0.06
15.85	239.27	Scorpio	239.94	Scorpio	– 0.67
15.90	239.24	Scorpio	240.66	Sagittarius	– 1.41
15.95	239.21	Scorpio	241.37	Sagittarius	– 2.17
16.0	239.15	Scorpio	242.09	Sagittarius	– 2.94
16.5	237.3	Scorpio	249.2	Sagittarius	– 11.9
17.0	231.3	Scorpio	256.2	Sagittarius	– 24.9
18.0	180.0	Libra	270.0	Capricorn	– 90.0
19.0	128.7	Leo	283.8	Capricorn	–155.1
19.5	122.7	Leo	290.8	Capricorn	–168.1
20.0	120.85	Leo	297.91	Capricorn	–177.06
20.05	120.80	Leo	298.63	Capricorn	–177.83
20.10	120.76	Leo	299.35	Capricorn	–178.59
20.15	120.74	Leo	300.07	Aquarius	–179.33
20.20	120.73	Leo	300.79	Aquarius	179.94
20.25	120.74	Leo	301.51	Aquarius	179.23
20.30	120.76	Leo	302.23	Aquarius	178.53
20.4	120.84	Leo	303.69	Aquarius	177.15
20.5	120.97	Leo	305.15	Aquarius	175.82
21	122.2	Leo	312.5	Aquarius	169.7
22	126.2	Leo	327.8	Aquarius	158.4
23	131.5	Leo	343.7	Pisces	147.8
24	137.5	Leo	360.0	Aries	137.5

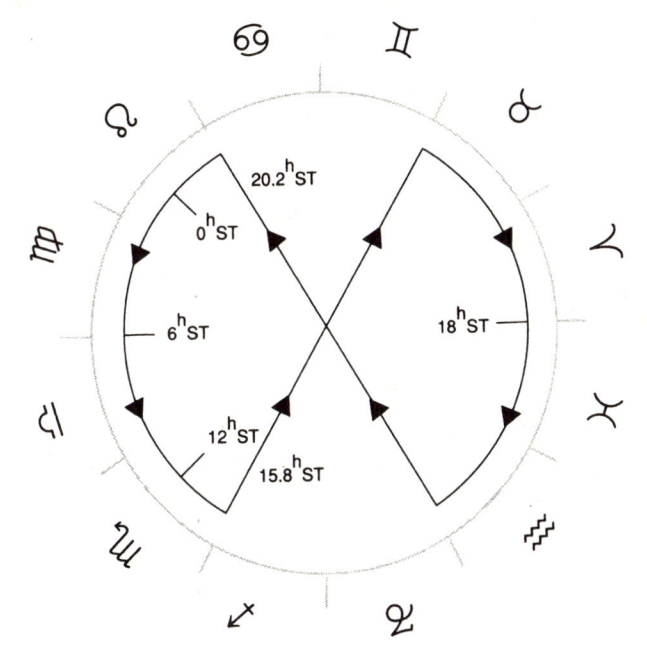

Intermezzo VI: *Weird House Situations in Arctic Horoscopes*   155

Figure VI.4. The course of the ascendant at 70° N.

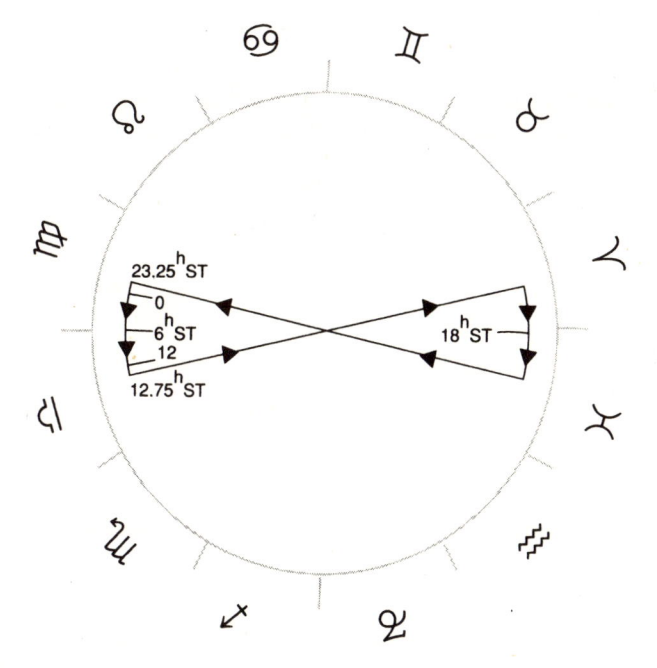

Figure VI.5. The course of the Ascendant at 85° N.

156 Making Sense of Astrology

Notice that the sequence of the houses in the zodiac changes at 15.80h
   from X(239.**21**°) – XI – XII – I(239.**27**°)
   to I(239.**27**°) – XII – XI – X(239.**94**°) and
   at 20.15h from I(120.**74**°) – XII(127.4°) – XI(299.7°) – X(300.**07**°)
   to X(300.**79**°) – XI(300.8°) – XII(120.3°) – I(120.**73**°).

And if all of this were not enough, it is evident that with this "new" Ascendant something else remarkable happens: *The zodiac rises in reverse order!* The normal sequence of the rising signs is Aries–Taurus, here this becomes Taurus–Aries–Pisces, etc. The course of the Ascendant is graphically represented in figure VI.4. From this figure it can also be deduced that the Ascendant remains much longer in the zone Leo–Scorpio than in the other signs: the 118° from Leo to Scorpio require 19.6h to run through, the 118° from Taurus to Aquarius (reverse order!) only 4.4h.

Figure VI.4 also makes another point clear yet: *Some signs never become Ascendant!* At 70° N (that is, for example, in northern Alaska or Siberia) the signs of Sagittarius and Capricorn *never* rise above the horizon, while the opposite signs, Gemini and Cancer, *always* remain above the horizon. In this area no people can be born who have Sagittarius, Capricorn, Gemini, or Cancer as the Ascendant. And since the astrologers claim that the Ascendant is one of the most important factors in a horoscope, the question can be asked if a noticeable number of people walk around in this region without the characteristics of the signs of these Ascendants.

At still higher latitudes all this becomes much worse yet: The parts of the horoscope that are forever below or above the horizon become larger and larger (see figure VI.5). In the extreme case, on the North Pole, an Ascendant is out of the question: The two intersections of the zodiac with the horizon remain for ever the same (the vernal and autumnal equinoxes) so that the signs Aries through Virgo are permanently above and the signs Libra through Pisces are permanently below the horizon. Not a single sign sets or rises. The idea of "Ascendant" has become meaningless. We also cannot look for signs on the eastern or the western horizon, because on the North Pole east and west do not exist.

Intermezzo VII

The Skeptics and the Mars Effect

As was discussed in chapter 6, in 1955 Michel Gauquelin announced that he had discovered correlations between planetary positions and the births of famous persons. From the many calculations he published since that time, it is evident that at the births of certain groups of eminent people some planets stood more often just above the horizon or were just past the south (MC). The strongest effect was found for the correlation between Mars and sports champions. If the heavens at birth were divided into twelve sectors, then Gauquelin found—in his most complete statistics—that Mars was present in sectors 1 or 4 in 22 percent of the cases, while according to chance only 17 percent (two sectors out of twelve) were expected.

In principle Gauquelin's work method was simple. He collected the places and dates of births of thousands of well-known (mostly French) sportsmen in reference works. (He mainly used two: *Dictionnaire encyclopédique des sports, des sportifs et des performances* and *L'athlège*.) He then asked for the hours of their births at the registry of their birthplaces and then calculated the corresponding planetary positions. Of course this work was not all that easy. For instance, the official time that had been used had to be taken into account. Wrong data had to be removed. In this way he arrived at the group of 2,088 champions.

Since that time Gauquelin's research has been studied diligently, dissected, criticized, and repeated by skeptics. It was clear that Gauquelin had found something extraordinary, if not "impossible." Earlier statistical "proofs" of astrology had been thrown into the wastebasket because of elementary errors, but the work of Gauquelin was of quite a different level. His methods appeared to be sound and his material was so extensive that a verdict could not be passed on it right away.

Convinced opponents of astrology, such as astronomer Paul Couderc and mathematician Jean Porte in France, acknowledged frankly that Gauquelin's statistics deserved further research. However, they pointed to the problem of the *expected* distribution (or the null hypothesis): The obtained distribution of Mars over the sectors of the heavens for sports champions must be compared with the distribution that could be expected theoretically if *no* planetary influences played a role. Gauquelin had originally supposed that Mars would be uniformly distributed over the sky, but this is not the case.

On the one hand the number of births during the day varies, and on the other hand Mars does not dwell in each sector of the sky for the same length of time. The orbit of the planet is not much larger than that of Earth (about 50 percent larger), which means that both planets can come quite near to each other. When that happens (about once every two years and two months) Mars moves relatively fast among the stars and is found in the opposite direction of the Sun (see chapter 4 and figure 4.2 [page 84]). This period of opposition however, when Mars shines during the whole night, is relatively short. Most of the time Mars is farther from Earth and, as can be deduced from figure 4.2, is nearer to the Sun in the sky as seen from Earth. On the average the angular distance of the planet from the Sun is less than 90° for three-quarters of the time, so Mars will be found in a horoscope much more often in the neighborhood of the Sun than far removed from it. Those demographic and astronomical effects can have an important influence on the distribution of Mars over the sectors.

Therefore Michel Gauquelin—together with his wife Françoise—corrected the expected values for each sector by multiplying them by two factors. One was a "demographic coefficient," based on the distribution of the births of the French population over the day, the other was an "astronomical coefficient" taking into account the distribution of the position of Mars.

The Comité Para Tests the Assertions

The first group of skeptics that answered the challenge to test the Mars effect was the Belgian Committee for the Scientific Investigation of Reputed Paranormal Phenomena (*Comité belge pour l'investigation scientifique des phénomènes réputés paranormaux* or, in short *Comité Para*). This committee was founded in 1948 to objectively test statements which appear to be contrary to scientific knowledge. The Belgian committee was the first organization of its kind, but it already had several tests on its account. (One set of tests involved locating missing persons through dowsing, passing a forked stick over the surface of a map so that the stick might dip suddenly when brought over the right spot, or by using a swinging pendulum over a map, where the movement of the

Intermezzo VII: The Skeptics and the Mars Effect

pendulum was interpreted as an indication of the missing person's location. The results were always negative.) After years of preparatory contacts with Gauquelin, the committee decided in the 1960s to proceed to do a test (in principle the committee only examines assertions which are introduced by someone).

Use was made of the birth data of 535 top champions born between 1872 and 1945. The test was applied to 430 Frenchmen who appeared in the *Dictionnaire encyclopédique des sports* together with 43 French and 62 Belgian soccer players (soccer players who had been chosen for a minimum number of international selections). The birth data were collected by Gauquelin (most of them had already been present in his database) and his Belgian supporter, Luc de Marré. The calculations were done by two members of the Comité Para, statistician Jean Dath and astronomer Jean Dommanget.

The distribution they found effectively agreed with what Gauquelin had discovered earlier: 119 sportsmen (roughly 22 percent) had Mars in sectors 1 or 4 at their births, where only 92 had been expected. The probability that this was due to chance was 1 out of 460 (Gauquelin, in his own work, obtained more spectacular probabilities, but he used a larger sample).

The data were collected in 1968, but it took until March 1975 for the Comité Para to make the results available and until 1976 for the committee to publish its point of view in its periodical *Nouvelles Brèves*.

The Comité Para admitted that the calculations for the distribution of the 535 sportsmen were correct and that the distribution did indeed deviate from the theoretical values. But these values (or rather, the formulas Gauquelin used to calculated them) were rejected as insufficiently accurate. The committee had drawn up a mathematical model in order to indicate which conditions such formulas had to satisfy and they refused to accept Gauquelin's assertions as long as he maintained his formulas.

Gauquelin saw little more in the committee's rejection than a loophole to deny the Mars Effect. He demanded that the committee propose its own formula, which did not happen. The attitude of the Comité Para came down to the opinion that the Mars Effect might be completely due to astronomical and demographic factors. Gauquelin thought that the committee had to show that itself, but the committee believed it was up to Gauquelin. Both parties stuck to their points of view.*

---

*In the discussion of this work it is often claimed that the Comité Para had indeed found the Mars Effect, but had refused to recognize this. This is a question of definitions. In many publications—and even in these pages—the deviation of the statistical distribution of the positions of Mars is called the "Mars Effect." In a more strict sense there can only be a "Mars Effect" if it can be shown that the *cause* of this deviation is due to Mars.

American Skeptics Try to Find a Way Out

In 1974 an article written by science journalist Lawrence E. Jerome opposing astrology and criticizing Gauquelin's discovery appeared in the American periodical *The Humanist*. Gauquelin replied and as an argument he quoted the confirmation of his results by the Comité Para. This lead to a discussion in *The Humanist*. The Comité Para also participated in this discussion; it repeated its point of view about the expected value. This discussion was one of the motives of the creation, in 1976, of the Committee for the Scientific Investigation of Claims of the Paranormal (CSICOP), with philosopher Paul Kurtz, then editor of *The Humanist*, as chairman.

As a reaction to Gauquelin's arguments, Marvin Zelen, later professor of statistics at Harvard University, suggested a control experiment to test the conjectures of the Comité Para. A sample of champions chosen at random from Gauquelin's statistics should be compared with a control group of "common mortals," born at about the same time in the same place. If about 22 percent of the control group also had Mars in the two "notorious" sectors, there would be no more question of a peculiar Mars Effect for sports champions. And in the case that the random sample scored still higher than the control group, the discussion about what statisticians call "the null hypothesis" (what to expect when no effect is present) would be settled. This test was performed by Zelen, Kurtz, and astronomer George Abell, three founding members of CSICOP.

Among a control group of 16,756 ordinary people, Mars was found in 16.4 percent of the cases in one of the two infamous sectors, but among the 303 top sportsmen (chosen from Gauquelin's list) this was the case for 22 percent. Roughly estimated, we might have expected 16.7 percent for the champions (two sectors out of twelve), but Gauquelin estimated that number, after astronomical and demographic corrections, to be 17.2 percent.

So the control experiment appeared to be to Gauquelin's advantage. But the three American researchers objected to the reliability of the sample of champions. In the first place Gauquelin had not chosen the data at random. Secondly, if the group of 303 top sportsmen was divided according to the region of birth, then only the group born in the region of Paris truly showed the "effect." This "remarkable conclusion" gave Kurtz, Zelen, and Abell reasons for distrust.

Gauquelin criticized this because the objections were stated after the test was performed: The reliability of an experiment should preferably be determined before the experiment is carried out (even more so in this instance, as the test was not intended to verify the distribution of the champions). On the other hand, Gauquelin stated that the subdivision of the sample of 303 champions could not be used to create doubts about the significance, since the significance can always be decreased by dividing an arbitrary group into smaller subgroups. By criticizing the sample splitting, Gauquelin and his defenders overlooked that Zelen used that argument to show that the sample was not chosen at random.

No Mars Effect among (Top?) American Athletes?

In two cases skeptics subjected Gauquelin's statistics to tests, in both instances with success for Gauquelin as well as a lot of controversy. To break the deadlock CSICOP decided to analyze a completely new sample, one not based on Gauquelin's research. As most of the sporting champions used by Gauquelin were French, the obvious choice for the Americans was to create their sample from U.S. champions.

Kurtz, Zelen, and Abell performed the test this time also, which is why the experiment is known as the KZA test. They selected 438 sports champions from a number of sports editions of *Who's Who*.

The result, published in 1979, was negative for the Mars Effect: Only in 13.5 percent of the cases did Mars appear to be located in the key sectors.

But this test also was criticized. According to Gauquelin far too few of the selected athletes belonged to the "best of the best of internationally known champions," so the Mars Effect should not apply to them. Kurtz maintained that his selection had been at least as rigorous as that of Gauquelin. If Gauquelin had been able to find 2,088 champions in France, why should he not be able to select only 403 champions in a much larger country in which sports and competition are so highly praised? A whole debate about selection criteria of sporting men arose. It was striking that Gauquelin rejected the whole selection of basketball players (basketball being nevertheless of a very high level in the United States), because his own results with basketball players had been—according to himself—"disappointing" for the Mars Effect. Indeed, among the thirty-four basketball players in Gauquelin's database only five (15 percent) had Mars in the "good" sectors.

When, the year after the KZA test, Gauquelin published new statistics of 432 European champions with (for him) favorable results, Kurtz and CSICOP reversed the roles. They claimed that Gauquelin had not even used the same criteria for his own test that he had required of them.

Gauquelin and his supporters now accused the skeptics of trying to "reason" the favorable results away. Dennis Rawlins, who cooperated in the test but who later thought that he had been unfairly treated by CSICOP, left the committee in anger. Rawlins had criticized the Zelen test, the one that had first been performed by CSICOP, as a totally superfluous and counterproductive confirmation of what any competent scientist could figure out on the back of an envelope. Rawlins saw the mere mention of the Zelen test as a serious stain on the otherwise excellent report of the second (KZA) test, for which Rawlins had done the astronomical calculations.

In a very colored account of the whole case in a pro-occult periodical, Rawlins went so far as to interpret the unwillingness to admit that he was perfectly right as a kind of cover-up. This is the origin of the story that the KZA test was fraudulent: Sporting people of lesser eminence were supposed to have been added systematically to the sample in order to reduce the score for the Mars Effect. In fact, CSICOP tried to include a large number of people in the test, but because of the strict American privacy laws it originally obtained data for only 128 persons, too low a number to obtain any significant results. In order to get enough data it was decided to ease the selection criteria, a decision that has never been denied nor kept a secret. It is a fact that the original sample of 128 champions "scored" better on the Mars Effect (namely 19 percent)—thus the accusation that "lesser gods" were consciously searched for and added to the sample in order to reduce the Mars Effect. This is a rather odd accusation, since it entails that researchers who a priori did not believe in Gauquelin's hypothesis used that hypothesis in selecting their data, in order to be able to reject it.

The Eminence Effect and the Nonpublished Athletes

The row about the KZA test was followed by a kind of truce between Gauquelin supporters and skeptics until 1987, when Suitbert Ertel, a German psychologist and strong supporter of Gauquelin, began to defend the hypotheses using the "Eminence Effect." Ertel derived statistics for all the athletes in Gauquelin's files; not only the 2,088 whose names Gauquelin had published, but also the control groups about whom he reported without mentioning their names and other data. When Ertel visited Gauquelin in Paris, he discovered that there were 1,495 other champions whose names had not been published, only 14.8 percent of whom had Mars in the key sectors. Ertel deduced from this that Gauquelin could *not* have been objective in his selection. In other words, *the position of Mars had sometimes played a role in his selection of the "good" champions.* For Ertel this was not a reason to doubt the Mars Effect. On the contrary, he tried to justify this bias using what he called the "Eminence Effect." Ertel established how often each champion was mentioned in several sports dictionaries; in other words: he applied a kind of citation analysis. He found that the Mars percentage went up with the number of citations. So each category of increasingly famous sporting men showed a stronger Mars Effect. For Ertel this appeared to be a strong confirmation of Gauquelin's hypothesis.

Intermezzo VII: The Skeptics and the Mars Effect

In 1991 the Dutch skeptics Carl Koppeschaar and Jan Willem Nienhuys put some question marks after the Eminence Effect. The whole effect relies on the foreign (non-French) champions in Gauquelin's files and on three reference works that Ertel had borrowed from Gauquelin. The Dutch researchers also emphasized that the Mars Effect was so minor that it would become questionable if it was shown that the selection of the champions had not been completely objective.

Ertel's argument also became questionable when he discovered that the Mars Effect slightly *diminished* at the "truly absolute top" of champions (Olympic champions scored less well than the winners of bronze medals). Apart from that he also found that famous scientists (who according to Gauquelin have Saturn in the key sectors) show a "reverse Eminence Effect": the Saturn Effect decreases with increasing fame. Because of these subtleties there are only a few people nowadays who take Ertel's Eminence Effect seriously.

A Decisive Test

Meanwhile people had been waiting for a long time for the results of a totally new test in France. This test found its origin in a discussion about Gauquelin in the French popular-scientific review *Science & Vie* in 1981. On this occasion the French skeptical organization *Comité Français pour l'Evaluation des Phénomènes Paranormaux* (CFEPP) agreed to carry out a new test.

The CFEPP tried to evade the problems of the previous tests. In order to avoid criticism the research protocol was published ahead of time in *Science & Vie*. The work would be done exclusively on French sports champions born before 1950 and be based on the same reference works which Gauquelin had used earlier. The sports disciplines and the level of champions were fixed in the protocol. The level ought to be the highest possible, but for statistical reasons the final list had to contain at least 1,000 names. First a list of 1,439 champions was created fitting the criteria in the protocol. Only after that was done could the birth data be asked for at the registries. Evidently in many cases these data were absent or could not be found, and, as a matter of fact, false data had to be removed. Yet in the period 1988–1990 the CFEPP was able to collect data from 1,066 athletes. It was only then that the CFEPP could begin to calculate the position of Mars for each of the births.

The protocol called for a kind of Zelen test to make a control group, but that turned out to be impractical. An alternative method was proposed, namely creating a fictitious group by shuffling the data of the champions many times. Such a method had been used already by Gauquelin himself. From the sample of 1,066 champions, a random mixing of the dates and times of births was made eighty times, resulting in a group of 85,280 fictitious births.

164 Making Sense of Astrology

The work had proceeded rather slowly and was sometimes halted for several years because of personal circumstances which struck the pace-makers of this research. Only in September 1994, twelve years after the publication of the protocol, did the first results become public: Of the 1,066 collected champions, 200 (18.76 percent) had Mars in the well known sectors, and in the fictitious control group this was 18.2 percent.* The final results became available in 1996 after the Dutch mathematician Jan Willem Nienhuys had reviewed the whole study (the final figures turned out to be 1,120 champions with 209 [18.66 percent] in Mars sectors, with a control group yielding 17.7 percent) with the same basic result. As the French committee concluded, "The results are clear and do not show the least evidence for the 'Mars Effect.' "[1]

In this case the differences between the selection of the CFEPP and that by Gauquelin and in particular the comments he gave to the CFEPP list, are interesting. All the work, including collecting the material, was done by the CFEPP, without Gauquelin, but Gauquelin was permitted to suggest modifications to the list before the statistical study was finished. In 1990 the committee sent Gauquelin the list of selected champions. He suggested some corrections, additions, and deletions to this list. The CFEPP was surprised with the suggestions (and therefore did not follow them) since most of them were favorable to the Mars Effect and seemed to demonstrate some bias in Gauquelin's selective process. After Gauquelin's death Nienhuys compared his files of sports people, published and unpublished, with the CFEPP sample. He found 131 champions for whom the birth dates and times were different. Gauquelin had reported only 39 deviations to the CFEPP, among them 20 of which were in his favor. He did not mention even one of the 16 deviations that were disadvantageous for the Mars Effect. In addition he proposed adding 105 champions to the list, 49 of whom (almost half) had Mars in a "good" sector. Sixteen of the names, however, did not have Mars in a "good" sector.

There were other quite remarkable deviations. The CFEPP had decided to exclude French champions who where born in foreign countries and French overseas possessions from the sample, since it wanted to determine the birth data unambiguously. Gauquelin wanted to include champions born in French colonies and overseas possessions. Was it purely accidental that, in Gauquelin's research, 42 percent of that group showed a Mars Effect?

The explanations that Gauquelin put forward for these changes were disputable. For instance he wanted to reduce the number of rugby players drastically because rugby was only a regional sport. On the other hand the top players of Basque pelote (a ball game) had to be included according to him.

---

*The results were:

Sector	1	2	3	4	5	6	7	8	9	10	11	12
Number of births	112	94	97	88	81	68	88	91	96	91	76	84

Intermezzo VII: The Skeptics and the Mars Effect

Now, France is an important rugby country, but that sport is mainly popular in the south, not in Paris. On the other hand, in France Basque pelote is, apart from the Basque region, played practically only in Paris. For Gauquelin this was no reason to label this typically Basque sport as a regional sport. However, while none of the debated rugby players had Mars in the key sectors, 30 percent of the Basque pelote players did. And those are only the most striking examples of what seems to be a highly subjective attitude.

In the course of discussions with Ertel, Jan Willem Nienhuys uncovered evidence that Gauquelin had been throwing data away. More specifically, the sports dictionaries are often not very accurate, and one often finds contradictions between what such sources say and what the registries report. It seems plausible that Gauquelin's judgment about when to trust data was influenced by his knowledge about the Mars sector. The evidence is that in data collected by Gauquelin himself, the Mars percentage is consistently high, about 30 percent, among champions whose data might induce feelings of doubt. In a corresponding group collected by the CFEPP but not found by Gauquelin the Mars percentage is absurdly low: 6 percent. As Nienhuys concluded, "Michel Gauquelin apparently could not keep exploration distinct from testing in his own research, and displayed a strong bias in a public and crucial test. I cannot see how anyone can continue to maintain that his data are worthy of serious attention."

Maybe the last word about Gauquelin has not been said. Today, Ertel and other supporters of Gauquelin still try to demonstrate the reality of the Mars Effect. They maintain that the effect can still be found in the CFEPP statistics if one replaces the twelve sectors by an alternate subdivision of the sky (with 36 sectors). That looks like saying that the results of a football game would be different if the lines on the football field were traced in a different way. But by trying this they seem to forget the fundamental objection to Gauquelin's work: The way in which he collected his data is too subjective to prove the reality of a planetary effect.

Note

1. Comité Français pour l'Etude de Phénomènes Paranormaux (CFEPP), "L'Effet Mars est-il réel?" *Science & Vie* (October 1982): 44. The CFEPP remarked in its report that there was a higher frequency of births of athletes with Venus in key sectors than Mars: 207 as opposed to 200. It added that this does not signify an undue Venusian influence but that it was amusing to note it!

7

THE ASPECTS

The last technical element that we will discuss is the aspects. When planetary positions, houses, and aspects are calculated, then all the elements of the horoscope are present and the figure can be drawn up in total. Just try to see it through, and the last tip of the astrological veil will be lifted.

Aspects are the *angular separations* between the planets, the Ascendant, and the Midheaven in the horoscope. The aspects are therefore partly of a cosmic and partly of a local nature. The aspects of the planets with respect to each other are cosmic, those of the planets with respect to the Ascendant and the Midheaven are local. An aspect of Mars with Jupiter is cosmic, an aspect of the Sun with the Midheaven is local.

The Geometrical Aspects

Which angular separations will be considered for the formation of an aspect? This question can be split into two parts: How are the angular separations determined and how large (in degrees) does the angle have to be in order to obtain the status of an astrological aspect?

In contrast to what an outsider might suspect, the angular separations that are used in astrology are not the real angular separations in the sky between the planets themselves or between them and the Ascendant and the Midheaven; instead they are the angular separations as they are seen on the figure of the horoscope. The difference between these two is due to the fact that the planets in the horoscope are drawn as *projections* on the ecliptic. Figure 7.1 makes the difference clear. Since the drawing of the planetary posi-

Table 7.1: The Classical Aspects (Major Aspects)

Difference in Angle on the Ecliptic	Aspect Name	Symbol	Astrological Influence
0°	Conjunction	☌	Variable*
60°	Sextile	✶	Favorable
90°	Square, quadratic	□	Unfavorable
120°	Triangle, trine	△	Favorable
180°	Opposition	☍	Unfavorable

*Depends on the planets forming the aspects.

tions in the zodiac was already done by means of that projection on the ecliptic (see also Intermezzo III and figure III.1, page 110), these data are already at hand when the aspects have to be determined.

On the basis of this projection the angular separations are then calculated between each element (planet, Ascendant, Midheaven) and every other element. The size of the angular separation determines whether or not one can speak of an astrological aspect. The astrologers assume that only a limited number of angular separations have to be taken into account. Which angles these are together with their exotic names such as quincunx, biquintile, or sesquiquadrate, is listed in table 7.1 and shown in figure 7.2.

The basic idea of the system of the aspects is the division of the circle in equal parts or, as it is shown in the figures, describing geometrical figures (square, triangle, etc.) inside the circle. That is why the aspects have been given certain names: A triangular aspect, or a trine, is given by the angle that is formed by the two sides of an equilateral triangle; the situation is the same for a square and a sextile (hexagon). The names of some of the minor aspects (see table 7.2) were derived in the same way: A quintile is formed by drawing a pentagon (*quinque* is Latin for five) in the circle; its angle therefore amounts to 360°/5 = 72°. A biquintile is then twice that angle, or 144°.

Strictly speaking an aspect is a configuration that is very rarely found in a horoscope. Just as each house division irrevocably collapses above the Arctic Circle at certain *indivisible* moments, so these aspects are there only at certain indivisible moments. At 16h34min12.37s the angular separation between Venus and Jupiter can be 120.000° (therefore a trine), but just a few moments earlier or a bit later this separation is somewhat smaller or larger. This would make the application of the aspects in astrology almost impossible.

In order to get around this problem the astrologers have mapped out a small area around each aspect, the so-called *orb*. Within this small area one might be able to observe the effects of the aspect. The size of the orb depends

168 Making Sense of Astrology

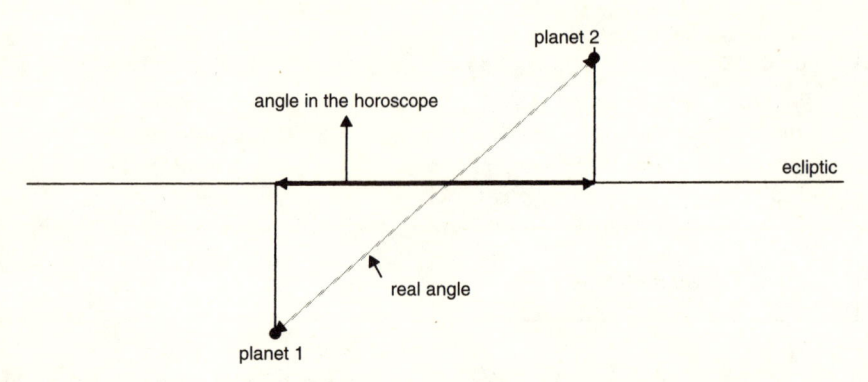

Figure 7.1. Angular separation between planets.

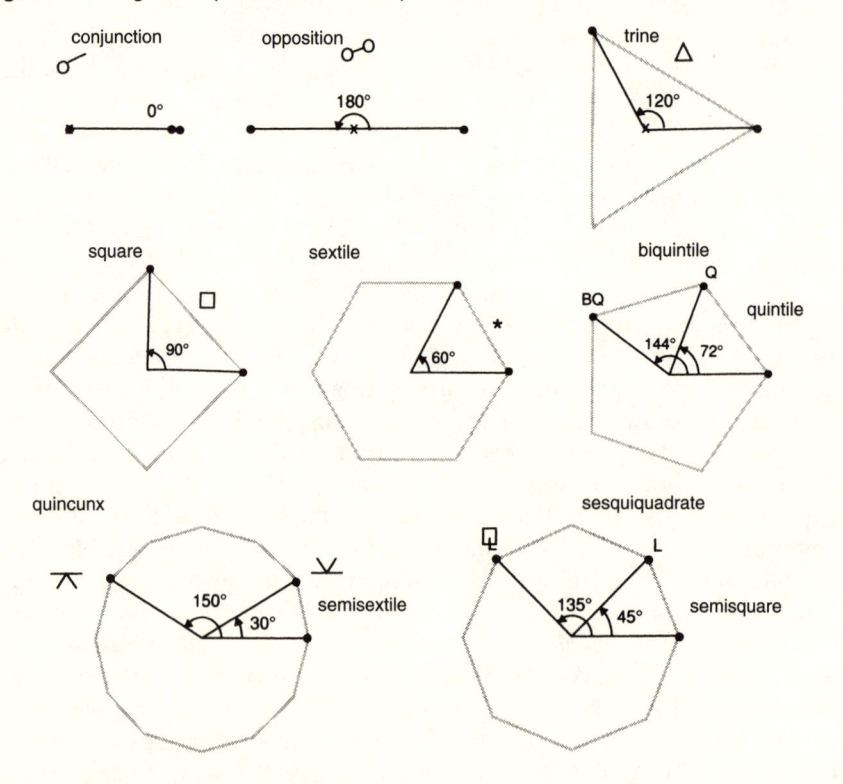

Figure 7.2. Some aspects as figures in the circle.

Table 7.2: Some Non-Classical Aspects (Minor Aspects)

Angular Separation on the Ecliptic	Aspect Name	Symbol	Astrological Influence
30°	Semi-sextile	⊻	Favorable
45°	Semi-square, semi-quadrate	∟	
72°	Quintile	**Q**	
135°	Sesqui-quadrate	⚼	Unfavorable
144°	Biquintile	**BQ**	
150°	Quincunx or inconjuct	⚻	
0°(*)	Parallel	//	Variable

(*) calculated in latitude above or below the ecliptic. Therefore this is an exception to the general rule that aspects are only angular separations *on* the ecliptic.

on the aspect and on the astrological planets involved. For the classical major aspects with the Sun or the Moon the orbs are usually larger than elsewhere: at least 5° and often much more, up to 12°; for the planets we find orbs of at least 3°. For the minor aspects a smaller orb (such as 1°) is applied. If, for example, Venus is square with Neptune and the orb used is 3°, then the first signs of the aspect would become noticeable as soon as the angular separation amounts to 87°. Between 87° and 90° the aspect becomes "more exact" and its effect increases after which it decreases again between 90° and 93°.

By assuming an orb, the chance to find one or more aspects becomes much larger, of course. The larger the orb, the more aspects in the horoscope. If only the classical aspects are considered and an orb of 5° is assumed, an average of ten aspects per horoscope is found. A horoscope without aspects then becomes a rarity.

The Astrological Meaning of the Aspects

In astrology it is assumed that the planets, the Ascendant, and the Midheaven, which are part of an aspect, influence each other's effect in the horoscope in a certain sense. The characteristics of the planets influence each other and share something of their nature with each other. An aspect between Mercury and Mars, for instance, will give the intellectual capacities of Mercury a militant, active, sharp turn (which, for instance can find its expression in debates), because this agrees with the astrological Mars.

Whether these influences turn out to be positive or negative is determined by the *type* of aspect that occurs. Aspects like *trine* and *sextile* are supposed to have a *favorable* influence on the mutual relationship. The *square* and the *opposition* on the other hand will emphasize the *unfavorable*, counteracting facets of the two planets. The conjunction is of a variable nature. It depends on the planets themselves if they reinforce each other's favorable or their unfavorable traits (see tables 7.1 and 7.2).

In this way "Venus square Saturn" points to an emotional life (Venus) which is gloomy and melancholic (Saturn), in which case love affairs tend to be not too successful. If the aspect is a trine instead of a square, however, then this points to the building of a stable, profound relationship (the favorable side of Saturn is concentration, profoundness). Aspects with respect to the Ascendant and the Midheaven are interpreted analogously: A relationship with the Ascendant says something (at least according to astrology) about the subject of the horoscope; the Midheaven points to a certain influence on professional life and one's social position. In this way "MC sextile Mars" is explained as energy (Mars) applied in the development of the social position (MC) with favorable prospects (sextile).

In looking at the aspects and considering the astrological adage that the horoscope is a totality one also has to have an eye for the houses in which the planets to be considered are located. An aspect of a planet with another planet indicates the *nature* of the mutual relation. The house from which the aspect originated then again points to the *area of life* in which the cooperation or obstruction can be expected. A square with Mars in House VII, for instance, suggests an active (Mars) opposition (square) from the side of business partners, spouses, and so on (House VII).

Taking all this into account, it is becoming clear that the interpretation of the horoscope is a rather complicated business. At the same time this complication also offers advantages: The more elements and relations are given, the more "astrological information" is available to draw from during the interpretation. The whole becomes much less surveyable, but it also provides considerably more possibilities and as a result a greater freedom of interpretation. Experience teaches that with hindsight just about *everything* can be found retroactively in any horoscope whatsoever.

Astrological Disagreement (Part IV)

As could be expected from the previous chapters, the astrologers do not show any large unanimity in the case of the aspects. Lucky for them the confusion in this instance is just a little bit less than for the houses or the planets. The disagreement primarily concerns the following points.

Aspects to Be Used

As mentioned earlier, there are two large groups of aspects: the major (classical) and the minor aspects. All astrologers do, as a matter of fact, use the classical aspects (conjunction, sextile, trine, and opposition), but that does not mean that they also use the minor ones. After all, these only began to be used around the beginning of the seventeenth century, due, among other things, to the influence of the famous astronomer/astrologer Kepler.

Why some astrologers reject the latter group totally or partly while others consider them indispensable is rather unclear for an outsider. Maybe there is some overwhelming evidence for one or the other.

The Determination of the Aspects

The Western astrologers determine the angular separation between two elements (planets/Ascendant/MC) that form the aspect. The exactness of the angle determines whether or not an aspect exists. In antiquity—and currently still in India—another system was applied; there the starting point was not the position of these elements, but the position of the signs in which they were found. The angular separation between these two signs determined the aspects. In this way Venus in Gemini always formed a trine with Jupiter in Libra, although the angular distance between the two planets in these signs could vary between 90° and 150°! The contrast between these two methods is striking.

We know that Western astrologers are convinced that it is the exact angles which count. However, we do not know what their Indian colleagues think about it or how Ptolemy would have reacted.

The Starting Point

In calculating an aspect, a point of reference, the center of the circle in which the angles will be measured, is necessary. The traditional astrologer, who observes that, up until now, people are born on Earth, considers the aspects as seen from Earth. These are the *geocentric* aspects, as they are usually drawn in the classical horoscope. There is still some uncertainty in their calculation: Most astrologers calculate everything based on planetary positions which are valid from the center of Earth; others, however, calculate the angles formed with respect to the place of birth. The latter requires additional arithmetical work and it only provides a noticeable difference for the position of the Moon.

Another group, a minority which wants to adapt astrology to a modern worldview, uses *heliocentric* aspects: angles as they are seen from the Sun. Here one starts from the fact that the Sun is the center of our solar system and that, according to the partisans, the planetary influences do not reach Earth directly but make a detour via the Sun.

The results of these two systems of course vary widely from each other. Some aspects which are geocentrically impossible can indeed occur heliocentrically (such as Venus opposite Mercury), which can enrich the interpretation. In the heliocentric system, moreover, aspects with Earth are also formed. There is thus an additional planet! But then again in such a system the role of the Moon is strongly reduced and the Sun as the reference point cannot not form aspects anymore. Heliocentric aspects last a relatively long time (several days), so that they are valid for very many people. In the traditional system the duration of the aspects—except for the aspects that the outer planets form with each other—is rather limited. An aspect of the Moon with a planet lasts only a few hours, aspects with the Ascendant or the Midheaven even but a few minutes. Because of this aspects in the geocentric system are tied to the person more strongly.

The Size of the Orb

Astrologers who only consider aspects formed by the signs in which the planets are located (such as the Indian astrologers), do not need an orb. Their fellow craftsmen who work with real angles are by nature forced to take the orb into account. How large the applied orb has to be turns out to depend on the personal preference of the astrologer. The values used vary greatly: from less than 1° for some minor aspects to 10° or more for the major aspects with the Sun and the Moon (even up to 18° or one-twentieth of the total zodiac!). It goes without saying that, as the size of the orb increases, the number of aspects found in a horoscope also increases greatly. While an orb of 5° will supply an average of ten aspects, double that will be found for an orb of 10°.

No single system has been agreed upon, so very different horoscopes can be obtained, depending on the personal preference of the astrologer. The interpretation will certainly mirror this preference.

Astronomical Question Marks

In the area of astronomy the aspects are also open to criticism.

The way in which the angles are measured is not unique. Why does the planetary position have to be *projected* on the ecliptic? Why isn't the *real* angular separation determined? We do not have to look far for an answer: The projected angles can be read directly from the horoscope, but the determination of the real angles would require far more arithmetic, which in the

The Aspects 173

past would have been a serious handicap. For that matter, this systematic simplification of astronomy is characteristic of astrology (consider for instance the neglect of distances).

Most of the time the difference between the real angle and the projected angle will be very minor because the planets are more or less located in the plane of the ecliptic. However, this is not the case for the Moon or Pluto. The Moon can be located about 5° above or below the ecliptic, Pluto up to 17°. This will be sufficient, when a relatively small orb is used, to cause the difference between the absence or presence of an aspect.

A problem related to this is the status of the conjunction. In the strict sense of the word a "conjunction" should mean that the two planets approach each other very closely and "fall on top of each other," so that one planets eclipses the other. In reality this occurs very rarely; the most frequent ones are the Moon occulting a planet. However, if the *projections* of the planets are considered, a conjunction is a relatively frequently occurring phenomenon. As figure 7.3 makes clear, it can happen that a planet which is in conjunction with another is in reality at a larger angular displacement from it than from a third planet which will not get into a conjunction with the first one. The objective foundation for the determination of the aspects is therefore not very consistent.

In the criticism with respect to the planets (see chapter 5) it was mentioned that distances do not appear to play a role in astrology. A planet is located in a sign or in a house and that is it. Whether that planet is close to or far removed from Earth is of no importance. An analogous situation also occurs for the aspects; here too only the angular displacements between the planets are considered and the distances are not taken into account. Those who only contact the planets via a horoscope, like most astrologers, will hardly experience this as a problem.

However, neglecting the distances can lead to the following curious situations:

- Mercury in conjunction with Venus. As is shown in figure 7.4 this can happen in four different ways. Astrologically there is no difference between them.
- Mercury sextile Venus (figure 7.5). Here too there are four possibilities, two of which are shown in the figure. According to the astrologers there is not the least amount of difference between them.
- Mercury or Venus in conjunction with the Sun, shown for Venus in figure 7-6. The differences in distances between these two possibilities are in reality very large, but for the astrologer they do not exist.
- The Moon in conjunction with Mars (figure 7.7). Here too the same remark can be made. The distance from Mars can vary in a ratio of 1 to 6. The aspects of the horoscope do not mirror this simple but important astronomical fact.

174   Making Sense of Astrology

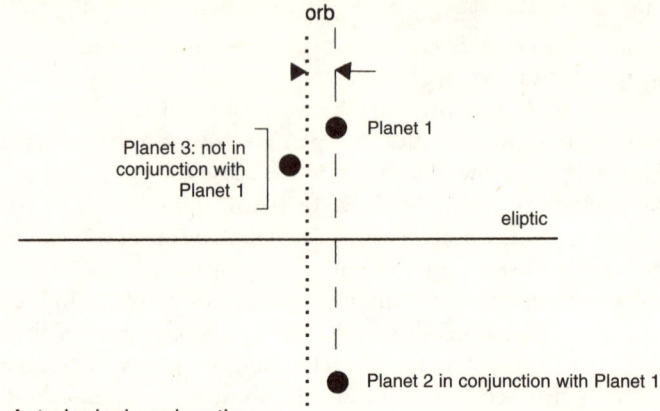

Figure 7.3. Astrological conjunction.

The astrological worldview, more than 2,000 years old, is shown to deviate so strongly from the astronomical reality that every effort toward a realistic interpretation in terms of "forces" appears to be meaningless.

We will spare the reader the explanation about some more possible objections, such as the origin of the aspects, or why some aspects are considered favorable and others unfavorable (for one thing, Greek number mysticism has something to do with it). The reader, meanwhile, will understand that here too questions can be asked about the "experience" that led to the knowledge about the aspects. Moreover, the value of the aspects stands or falls with the reality of the planetary influences. Next we will discuss the question of the statistical indications for the activity of the aspects.

Aspects, Statistics, and Radio Disturbances

Like the other elements of the horoscope, the aspects have been studied statistically. Here too, the results turned out to show the same tendencies that had been found many times before for this type of research: Most of the studies have a negative result and the few that are positive are either not repeatable (either too few data about the test are known to repeat it or the repetitions turn out negative) or they had been executed in the wrong way.

For instance, James Randall Noblitt looked for a possible connection between the presence of the type of aspects (favorable/unfavorable) in a horoscope and personality. Besides the number of aspects the character of the planets that formed the aspects was also considered. Not a single one of the two sets of tests resulted in a benefit for astrology.

Michel Gauquelin also tried many, many times to find a reality to the aspects, but to no avail.

The Aspects 175

Aspects and Distances

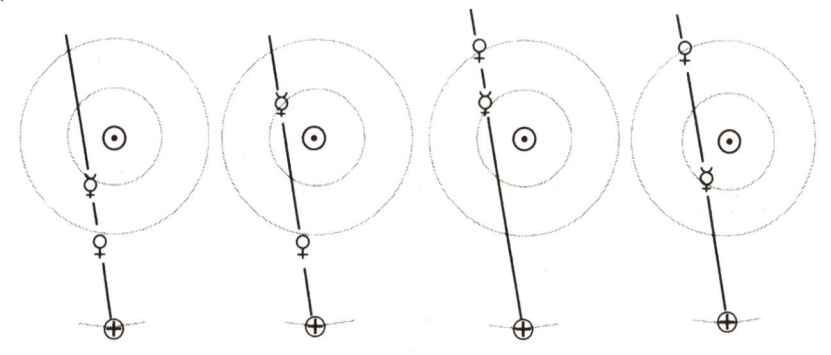

Figure 7.4. Conjunction Mercury—Venus.

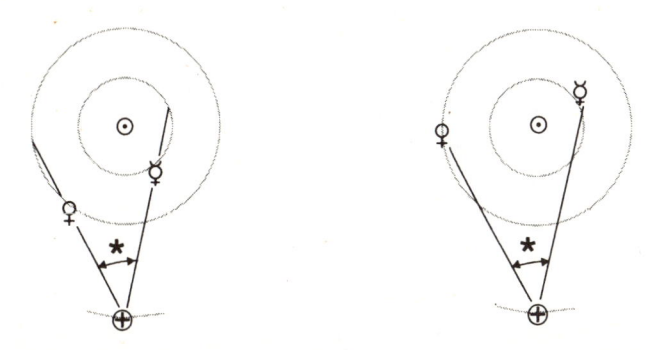

Figure 7.5. Sextile Mercury—Venus.

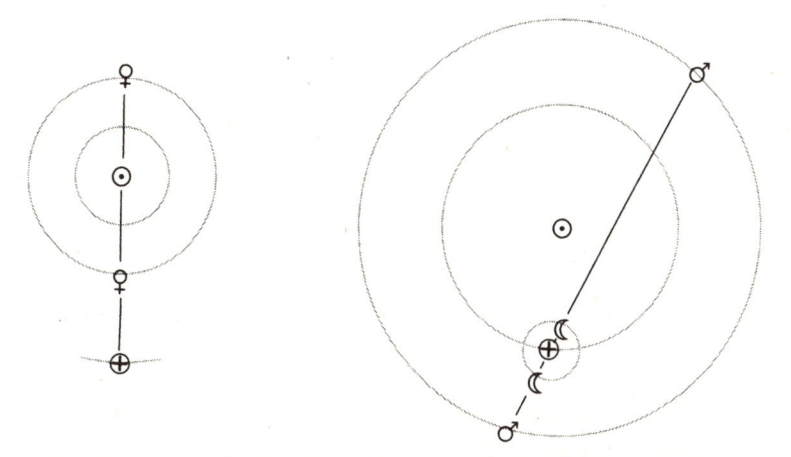

Figure 7.6. Conjunction Venus—Sun.

Figure 7.7. Conjunction Moon—Mars.

176   Making Sense of Astrology

In earlier discussions of statistical studies we have mentioned a "successful test": the research by Eysenck and Mayo in the chapter on the zodiac and the work of Gauquelin for the houses. The aspects also have, or rather had, such an "ultimate proof": the 1951 claims of John Nelson.

John Nelson was an American engineer who studied short-wave radio disturbances. He was looking for a factor that would help to improve the predictions of these disturbances. According to him the methods used, which are based on solar magnetic activity (see Intermezzo IX), were not satisfactory.

In his research he proceeded as follows. He used an eight-hour period of time as a unit for his observations (the radio connections were checked for disturbances by teams which each worked eight hours, hence the selection of that unit of time). Depending on the quality of the reception during the period of observation these units of eight hours were divided into "disturbed" and "undisturbed" periods.

During his investigation Nelson got the idea to check the planetary positions during periods of disturbed radio reception. In this case he looked at the angular separations of 0° (conjunction), 90° (square), 180° (opposition) and 270° (square, but in the opposite sense: –90°) between the planets as seen from the Sun, i.e., the heliocentric aspects. His procedures and reasoning are in this case interesting enough to follow them closely.

In this investigation each day was allotted a number that indicated the position of that day with respect to the *nearest* aspect.* The day in which an aspect occurred was indicated by "day 0." The days before that then became –1, –2, –3, and so on; in the same way the days following the aspect obtained the numbers +1, +2, +3 (figure 7.8) until any occurred that was closer to the next aspect and which therefore received a negative number. In this way one could, for instance, obtain the order –1, 0 (aspect), 1, 2, 3, –4, –3, –2, –1, 0 (aspect), 1, 2, during a certain period.

Nelson then prepared a graph which showed the number of disturbed periods per day number (figure 7.9). He discovered that this graph had a triangular form: it was obvious that more disturbed periods occurred at day number 0 (the days on which there was an aspect) than on the other numbers. As the day was farther removed from "day" 0, fewer disturbances occurred.

According to Nelson this could mean only one thing: The appearance of the radio disturbances depended on the heliocentric planetary aspects. The proof was thereby supplied that the planets by means of their mutual positions influenced Earthly events!

As was to be expected the astrologers annexed these conclusions to their own system. The fact that the investigated aspects were heliocentric and therefore contradicted the astrological tradition was ignored, as was the fact that radio disturbances are not exactly connected with human characteristics.

---

*In this discussion of the work of Nelson we mean by "aspects" only the angular displacements of 0°, 90°, 180°, and 270°. As already mentioned these are always heliocentric aspects.

The Aspects   177

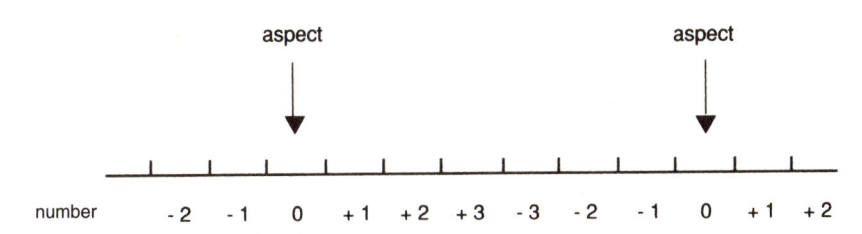

Figure 7.8. Day numbering according to John Nelson.

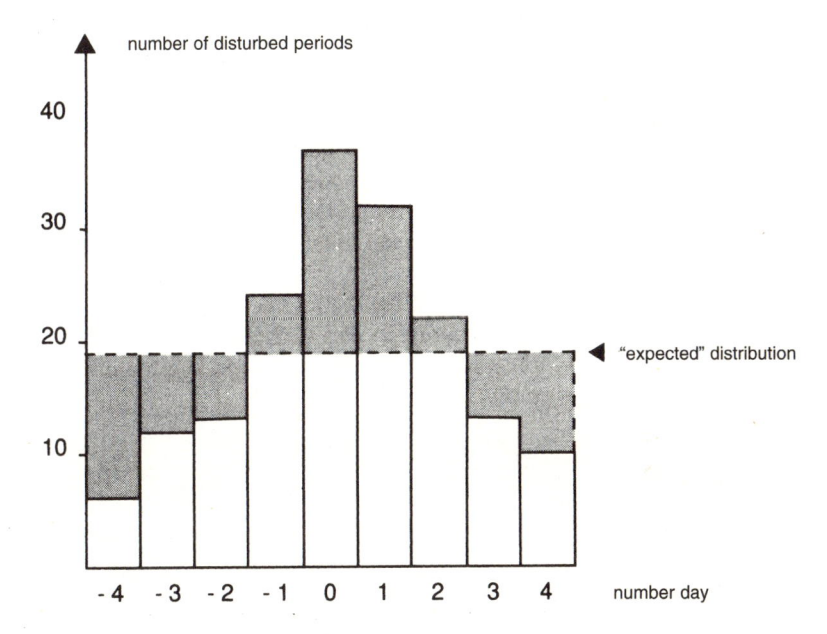

Figure 7.9. John Nelson's 1942 observations.

Whatever the case might be, Nelson's conclusion was sensational. In doing his calculations, however, he forgot to ask one important question, and the answer to that question was going to destroy his thesis completely.

This kind of statistical investigation is based based on comparison, the way in which a series of data (in this case, the number of disturbed periods) is distributed is compared with another distribution, the distribution to be expected if the investigated effect was *not* present. This distribution is either derived from theory or from observations of a control group. We came across this principle previously when we discussed other statistical studies.

178   Making Sense of Astrology

In order to understand the meaning of the triangular distribution of the disturbances that Nelson obtained, the first important question therefore is, What can be expected theoretically? What is the "normal" distribution for such a case? And how strongly does what was discovered deviate from that?

Nelson started out with the assumption that for each day number (–4, –3, ... +3, +4) about the same number of disturbed periods could be expected; instead of the triangular distribution that was found, there should have been a flat, rectangular distribution. But the observed figure deviates very strongly from this (figure 7.9). The probability of finding such a large difference by chance amounts to about 1 out of 10 million. It is therefore right to assume with great certainty that what Nelson found deviated strongly from the proposed distribution. Thus, he concluded that another factor played a role, and the connection with the heliocentric planetary aspects was the obvious choice.

But wait a moment! Concerning the first distribution—with what was observed, that is, the triangular distribution—there can be no quarrel. But what about that second, theoretical, rectangular distribution? Is it so certain that for every type of day the same number of disturbances can be expected? There are two possibilities that can influence this distribution:

- other factors—besides the aspects—influence the occurrence of disturbed periods;
- the different *categories* of days (–4, –3, . . .) do not occur equally often.

The second possibility turns out to offer the correct explanation. There exists a pronounced irregularity in the number of days in each category that appears in the course of a year.

In order to understand this we have to give some serious thought to the definition of the "day number." Each day on which two planets showed a mutual angle of 0 percent, 90 percent, 180 percent, or 270 percent obtained the number 0, each day which occurred N days before the nearest aspect obtained the number –N, each day N days after the nearest aspect got the number +N. Nelson assumed implicitly that each number would occur about equally often, but this is not the case. It is clear that the series of numbers cannot increase or decrease without limit: As the number of days since the last aspect increases, the probability increases that a new aspect will appear soon. And heliocentric aspects occur more often than we might presume intuitively.

Consider the fastest planet, Mercury. This planet makes one turn around the Sun in eighty-eight days. After about 115 days, Mercury "catches up" with Earth and all six planets farther from the Sun than the Earth have been "passed by." During these 115 days Mercury and each of these seven planets (six planets plus Earth) were at least once in conjunction, once in opposition, and twice square. That gives at least twenty-eight aspects in less than four months or, on the average, almost one every four days. If this is calculated for all the planets (and the fact that several aspects can occur on the same day is taken into account), an average is obtained of *one aspect every 3.5 days*.

The periods between two aspects are therefore relatively short. Mathematically it can be shown that there are fewer days with number −3 than there are days with number −2, fewer days with +3 than with +2, and so on. The days with number 0 are the most frequent. That is why the number of disturbances in category 0 is larger than in any one of the other categories.

If we use this insight to correct the expected distribution, then not a trace of any planetary effect can be noticed any more. The strange distribution that Nelson found is therefore not due to planetary influences on the radio waves, but to a wrong way to count the days!

Maybe Nelson would not have been caught in this trap if he had compared his data with those of a group of events that really happened randomly. In that case he could have ascertained that, with his method, such a control group always comes up with a similar triangular distribution. The American researchers P. A. Ianna and C. J. Margolin did something like that. They let a computer randomly determine a number of days in a year and compared these with the heliocentric aspects on those days in the same way that Nelson did with his disturbed days. Their results showed the same triangular graph. The British astronomer Hunter set to work in a somewhat more frivolous way: He applied Nelson's method to the days on which there was an afternoon show in the Parisian cabaret Folies-Bergère. Here too he found a similar triangle with a large peak on day 0. In this case nobody has suggested that the planetary positions have anything to do with the shows of Parisian cabarets.

And the astrologers? It is obvious that it dawns on them very slowly that Nelson was mistaken. In 1987 his "discovery" was still mentioned in a pro-astrology article in the Belgian weekly *Knack*. No mention was made of the mistake; the only mention was that he was laughed at because his conclusions were reminiscent of astrology (the almost mythical picture of the "unrecognized genius"). One year later a well-known Flemish astrologer, Daniël Van Ooteghem, Ph.D., mentioned—in a television debate with the authors of this book—the investigations of Nelson as a possible proof of astrology. Very recently the "proof" was mentioned in a book by the French astrologer Elizabeth Teissier (known, among other things, for her plea to allow astrology to be taught again at the university). What is the sense of looking for the truth if some people do not want to know that truth?

Conclusion

It is becoming monotonous, but for the validity of this last building block of classical astrology, the aspects, there obviously are no clear proofs available.

180   Making Sense of Astrology

In some sense this was more or less to be expected: systems which are developed on the basis of mystical considerations—in this case Greek number mysticism—are very rarely in agreement with the reality of nature. Why should nature prefer certain angles if there are no compelling reasons for it?

Here our review of the four most important parts of astrology ends. Quite a few astrologers take yet other elements into account, such as:

- the *Part-of-Fortune* or *Pars Fortunae*, a point on the zodiac that is calculated by adding the longitude of the Ascendant to the longitude of the Moon and subtracting from this the longitude of the Sun. The result is an arithmetical point on which nothing real is located. However, it is nevertheless considered important by some astrologers (see also chapter 9);
- the *nodes of the Moon* (the intersections of the orbit of the Moon with the ecliptic);
- the location of the *last New Moon;*
- the *Black Moon*, an astrological name for the perigee of the orbit of the Moon (the point where the Moon is closest to Earth);
- the location of some *fixed stars* in the zodiac—usually the brightest ones—or a star cluster such as the Pleiades (as we have already seen stars play a negligible role in astrology).

In addition to these, things known as dwads, harmonics, the ruler of the hour, and so on are also used. For several reasons we will not delve deeper into these factors. In the first place these elements are truly of minor importance; they vary so much that any description of them would be incomplete. Moreover their popularity differs from time to time, from place to place, and from astrological school to astrological school. Some factors such as the fixed stars appear to have fallen somewhat into disuse, whereas the use of the Black Moon is supposed to be increasing. And last but not least they do not provide new facts or arguments in the discussion about the validity of astrology.

The criticism of the major building blocks (the astronomical absurdities, lack of an experimental base, astrological disagreement) is also valid, and sometimes to a much larger extent, for the minor factors. Anyone strongly convinced of the influence of the Black Moon may reproach us that we do not pay attention to it. Maybe we can do that once there is more certainty about the influence of the real Moon.

What now remains of this complicated system? Very little, in our opinion. Astrological theory appears not to agree with observations; everywhere we looked in our search for proof we found nothing. The conclusion appears to be unavoidable: Apart from all the speculations about the relation between Man and the Universe, *there is not a single indication that the astrological system,* as it is applied daily by the astrologers, *is based on anything at all.*

Astrology arose in antiquity as a religio-philosophical system which was in agreement with the then accepted ideas of its developers. One should not think poorly of them; in those times the knowledge and the methods were too limited and imperfect to allow one to obtain a better insight into the universe. What the present-day astrologers may well be reproached for are their claims that their theses are scientifically justified or even proven. Astrology during its whole evolution never cared all that much about reality, and testing its claims has never been its strongest point.

After all these objections we may ask why astrologers are still occupied with their subject. Are they cheats who see it as a profitable activity, or simply souls who cannot tell correct from incorrect? In order to find out we will have to enter the area of psychology in the next chapter.

Intermezzo VIII

☉ ♆ ☾ ☊ ☋ ☌ ⚺ ✶ □ △ ⚻ ☍

THE ASPECTS IN THE HOROSCOPE OF A. S. TROLOGER

In a number of intermezzi the horoscope of A. S. Trologer was built up step by step. Now the last little piece of this astrological puzzle follows; according to classical astrology the figure is then complete and ready for interpretation. However, there also exist astrological schools who at this point start with a complex juggling of numbers. But in order not to put the readers through a useless trial, some frugality is practiced in this part of the book...

In Intermezzo III the following values were found for the planetary positions:

Sun 19.5° Capricorn =	289.5° (ecliptical longitude)
Moon: 4.6° Libra	184.6°
Mercury: 3.9° Aquarius	303.9°
Venus: 18.8° Aquarius	318.8°
Mars: 5.4° Libra	185.4°
Jupiter: 8.6° Aquarius	308.6°
Saturn: 19.3° Virgo	169.3°
Uranus: 2.3° Cancer	92.3°
Neptune: 17.3° Libra	197.3°
Pluto: 17.6° Leo	137.6°

In Intermezzo V the Ascendant and the Midheaven were added:

Asc 6.2° Capricorn = 276.2° (ecliptical longitude)
MC 11.1° Scorpio   221.1°

In order to facilitate the calculation of the aspects all the positions were converted to the ecliptical longitude, the angle on the ecliptic measured

Intermezzo VIII: Aspects in the Horoscope of A. S. Trologer

from the vernal equinox (or the beginning of the sign Aries). This was done in order to avoid a further juggling with the signs.

In this example a value of 5° was assumed for the orb (the small area around an aspect inside of which the aspect is considered "active") if an aspect was formed with the Sun or the Moon, and 3° for aspects between the other elements (planets, Asc, MC). For the sake of simplicity we will consider only the major aspects.

To determine if two of the above elements (planets, Asc, MC) form an aspect with each other, their difference in longitude is calculated. If this difference lies within the orb of a certain aspect, then that aspect is present. For the sake of clarity a small table of these areas around the aspects follows.

Angular Difference (°)	Aspect	Area Orb 5°	Area Orb 3°
0°	conjunction	−5° − +5°	−3° − +3°
60°	sextile	55° − 65°	57° − 63°
90°	square	85° − 95°	87° − 93°
120°	trine	115° − 125°	117° − 123°
180°	opposition	175° − 185°	177° − 183°
240°	trine	235° − 245°	237° − 243°
270°	square	265° − 275°	267° − 273°
300°	sextile	295° − 305°	297° − 303°

For the Sun the following angular differences are found:

Sun–Moon: 289.5° − 184.6° = 104.9°. This value is not found within the zones in the table. Therefore there is no aspect.
Sun–Mercury: 303.9° − 289.5° = 14.4°. Ditto.
Sun–Venus: 318.8° − 289.5° = 29.3°. Ditto.
Sun–Mars: 289.5° − 185.4° = 104.1°. Ditto.
Sun–Jupiter: 308.6° − 289.5° = 19.1°. Ditto.
Sun–Saturn: 289.5° − 169.3° = 120.2°. This value lies within the interval 115°/125°, so we have a *trine* here.
Sun–Uranus: 289.5° − 92.3° = 197.2°. No aspect.
Sun–Neptune: 289.5° − 197.3° = 92.2°. This value lies within the interval 85°/95°, so this is a *square*.
Sun–Pluto: 289.5°—137.6° = 151.9°. No aspect.
Sun–Asc: 289.5° − 276.2° = 13.3°. Ditto.
Sun–MC: 289.5° − 221.1° = 68.4°. Ditto.

All the possible combinations of the Sun with the other planets and with the Ascendant and the Midheaven were checked, which supplied us with two aspects. The same is now being done with the Moon and the rest of the table of the positions of the planets. After much comparing the following list is obtained:

184   Making Sense of Astrology

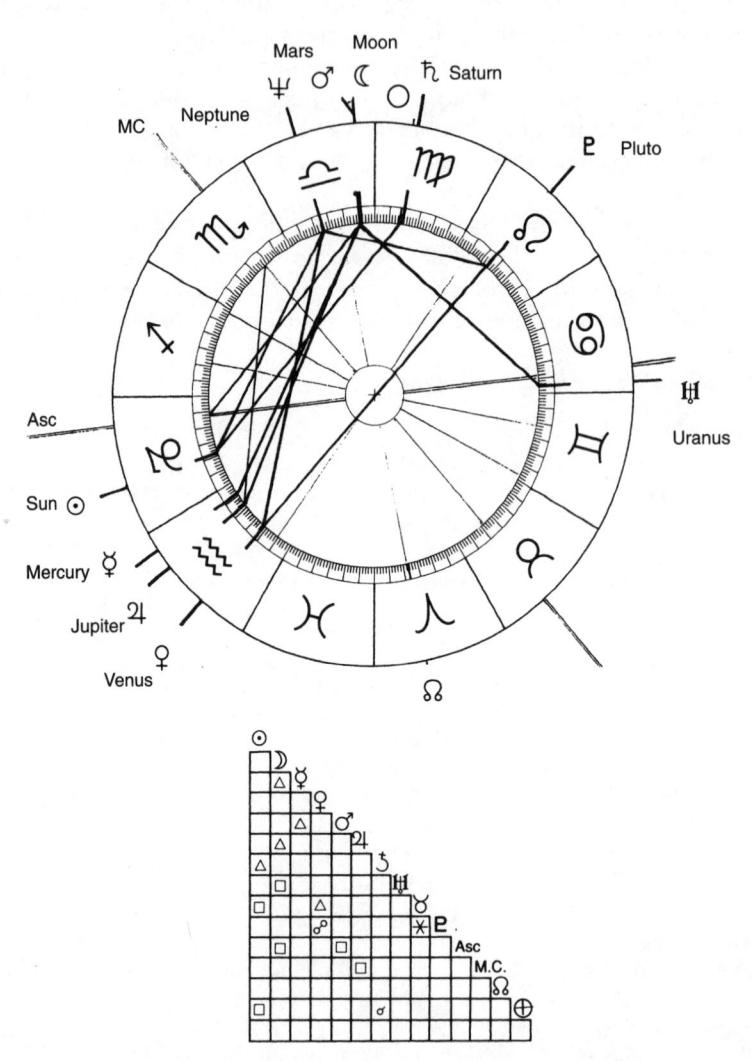

Figure VIII.1. The complete horoscope of A. S. Trologer. The diagram at the bottom describes the aspects depicted in the horoscope figure itself in bold lines. For the sake of completeness, the *Pars Fortunae* (⊕) and the ascending node of the Moon (☊) are also indicated. They too can form aspects, as in this case the *Pars Fortunae* with the sun (square) and the *Pars Fortunae* with Saturn (conjunction).

Intermezzo VIII: Aspects in the Horoscope of A. S. Trologer

Elements	Aspect	Angle
Sun–Saturn	trine	120.2°
Sun–Neptune	square	92.2°
Moon–Mercury	trine	119.3°
Moon–Mars	conjunction	0.8°
Moon–Jupiter	trine	124.0°
Moon–Uranus	square	92.3°
Moon–Asc	square	91.6°
Mercury–Mars	trine	118.5°
Venus–Neptune	trine	121.5°
Venus–Pluto	opposition	181.2°
Mars–Asc	square	90.8°
Jupiter–MC	square	87.5°
Neptune–Pluto	sextile	59.7°

Therefore, thirteen aspects were found. It goes without saying that if the applied values for the orbs had been larger or smaller, the number of aspects also would have been correspondingly larger or smaller.

All the data that have been found can now together be drawn on the figure of the horoscope (figure VIII.1). If done with some care, this can become an aesthetically attractive drawing which by its complicated shape alone strikes the layman with authority, even before the actual astrological work has started. And that is a nice little extra for the astrologer. Something that looks so complicated certainly must have a kernel of truth somewhere. Or perhaps not?

8

ASTROLOGY AND PSYCHOLOGY

It should have become clear by now that there are no irrefutable proofs for the foundation of the astrological statements. The origin of the system is unclear, astrologers contradict each other on essential points, and scientific proofs for the validity of the building blocks of the horoscope have not been found. Our critical objections were for the most part of a scientific nature; that kind of argument may a priori be rejected by quite a few astrologers, but nevertheless they ought to carry some weight.

In spite of all this, one thing remains clear: A large number of people firmly believe in the correctness of astrology. How can this be explained? How is it possible that so many people attach so much value to an unproven system based on hopelessly obsolete ideas? Why do thousands of people not only read their daily newspaper horoscope, but why are there also many who at regular times personally consult an astrologer for assistance with their life's problems?

The same answer is almost always obtained from the astrologers themselves when they are questioned as to why they actually practice astrology, in spite of all the arguments against it—assuming they know them. This answer can be condensed into one short sentence: "I have the *experience* that astrology *works*."

And, from our own experience we have to admit that in this respect astrologers are right. Astrology "works," if that means that the astrologer gets positive reactions from his or her customer when interpreting the horoscope. If the customer is satisfied with the result of the work, he or she has the experience that the directions of the astrologer are right. And because of that the astrologers's conviction that astrology is true will be reinforced. After all, how could the clients possibly be satisfied if astrology did *not* work? Next to that

Astrology and Psychology 187

experience, discussions about contradictory house systems, moving zodiacs, or whether planetary influences exist or not are totally beside the point: The experience of the daily practice always turns the scales.

If one takes a skeptical point of view, he is in for a dilemma: Either the previous critical remarks about the senselessness of the astrological elements somehow missed the boat, or there is something fishy about the much-praised experience. But can that experience be pushed aside without much ado? Can the statement that astrology works in practice be attributed to something other than the obvious explanation of the correctness of the methods used?

In order to solve this dilemma, it is necessary to judge human experience on its reliability. If it turns out that it is after all not such a good guarantee of correctness, then, at the same time, the direction in which a satisfactory explanation for this phenomenon has to be found is indicated. And, as the intelligent reader will have surmised already, it can be shown that not every experience rests on solid ground. A few examples in a borderline area of astrology will allow us to show this.

Most people are familiar with the popular belief that during the Full Moon more children are born than during other phases of the moon. There are enough witnesses (nurses, midwives) who from their own "experience" can testify to the correctness of that claim. Nevertheless, a closer examination makes it obvious that this "experience" *cannot* be confirmed. Sure, there are periods during which more children are born around Full Moon than during other phases of the Moon, but there are also periods in which, as a matter of fact, there are *fewer* births in this interval, or during which the maximum number of births occurs around New Moon, First Quarter, or somewhere in between. If all the studies on this subject are combined it turns out that in the long run the number of births is equally distributed over all the phases of the Moon (see Intermezzo X).

Also widely accepted is the opinion that around the Full Moon some people show unusual behavior. The best-known example is the myth that psychiatric patients are more restless around the Full Moon. Some people associate this with an increase in the number of crimes or a higher number of suicides. Each tendency toward abnormal behavior is supposed to be expressed during that phase of the Moon. But, as explained in Intermezzo X, this also cannot be proven.

These two examples show that the *conviction* that something is true offers no guarantee. The "experience" can simply be wrong.

Astrologers used to attribute their positive experiences to the "synthetic" character of the horoscope. According to them the effects of each element separately are so subtle that in an extensive statistical investigation they simply disappear in the variations of the background. Hence the failures of the statistical investigations. A horoscope is a totality, as we are told over and over again, and can only be judged and interpreted as a totality. It is a complex collective interaction of the astrological elements in a unique relationship that is different for each person. Understanding and acknowledging this "fact" leads to the correct interpretation of the horoscope. Overlooking this must lead to negative results.

Is this argument valid? Are astrologers able to obtain better results when using the complete horoscope than the previous chapters would lead us to suspect?

Until about fifteen years ago it was quite difficult to answer that question; after all hardly any material existed that could throw some light on the problem. Fortunately the renewed interest in astrology beginning in the 1970s has also resulted in a number of experiments with extremely interesting results.

In order to judge the value of the *practice* of astrology, the following questions can be asked:

- are the *clients* of the astrologer able to distinguish between different horoscopes?
- are the astrologers themselves able to distinguish between different horoscopes?

The first question measures the reliability of the judgment of the horoscope by the client, the second the value of the experience of the astrologer.

The Client as Judge

Imagine the following experiment. The birth data of a number of people (let's say five) are looked up. These data are handed to an astrologer who casts the horoscope of each person and interprets it. The result consists of five astrologically composed psychological portraits. Now these portraits are shaped into an anonymous form: The names are omitted, as are the birthdates and explicit references to the sunsign. All five reports are then given to each of the five participants with the instruction to pick out the description that best fits them. A simple experiment that, if astrology really "works," should result in more than one-fifth of the persons in the experiment being able to point out their own horoscope as the best one. Does this happen in practice?

Since 1978 this kind of experiment has been performed at least seven times. In all a total of about 230 persons were tested who, depending on the experiment, had the choice between two to six personality descriptions. If only chance played a role in the choice, then 83 correct choices would have been expected. The "right" horoscope was selected only 80 times.

The implicit assumption of astrologers that their experiences are reliable because, if astrology did not work, then the customer would notice this and would not accept the offered profile, is therefore completely incorrect. That the customer recognizes a horoscope interpretation as "correct" is absolutely no proof for the correctness of the delivered product, but rather proves that most of the people are able to find themselves in most of the descriptions. The astrological experience is built on quicksand.

The inability of astrology to provide convincing character profiles goes, however, further yet. Geoffrey Dean, an Australian (ex-)astrologer who performed a lot of research into the validity of astrology, gave an astrological reading to a limited number (twenty-two) of people. However, for one-half of them he used the real horoscope as his starting point and for the other half the "inverted" figure, obtained by changing the figure in such a way that its interpretation provided the opposite results. For instance, if in the original horoscope a certain aspect was interpreted as "impatient, opinionated," then it became "very patient and is easily influenced by others." The test subjects did not know that they had participated in a test, but thought that they had received an accurate horoscope. The circumstances were therefore identical to those in normal practice. Both groups were equally satisfied with the results.

The first question can therefore be answered in the negative: *The customer is not able to recognize his own horoscope.* In principle this does not mean that astrology is incorrect; all this may well be due to a lack of self-knowledge of the subject of the horoscope. If the astrological interpretation is replaced by a classically composed psychological profile, the subjects are also often not able to pick their own description. The favorable reactions which the astrologer receives from his customers therefore do not say anything about the value of the theory that was used to compose the profile.

The Astrologer as Judge

The customer cannot judge the value of his horoscope, but can the astrologer do any better? Maybe the astrologer, as a less directly involved person, is better placed to pass an objective judgment on a psychological portrait. In order to test this, the previous example has to be reversed. Let us assume that we let five persons fill out a psychological questionnaire, so that the customer provides the psychological profile himself. Then we give these profiles to the astrologer together with the birth data of *one* of these persons. Can the astrologer, guided by the horoscope of that one person, determine which profile goes with it?

Another variant is also possible: A psychological profile is composed of *one* person and given to the astrologer together with the birth data of five persons, among whom is the subject of the horoscope. Can the astrologer select the right horoscope? Since astrology does not apply itself exclusively to the psychological side of the matter but also claims to be able to make statements about the course of life, important events, and other facts of someone's life, these data can also be used in an experiment.

Through the years about twenty reports have been published of such investigations. They are often called Vernon Clark tests, after the man who first performed this kind of test and who obtained very favorable results for the astrologers. In most of the cases the astrologers were given as basic materials two horoscopes, together with one or more characteristics of the subjects. In this way they were asked to tell the difference between

- suicides and random control subjects;
- alcoholics and random control subjects;
- intelligent and less talented subjects;
- people with an IQ of over 140 and persons with brain damage (cerebral palsy).

In other experiments the information given consisted of

- some important life events (case studies);
- characteristics from psychological tests;
- a complete psychological profile.

The results of these tests were rather variable. Clark performed three studies and obtained correct answers in respectively 72 percent, 59 percent, and 59 percent of the cases, although in each case only a score of 50 percent was expected. Three other studies also obtained scores of more than 60 percent. Although the practical value of these results is minimal—in practice it would mean that the astrologer still misses out in 4 cases out of 10—the deviation from the expected score of 50 percent is, statistically speaking, highly significant. However, when looking further into these results, it becomes clear that the excess of positive results is not necessarily attributable to astrology. There exist a number of non-astrological factors which can explain the preponderance of the favorable results.

One of these factors is the well-known tendency among experimenters not to publish negative results. If an investigation of which much is expected is performed and it turns out that the result does not agree with the stated expectations, then there is a tendency to presume that something went wrong so that the final result became worthless. In this way the number of published negative results will become smaller. On the other hand, an investigation with results in accordance to the expectations is much more likely to be published. Possible errors in the latter case may then be considered as unimportant for the final result. The consequence is that more positive studies are published. These two factors together then create a too optimistic picture of the whole.

Astrology and Psychology

Another problem is that some of these studies have not been performed double-blind. In a double-blind investigation not only the final judge—here the astrologer—but also the organizer is unaware of the correct solution (the correspondence between subject and horoscope). The choice of the data to be used (which subjects will be selected and which data the astrologer will obtain about them) will be left to a third experimenter, who is himself not acquainted with the purpose of the investigation. In this way the organizer's knowledge of the purpose of the study cannot possibly influence his choice. For the tests that we are considering now the criteria used were sometimes determined by the astrologer, so it is not impossible that unconsciously the "astrologically best" cases were selected for the experiment. If this has happened, the final result tells more about the amount of mutual agreement among astrologers than about the validity of practical astrology.

Eysenck and Nias in their book *Astrology, Science or Superstition** point to still two other possible explanations. The first one is that the data which had been given by the subjects of the horoscope could have been influenced by their prior knowledge of astrology (as we saw for the test of Eysenck in Intermezzo II). The other, somewhat more involved argument that they discuss is the problem of the choice of the number of subjects.

Most of the studies had been performed with about ten horoscopes which were judged by different astrologers. As a matter of fact ten is actually too small a number to be sure that the basic material itself does not already show a tendency in a certain direction.

If one presumes that no astrological influences exist and that any agreement between the horoscope and the psychological profile is purely due to chance, then one can expect that for such tests the chances are 50 percent that the horoscope (i.e., the "standard" astrological interpretation) agrees with a specific character trait of the test person (taking into account the frequency of that trait in the population, of course). For a test with a large number of horoscopes it can therefore be expected that—if astrology plays no role—roughly half of them agree with the profile. But if only ten horoscopes are selected, there is a considerable chance that the number of "agreements" is not exactly five, but, for instance, four or six (if you toss a coin ten times it is not at all surprising that tails turn up six times). In the case of six agreements out of ten the participating astrologers—if they at least interpret the horoscopes correctly according to their own rules—will score more hits than expected, even if astrology itself is wrong. The favorable results can then easily be taken for a confirmation of the tested astrological thesis.

In order to avoid such misleading results, it is recommended that the number of horoscopes be increased, if necessary at the cost of the number of participating astrologers. A minimum of twenty horoscopes is advisable. But,

---

*(Harmondsworth, England: Penguin Books, 1982)

of the published studies only one-fourth turned out to fulfill this minimum requirement, and the highest score obtained in this group was 58 percent (an investigation by Steffert, but other errors were made with it). The other scores in this group varied between 45 and 55 percent.

Because the above-mentioned factors had not been taken into account, the results of the positive studies cannot be accepted as proof for the validity of the astrological practice without further considerations. The reverse is also true; for the same reasons some studies with negative results cannot be used as proof against astrology. In order to get a more solid foundation we now have to discuss the better work.

In 1985 American physicist Shawn Carlson tested twenty-eight astrologers who had been considered the best in their field by their colleagues. For that test 116 horoscopes were used which were accompanied by three psychological profiles, drafted with the help of a questionnaire known as the California Personality Inventory (CPI). The obvious question asked of the astrologers was, Which of the three profiles belongs to each horoscope?

Although the astrologers did not voice any objections to the way the investigation was conducted and assured the experimenters that they would make the right selection in at least half the cases, it turned out that barely one-third of the given solutions were right—the same as the expected score from chance alone. Moreover, the results were shown not to be dependent on the confidence that the astrologers had in their decisions. Assignments in which the astrologers had great confidence were definitely no better than those about which they were less certain.

Here the astrologers failed. After the fact criticism was aired as to the use of the psychological test. The instructions of the CPI mention explicitly that this test is only valid if interpreted by a competent psychologist who is sufficiently familiar with it. This happened not to be the case here, although the participating astrologers themselves thought that they were sufficiently familiar with it. It is therefore possible that the astrologers were misled by incorrect psychological profiles. Yet it is remarkable that with all the precautions taken (a large number of horoscopes, double-blind tests) the results agreed exactly with what was to be expected according to chance. If the error had been caused exclusively by the interpretation of the questionnaire, then that would mean that this had not only been done incompetently, but had also been done arbitrarily.

Whatever the case may be, all the other tests discussed are overshadowed by the investigation of Geoffrey Dean, which is unequalled in its range, carefulness, thoroughness, and extensiveness.

The Investigation by Geoffrey Dean

Dean's study concentrated on two important psychological parameters which are characteristic of every one of us: extroversion/introversion and the extent of emotionality. An introverted person is more self-directed and does not seek much contact with other persons, rather, he draws back from social life, is reserved and quiet. An extroverted person, on the other hand, is socially directed, looks for the presence of other people, is rather impulsive, etc. Strongly emotional people have varying moods, worry a lot, and cannot stand stress, while the other extreme, emotionally stable personalities, are calm, not easily upset, and handle stress easily. Most people are somewhere in between these two extremes.

These psychological characteristics (extroversion/introversion and emotionality) are very suitable for astrological research for the following reasons (among other things):

- Both can be determined quite easily by means of the Eysenck Personality Inventory (see Intermezzo II);
- Both belong to the most important psychological characteristics of a person and remain stable during the whole life (extroverted babies never become introverted adults);
- A clear connection exists between the description of these characteristics and certain astrological rules, so that these characteristics can easily be derived from the horoscope (traditionally extroversion/introversion is connected with, among other things, the positive/negative signs and an excess of planets above/below the horizon, while emotionality is connected with the so-called water signs, Cancer, Scorpio, and Pisces).

In order to avoid doubtful cases only those subjects were selected who obtained extreme scores for both psychological characteristics. Only data from extremely introverted, extremely extroverted, extremely emotional, and extremely stable persons were then used. The selection of these extremes ought to have made the judgment of the total horoscope easier. After all, the expectations were that for these persons the relevant factors in the horoscope would stand out like a sore thumb.

The final version of the experiment consisted of the birth data of 160 persons who had extreme scores in one or more of these factors. In total 45 astrologers had to make 240 judgments about extro-/introversion and emotionality (some persons had extreme scores for both factors). The astrologers differed quite a bit among themselves as far as sex, nationality, work methods, experience, and so on were concerned. Besides their judgments about the subjects, they were also asked about their confidence in the result and the method used.

194 Making Sense of Astrology

From an astrological point of view, the results were disquieting to alarming, not to say catastrophic: *In not a single case was the chance expectation surpassed!*

For extro-/introversion an average of 60 correct results out of 120 attempts could be expected by chance; the obtained average was 60.2. For emotionality an average score of 60.6 was obtained where 60 had also been expected. Moreover, the deviation of the results of the individual astrologers around the average was also normal. A comparison with the results of a group of astrologers who only had guessed the results (that is without the use of a horoscope) showed no differences. Guessing therefore worked just as well (or as poorly) as astrology.

Because of the voluminous design of the investigation some other interesting data came to light.

For instance, the 120 answers of each astrologer were divided into two groups of 60 and a search was made whether the results of these two sets ran parallel, i.e., whether a high/low score of the first 60 responses was followed by a high/low score for the second 60. In this way it was possible to find out if some astrologers systematically obtained better or worse results (by, for instance, a better method or more experience). The connection that was looked for was not found: A high score for the first 60 turned out to be no guarantee at all for a high score for the next 60.

The extent to which the astrologers agreed with each other was also looked into. A priori a high level of agreement should have been expected: after all, astrologers learn their trade from the same manuals. In the judgment of extro-/introversion there appeared to exist a certain agreement; if an astrologer judged a certain horoscope as extrovert, then there existed a somewhat better than average chance that this same horoscope would be classified as extrovert by another astrologer also. The connection was, however, not as strong as had been expected. In an arbitrary judgment by 60 astrologers the interpretations can be divided into about thirty-three for one choice and twenty-seven for the other. And that occurs in spite of the common textbooks.

Next question: How much confidence did the astrologers have in their choices? If an astrologer found a certain horoscope very easy to interpret and another terribly difficult, did his colleagues agree? This was very clearly not the case; what for one astrologer is a simple horoscope turned out to provide insurmountable difficulties for another.

And as far as the connection between confidence and success is concerned, a great confidence in the correctness of the judgment turned out to be totally unjustified. Much or little confidence, the score remained stubbornly at about 50 percent.

Finally it was also investigated if certain groups of astrologers scored better than the rest.

- Do men score higher/lower than women?
  Answer: no.
- Is there a difference in score among American, British, continental-European (mostly German), and Australian astrologers?
  Answer: no.
- Do astrologers who are pronouncedly extroverted score better or worse than the introverted ones?
  Answer: no.
- Do the emotional astrologers score higher/lower than the more stable ones?
  Answer: no.
- Do astrologers with more experience get better results?
  Answer: no.
- Do astrologers who spend much time judging the horoscopes score higher than those who finished the job quickly?
  Answer: no.
- Do astrologers who found the experiment easy score higher than the ones who found it difficult?
  Answer: no.
- Do astrologers who used their intuition score better than those who had been guided exclusively by the horoscope?
  Answer: no.
- Do astrologers with a large practice (on the average fifteen customers a month) score higher than astrologers without?
  Answer: no.
- Were the results of astrologers who found this a fair test of astrology better than the results of those who could not agree with this opinion?
  Answer: no.

It was a complete disaster all over; astrologers were not able to derive important psychological characteristics from the horoscope. If this does not succeed for the extreme cases of introversion/extroversion and emotionality, how then can one trust horoscope interpretations that claim to expose much more subtle aspects of human behavior? The most alarming fact—at least for astrologers—is that this investigation brought *not even one single factor* to light that caused results better than pure chance. The failure of the astrologers could not be ascribed to the presence of less competent astrologers in the group; each subgroup in which the participants could be divided turned out to be equally bad. For this there is only one explanation: The fiasco is due to the astrological system itself and not to the competence of the individual astrologers.

The question may be asked whether in all those horoscopes any astrological factors could have been present that correlated with the extreme char-

196 Making Sense of Astrology

acteristics, but which are not included in the classical astrological theory. Maybe an analysis disconnected from the classical astrological rules could produce something interesting?

Geoffrey Dean performed such an analysis on his material, but he could find no astrological effect for any element whatsoever. Neither the position of the planets in the signs nor the positions of the planets in the decans produced anything. The use of another zodiac (sixty different ones were tested, among them the sidereal one) gave no improvement, any more than a check on the aspects present did. Also, the use of the sectors according Gauquelin was in agreement with chance expectations, again illustrating the uselessness of this theory.

In short, astrological practice fails simply because no relationship exists between the psychological characteristics investigated and the horoscope.

The representativeness of the tested astrologers, the carefulness of the whole experiment, as well as the honest intentions of Geoffrey Dean (he had nothing but sympathy for astrology) make this experiment ironclad and the results impressive. This study simply cannot be negated.

The astrologers did not give up that easily. Maybe, some thought, the validity of astrology cannot be tested by means of character profiles only. Maybe additional information is necessary. Although it is not clear at all why this ought to be the case, later tests were done to try to answer this objection. This was the case with an experiment in the Netherlands in 1994.

The test was designed by Rob Nanninga, secretary of the Dutch skeptical organization *Skepsis*, in cooperation with the Dutch Society of Practicing Astrologers. Forty-four astrologers from mostly experienced to very experienced were tested. Besides the birth data of seven anonymous subjects they also obtained answers to a series of questions asked of each subject. The questions had been suggested by the astrologers themselves and covered matters like the test person's sex, education, profession, recreation, family, religion, relations, interests, and life problems. Answers to a personality test were also included in each subject's file.

The forty-four astrologers also received a set of seven horoscopes and were asked to match them with the data for the subjects. Because the answers to some questions could possibly give a clue to the age of the person, all seven subjects were of about the same age. Also, no subjects were chosen for which the Ascendant at birth was close to the border between two signs, to avoid any uncertainty about the moment of birth causing doubt about the correct sign of the Ascendant.

This test too was a complete fiasco for astrology. Not less than eighteen of the forty-four participating astrologers had believed themselves able to identify all seven horoscopes correctly. In reality nobody succeeded in doing this. Worse, half of the astrologers did not make one single correct identification! Not a single astrologer scored better than three hits (therefore not even one-half). The results agreed completely with what could be expected by chance. More experienced astrologers did not do any better than the dilettantes. And finally, the results of the astrologers did not agree with each other; only two astrologers came, independently of each other, to the same—wrong—result. It looked as if each astrologer had been working completely arbitrarily.

With hindsight quite a few of the astrologers were of the opinion that the questionnaires contained insufficient information. Still, by far most of them had not stated any objections beforehand. Also, the horoscopes were supposed to be too much alike. Because all subjects were of roughly the same age, the slowly moving planets (Uranus, Neptune, Pluto) were often located in the same sign. But for the rest there had actually been very large differences in the horoscopes. And don't the astrologers state that each horoscope is unique?

Except for a few who have lost their trust in astrology because of the tests, the astrologers do not have a reasonable explanation for their failure. They often claim that astrology cannot be tested by means of questionnaires, but only by means of a personal conversation with the subject of the horoscope. And that person should preferably be not an arbitrarily chosen individual but someone who consults the astrologers of his own accord. And indeed, they have very solid reasons to believe this.

And Still They Do Believe: Why?

An objective judgment of the value of the astrological *practice* (this is what the astrologers *do* and what they claim to be able to do, not what should be possible according to their theory) turns out to be negative. Yet the customers of the astrologers are obviously satisfied with a practice that is based on not a single objective reality. How can this be explained?

We already pointed out that the customer is obviously not able to judge his psychological profile correctly. This is connected with a number of psychological processes that are active during the consultation of an astrologer—and not only there—and which allow even coarse inaccuracies in the supplied product to be accepted without much trouble.

Around 1975 the American psychologists C. R. Snyder and R. J. Shenkel looked into the factors that led people to accept a description of themselves as correct. Interesting in this context is the following "astrological" experiment:

A first group of people was asked to provide their year, month, and day of birth. These data would be used to draft a short astrological description of their personality, which they had to judge on its value. For the judgment, a scale of 1 (very bad) to 5 (perfect) was used. The description provided obtained an average score of 4.38 for this group—a very good grade.

The second group was only asked for the year and month of birth. They too received an astrological profile and this time the average score was 3.76, a little bit less than very good.

Finally a control group was given a description. The subjects were told that the description fitted the majority of the population. They too, were asked how well this was applicable to them. Here the average score was 3.2, just a little bit more than good.

We notice that the appreciation of a description is proportional to the amount of data requested. And notice, in reality no astrologer was used at all: *Everybody had received the same profile!*

In this case the different scores can clearly be attributed to a nonastrological factor. As the subjects were more and more convinced that the "horoscope" was especially composed for them, it was judged more favorable. The third group knew that the description was general and because of that they were much more critical than the second group, who understood the experiment to be personal, but took the fact into account that the description could apply to quite a few people. The members of the first group had an even stronger conviction that they belonged to a limited group (people born on the same day), and that made their judgment more favorable yet. What made the "horoscope" for the last group a success was therefore not its content, but the *conviction* of the "customer" who had to interpret it. It is obvious that, the more someone is convinced that the reading provided can only apply to him, the more he will experience it as unique and personal. The accuracy of the description is of little importance.

If one takes into account that the astrologer asks not only the year, month, and day of birth, but also the hour, minute, and place of birth, then it becomes obvious that the uniqueness of the horoscope will be emphasized and that the receptiveness for the astrological statement will increase further.

This is only one of the many psychological processes that are all more or less at work during an astrological consultation. Their net effect is that the positive experience the client has after the session is either consciously or unconsciously accepted as proof for the validity of astrology. Among psychologists this phenomenon is known as the "*fallacy of personal validation*": the tendency (and the mistake) to take one's own personal experience as the measure for judging the validity of something.

We give here a few other processes which can play a part during a conversation with an astrologer and make his pronouncements more believable for the customer, whether these pronouncements are correct or not. These processes are also valid for every predictive technique, not only for astrology, but also for reading coffee grinds, palm reading, reading (tarot) cards, crystal gazing, and clairvoyance:

- *Cold Reading* or responding to the reactions of the client. Spoken answers as well as body language, which is much more spontaneous and therefore can betray much more, come under this label. This technique is particularly useful for zooming in on problems and sensitive items, so that the client gets the impression that the astrologer knows how to reach the heart of the matter in an unnaturally quick way.

- *The Barnum Effect.* People are much more alike than usually is assumed. Because of this, pronouncements which are actually applicable to most of us are quickly presumed to be exclusively applicable to the unique, personal attitudes or experiences of the client.
- *Belief.* It goes without saying that whoever already believes in astrology does not have to be convinced further. As the belief increases, the critical sense decreases. Curiously this does not prevent the customer from being categorically convinced that he judges the pronouncements of the astrologer critically.
- *Persuasion.* With some flair the client can be forced to accept the given interpretation, if need be with the argument that she does not know herself all that well or that possibilities are being discovered of which she is not aware. The horoscope is always right!
- *Selective Memory.* Hits make a deeper impression than misses, particularly because one talks about the former much longer and with the latter the subject will be changed rapidly. Because of that hits are remembered much better and appear to be much more striking than misses. Of course, this increases the score for the successes.
- *Vagueness.* Some astrologers are keen to "raise" an interpretation to an uncontrollably high level, for instance by making ample use of psychoanalytical jargon. To the uncritical listener this must give the impression of a sequence of extremely profound truths—the psychological emperor's clothes, so to speak.
- *Interpretation-after-the-Fact.* If you search long enough you will always find an astrological factor that is applicable to the problem at hand. This is a logical result of the complexity of the horoscope.
- *Cognitive Dissonance,* or escaping disappointments. He who pays—and sometimes a considerable amount—wants his money's worth in any case. In order not to admit that one bought a pig in a poke, one unconsciously attributes a high value to the delivered product and emphasizes all positive characteristics of the buy.

To illustrate how some of these processes play a role (not only in astrology) we will give an example.

With high expectations a client goes to consult a trustworthy person: the astrologer. Most of the time the client is convinced in advance that there is "something" to astrology, otherwise of course, he would not have come (*belief*). That conviction is reinforced by the actions of the astrologer; a horoscope is constructed for which very precise personal data are required. In some countries some astrologers even go so far as to require an official birth certificate. The customer is right away duly impressed by the required exactness and the personal character of what is coming. The astrologer turns over the leaves of heavy tomes full of tables, executes complicated calculations, and finally produces a complex, mysterious figure (nowadays a computer is often used, which for some people is still quite impressive). Most of the time the client is not present when this is done—making it even more mysterious—but has to return later. Drawing and interpreting the horoscope after all requires "hours" of work from the astrologer. All this duly impresses the client and paves the road for the most important phase of the whole work: presenting the interpretation, during which the client is assured again how unique his horoscope is.

An experienced astrologer does not need many hours at all to interpret a horoscope, unless he desires to produce literature and therefore details everything on paper. A few minutes are sufficient for a trained eye to discover the main lines that can serve as a guiding thread for the interpretation. The practically unlimited number of combinations of factors that can be found in any horoscope makes it possible to develop the main lines in any direction. At the beginning of the interpretation a few general tendencies are sketched and most of the time the reactions of the customer soon make it clear which areas have to be expanded and which ones offer little hope of success (*cold reading*). In this way the astrologer gets a general idea of the problems with which the clients wrestles (health, relations, family, profession). By putting the emphasis on these subjects in the further interpretation, he creates the impression that the horoscope itself points to these problem areas.

During the presentation of the finished product most of the activity actually comes from the client. He after all has to interpret the assertions of the astrologer: He has to search in his memory for events, situations, remembrances, opinions, expectations, and interests that can be made to agree with what the astrologer says. The astrologer dishes up general statements dressed up in rather personal terms (*Barnum Effect*). Because of the situation in which the receiver of that message finds himself—particularly because it is stated very explicitly that the explanation is extremely personal—he will try to fit the message into the situations of his life; he is the one who interprets. As soon as an appropriate event, situation, or whatever has been found, the memory of the way in which the pronouncement was worded fades away. In its stead comes the conviction that the astrologer was the one who provided that interpretation!

Let us make this last statement clear with an example. Assume that someone consults an astrologer. After the necessary preparation (a horoscope is cast) the astrologer asks, "Have you recently had any emotional problems?" The customer remembers all of a sudden that a few days earlier he had a quarrel at work and that this left a strong impression on him for several days. The emotional problems have been found! (Just to make sure, dear reader, did *you* really not have any emotional problems recently? Have you truly not been up or down?). If someone sometime later asks that person what the astrologer told him, she will hear: "He told me I had had problems at work." The reality however was different: The astrologer was not the one who began to talk about the work and moreover he only started out by asking a question. The customer himself made the connection with the quarrel at work. Had the question not produced any remembrance, then the astrologer would have moved to another subject. But now that the nature of the problem has been found, the astrologer will analyze any possible connections with the sixth house (work as a subordinate) and with the Moon (emotions) to "prove" that the suggested problems are indeed to be found in the horoscope.

The astrologer, too, will be quite happy when he finds out that the customer is pleased with his pronouncements, which strengthen in both their convictions that the technique works, the basis for the subjective strength of the validity of astrology (*fallacy of personal validation*). Even the astrologer is the victim of the psychological processes which he, who learned them from the experience of many years, applies unconsciously. For that reason it is not at all miraculous that quite a few people who started to explain horoscopes just for fun are honestly convinced after some time that they have discovered a valuable system that proves its worth time and time again.

During the consultation the client participates in the process by asking questions ("How come I recently...?") to which the astrologer, without much trouble, gives an astrological answer ("In your horoscope I see that your Mercury in the tenth house makes an unfavorable aspect with Saturn") (*interpretation-after-the-fact*). The client also expands on the question of the astrologer ("Do you mean, perhaps...?") and tells much more about himself than he thinks.

And even if something goes amiss, nothing is lost: Astrology has access to an inexhaustible arsenal of excuses which "explain" errors. If the error is made in the psychological description of the client, then the error does not even have to be admitted: The horoscope is correct but the customer does not know himself! Or here and there some subtle distinction has to be taken into account. Or the pronouncement is concerned with "not-yet-actualized potentials" which just wait for expression (*vagueness*).

At more flagrant blunders the indistinctness of the horoscope can be called upon: Is the time of birth accurate enough? A few minutes earlier or later can, after all, make quite a bit of difference! Curiously that argument is never used if the pronouncement meets with approval, then the time of birth does not cause any problems. Another solution exists: The astrologer is only human and did err. Astrology is not being blamed, but the practitioner is: He did not take into account one of the many factors in the horoscope, or he did not take the hereditary characteristics or the upbringing of the client sufficiently into account.

At the end of the consultation the client pays the agreed upon amount (which, among other things, pays for the "large number of calculations").

202 Making Sense of Astrology

Now, nobody likes to admit that he spent his money on something worthless. If the client had not been completely convinced of the value of astrology upon entering the office of the astrologer, then this is an argument to strengthen his conviction (*cognitive dissonance*). On the way home the recent experience is again digested: The hits are put in order (*selective memory*) and simplified; questions become striking pronouncements; hesitations become noticeable disclosures; and the ballast of suggestions that led nowhere are thrown overboard. There remains a polished memory that will resonate for a long time. Astrology has booked another success.

The value of astrology can also be confirmed by a *self-fulfilling prophesy*. In this case the client is so strongly convinced that the astrologer is always right, that he (un)consciously arranges his life according to the pronouncements of the astrologer and adapts his behavior in accordance with the horoscope. As we saw in Intermezzo II this factor played a role in fooling the investigators in the studies of the effectiveness of the zodiac. An extreme example is the (probably apocryphal) anecdote about the famous Italian astrologer, mathematician, and physician Girolamo Cardano (1501–1576; particularly known as the inventor of the Cardan joint). "The rumor went around that he had allowed himself to die of starvation so that his date of death would not contradict the one that was pointed out in his horoscope—which he had cast himself."*

The above description of an astrological consultation is not quite fiction; with the exception of the financial side of the matter one of the authors of this book has seen all these processes work when many years ago he cast horoscopes for friends and acquaintances. And the reality often surpasses fiction. There were persons who for half an hour exposed themselves completely and the day after remained absolutely convinced that they had not said a word; there were also those who suddenly changed their behavior in order to bring it more into agreement with their horoscopes. Although the authors personally do not think highly of the moralizing arguments against astrology, the latter phenomenon is certainly a cause for second thoughts.

The example used is therefore rather typical for the psychological interpretation of the horoscope. In many cases, though, people do not go to the astrologer in order to get a lecture in psychology. Instead they have a problem for which they want to find a solution. Especially in this type of case the customer is not a passive listener who resigns himself to follow the advice of the astrologer. Most of the time the possible solutions to the problem have already been considered carefully, but the decision about the action to be undertaken has not been made. The duty of the astrologer consists in

---

*M. Milani, *Girolamo Cardano, mistero e scienza nel Cinquecento* (Milan: Camunia Ed., 1990). By the way, it seems he survived his predicted date of death by three years. Cardano had been embarrassed earlier when he predicted a long and happy life for the very young English king Edward IV. Edward died less than a year after the prediction.

removing the indecisiveness via the horoscope. Most of the time the client has already unconsciously decided what the best solution is, but what he wants from the astrologer is that little push, the confirmation that the selected action is the right one. The way in which the client explains his problem to the astrologer, the reactions to the suggested tendencies of the horoscope, the questions asked, the explanations the astrologer desires, all of this limits the role of astrology proper to an absolute minimum. Here the astrologer has to have a good knowledge of human nature in the first place and his advice has to be dressed up in astrological language. Mrs. Soleil (a famous French media astrologer who died recently)—did nothing else and achieved much success.

For people with psychological problems the use of the horoscope has an enormous advantage over the classical psychological consultation. During the consultation with the astrologer the attention is aimed at the horoscope and not at the client himself. Personal faults and shortcomings are projected on a drawing, problems and responsibilities are due to "the stars" and not the person. Classical psychology analyzes the person, astrology analyzes the horoscope. In this way it is much easier for the person in question to distance himself, which can only help in the solution of the problems. Astrology becomes a cheap—but often no less effective—form of psychotherapy. The psychological processes which promote the acceptance of the horoscope also work for written horoscope interpretations. The personal exchange between astrologer and client is then, of course, not present, but it is obvious that this does not prevent a favorable final appreciation. An illustration of this is the following experiment by Michel Gauquelin, which also sheds an interesting light on commercial astrology. (It also shows that Gauquelin, who was looking for cosmic influences all his life, was very critical of the existing astrology.)

In 1968 French astrologer André Barbault started to make use of the computer to produce horoscopes. Everybody who sent him—accompanied with the suitable amount of money, of course—his or her birth data, could receive a personal horoscope which was drafted by a computer (which at that time was something very new). Michel Gauquelin took advantage of the opportunity and mailed in a number of birth data. However, he was so sneaky as to provide the birth data of a number of notorious murderers. The most infamous among them was Marcel Petiot, a physician who had been decapitated in 1946 for committing at least twenty-seven murders. The personality descriptions which he received from Barbault were all exceptionally favorable for the people involved! For Dr. Petiot, for instance, there were no suggestions whatsoever that problems with justice were a possibility or that a violent death (the guillotine) was waiting for him. The computer also failed to mention that the person in question had been dead for more than twenty years.

This horoscope of Dr. Petiot was used by Gauquelin in another experiment. In a French gossip magazine loaded with occult advertisements and nonsense (a French *National Enquirer*) he offered readers a free horoscope. Whoever responded to this received a "personal" horoscope (in reality it was the one for Petiot), together with a questionnaire to check the correctness of the personality description (after all it was only proper to do something in return for a free horoscope). The first 150 forms that were returned showed that more than 90 percent thought that the text accurately described their character, personal problems, and life histories, and that this was supported by the opinion of family and friends. Psychology had done its work. It is only too bad, as Gauquelin remarked, that the only person for whom this astrological personality description was *not* valid was the real subject of the horoscope.

Order in Chaos

What kind of people consult astrologers? It is often said that astrology is particularly attractive to people who do not keep both feet on the floor, those who have "spacy" ideas. This kind of person is supposed to be less able to handle problems and would therefore seek support in astrology and other occult practices. They are more or less queer birds who can now be found mostly in the "New Age" movement.

This is an exaggeration. There are certainly people who answer to that picture, who show a real tendency for the mysterious, the occult, the esoteric—so-called hidden or secret knowledge—and for that reason alone show much interest in astrology. But that is not a true picture of the average adherent of astrology. Such a person turns out not to differ much from the average citizen. It is not true that somebody who believes strongly in astrology would not be able to function socially. The average astrologer is not a socially maladapted individual who walks with his head in the clouds (the more so because very few astrologers would recognize anything in the sky). As long as astrology is not the subject of discussion, the "astrological" army does not differ in any way from other people.

Still, there seem to be characteristics common to adherents. Psychologically, astrology is shown to fulfill the need to provide *order* in our life and our personal experiences. We want to see connections between experiences, we look for order in our experiences so that we can understand them better.

Each of us has a psychological worldview, a vision of how the world is put together, where our place in it is and how events and experiences fit into this context (A happens because B causes it). That worldview makes life understandable; we obtain psychological control over our life, we feel ourselves less a toy of fate. But these efforts to obtain control do not always succeed. After all, there are events which happen by chance and for which there is no sense in looking for an explanation. Assume someone gets hit by a roof tile on a stormy day. Why did this happen? Of course, it is possible to offer explanations such as because there were loose tiles or because there was a sudden gust of wind. But these explanations are psychologically very unsatisfactory; they only describe a number of facts which led to the accident. The victim would rather ask questions like: "Why exactly me?" "Why didn't that tile fall ten seconds earlier or later, then I would have gotten off with a good scare?" "Why was that gust right then?" There are a very large number of factors involved and if only one of them had been somewhat different, the accident would never have happened. This complex interplay of factors makes the event incomprehensible and makes the victim feel like a defenseless plaything of fate, given up to senseless suffering. The event was "by chance," unpredictable, and there is no single reason the victim can relate exactly to why the accident happened there and then. The "sense" of it escapes all understanding.

But most people have an almost inborn aversion to the idea of "chance." They usually state very clearly that according to them "chance does not exist." For them everything has a reason, and not just *any* reason, but one which fits the fact into the order of things. The fact is subjected to an explanation which makes the sense, i.e., the meaning of the event clear and which is therefore psychologically satisfactory. They demand, so to speak, an understandable connection between events, *even if that cannot be found in the objective reality.* They do not want to be a toy of chance, but, on the contrary, autonomous individuals who have the impression that they hold their fate in their own hands. For them astrology, palm reading, clairvoyance, card reading, and similar practices have an undeniable attraction. They offer the possibility of creating structure in what is unstructured, detecting rules and laws in what is accidental. With the help of the horoscope everything can be explained after the fact. The astrologer can make sense of every event with unwavering certainty with the aid of the innumerable relations between the cosmic factors in the horoscope. Man is no longer the helpless toy of unpredictable fate, but of predictable planets. The personal experience becomes part of a larger cosmic whole: The traumatic experience suddenly has obtained some meaning (the horoscope predicted the "possibility of an accident from higher regions"). What difference does it make then that the connection found is nothing but make believe? Psychological peace has been restored and that is for the person involved usually much more important than reality.

A second characteristic of quite a few practitioners of astrology is indeed their tendency toward the occult. Most of the time this is not limited to astrology; without any difficulty connections are made with other techniques of prediction, such as palm and card reading. The ease with which astrology was included in all kinds of esoteric systems such as theosophy, anthroposophy,* and the Rosicrucians promotes the acceptances of these systems. Theosophy, an odd mixture

---

*A spiritual and mystical philosophy based on the teachings of Rudolf Steiner.

of Western and Eastern mystical philosophy, founded near the end of the last century by the colorful figure of H. P. Blavatsky, has, to be sure, played an important role in the revival of astrology. The result of this interweaving of ideas is that many occult matters are explained in an astrological way and, conversely, astrological factors are interpreted in an occult way. Hence all those books about astrology and reincarnation, astrology and crystals, esoteric astrology, the horoscope of the Messiah of the Age of Aquarius, and more of such uncritical and often incomprehensive nonsense. Astrology has always been a constant value in the occult culture and this will probably remain so for quite a while.

Conclusion

One may ask, If we cannot trust our own experiences, what can we trust? We should not make this statement too extreme: Not all our experiences are unreliable, otherwise we could not handle our daily problems. The false experience, to call it that, is most clearly present in the cases where a lack of good information plays a role. Anyone who consults an astrologer surely does not have enough information to make the decision all by himself (at least consciously, unconsciously the decision may already have been made). Several different ways are available and some good practical advice by the astrologer can then rapidly be interpreted as a cosmic hint.

In judging a personality description the case is rather the reverse; here we have an abundance of information from which one only has to choose. The human personality is not unchangeable. Everybody experiences a permanent evolution, in the long as well as the short run. Now and again one is elated and looks at things through rosy glasses; sometimes later one can be rather discouraged and depressed. The attitude that we have toward others changes in accordance with that. The result is that everybody can find something in his past that fits most of the elements in the personality descriptions presented by astrologers.

As an example, take an astrological handbook in which the characteristics of the signs are described in detail. Little imagination is needed to find some sentences in the description of each sign that are applicable to the reader. If one then realizes that an almost inexhaustible arsenal is available to the astrologer, it is not at all astonishing that most people think that their horoscope is correct. And the stars (or coffee grinds) take the credit.

Subjective experience therefore is not an argument for the validity of astrology (or of anything whatsoever). The human personality is so immensely rich in characteristics, counts so many aspects, that each description has to have some items that agree with it. Hence the lasting success of all kinds of pseudopsychological systems which try to encompass that personality.

Intermezzo IX

☉ ♆ ☽ ☊ ☋ ☌ ⚹ ✶ □ △ ⊼ ☍

Cosmic Influences

In a discussion about the validity of astrology some opponents sometimes deny that we on Earth are exposed to cosmic influences. Of course this is a blunder, although the term "cosmic" sounds a little bit bombastic for what we could better call "extraterrestrial." The word "cosmos" after all means the whole universe, while in astrology only the influence of the planets should play a role.

It may be useful to take a moment to check which extraterrestrial influences could give a *possible* explanation for the relationships the astrologers claim to work with. Not that the astrologers are at all interested in them. For a number of them astrology is based on relations of an occult nature for which there is supposed to be no place in the modern "materialistic" worldview. But most of them simply do not ask any questions about it. For them only the results count.

Gravitation

Gravitation, which is defined as the force of mutual attraction between all bodies, is "the cosmic force" par excellence. It is the only force to play a role of importance on the scale of the universe, and by its nature it is an exceptionally weak force. All objects are attracted to each other by gravitation, but for objects in our daily life this force is completely negligible. Only by means of very sensitive instruments can it be observed. Only celestial bodies contain enough matter (mass) to make gravitation work noticeably. The relatively enormous mass of Earth attracts us and causes what we call "weight."

Each body has a gravitational field proportional to its mass and this field in principle extends to infinity. Still, in practice we do not notice the attraction of, for instance, the Sun, although it has a mass 332,000 times larger than the mass of Earth. This is due to the fact that the force of gravitation decreases with the square of the distance between the two bodies. If this distance doubles, then the mutual force the bodies exert on each other decreases to one-fourth. At a tripling of the distance, the force of gravitation decreases to one-ninth; at ten times the distance, the force remains only one-hundredth. The Sun is about 23,000 times farther away from us than the center of Earth. This distance compensates more than needed for the much larger mass of the Sun, with as a net result that the force of gravitation the Sun exerts on us is 1,600 times weaker than that of Earth. For planets—which have a much smaller mass than the Sun and are often also farther away—the effect is still slighter.

Tidal Effects

Still, there exists a noticeable effect on Earth that is due to gravitation. We all know that the oceans move up and down twice a day because of the forces of attraction of the Sun and the Moon. This phenomenon is rather easy to explain. The part of Earth that is closest to the Moon is a little bit more strongly attracted by the Moon than by Earth's own center. The part that is farthest removed is attracted a little bit less. For a fluid surface such as that of our oceans this causes a protuberance at both sides, like a lemon. Because Earth rotates about its axis, these protuberances move over the surface of the water. Not only the Moon but also the Sun exerts a tidal force. Both forces reinforce or weaken each other depending on the relative positions of those two celestial bodies. If the Sun and the Moon are located in one line with Earth (at Full and New Moon), these protuberances become extra large.

The connection between the phases of the Moon and the tides works as an inspiration for some astrologers. Why shouldn't this cyclical influence exist in humans? After all, about three-quarters of the human body consists of water.

To begin with, this analogy, no matter how beautiful, is not an explanation for the presumed astrological influences. It is not clear how that could possibly be the case. Moreover, the magnitude of the ocean tides should not be overestimated. On the average the protuberance is less than one meter, not that much for oceans, which have a mean depth of 4,000 meters. It is only because the water does not flow freely over the surface of Earth that locally the tidal difference can be much bigger. The position of islands and continents causes deviations in the tidal movement. In narrow and shallow seas, estuaries, and bays the effect can be reinforced. At some places—such as the English Channel or the Bay of Fundy (between New Brunswick and Nova Scotia, Canada)—the difference in tides can be as much as ten meters.

The effect of the tides on human beings can be calculated in exactly the same way as that for the oceans. In the most extreme case our weight will decrease by 0.0000035 percent (or almost a thirty-millionth) when the Moon is standing straight above us, as compared with the position of the Moon at the horizon. For a person who has a fair weight that difference is equal to the weight of a postage stamp. If the weather changes, our weight can vary with 0.03 percent; if we move over the surface of Earth, with 0.5 percent. Nobody notices this and compared with these the tidal effect of the Moon is completely negligible.

For the Sun the tidal effect is much less because tides decrease with the cube of the distance. If a celestial body with a certain mass is removed to ten times its original distance from us, then the tidal effect it exerts becomes a thousand times smaller. Although the Sun's enormous mass still causes a noticeable influence, the influence of the planets is totally negligible.

And what about human beings? Because of the rapid decrease with distance the tidal effect of the planets on a human being is less than that of another human being at a few meters' distance. At birth—the moment that would determine the horoscope—the nurse-midwife exerts a tidal influence more than a thousand times stronger than that of the Moon and many billion times stronger than that of any planet whatsoever!

The Rhythm of the Oysters

Tides are important for a number of forms of life on Earth. Some scientists even assume that life could not have moved from the ocean to dry land without tidal differences. Many plants and animals are dependent on ebb and flood for their food and their propagation. In most cases there is no reason to assume that they experience the influence of the Moon directly; they simply follow the rhythm of the rising and falling water. But there has been an investigation which appears to point to such a direct influence.

We refer to an experiment American biologist Frank Brown performed with oysters in 1954. A number of oysters that had been raised in New Haven, Connecticut, on the Atlantic coast, were transported to Evanston, Illinois, nearly one thousand kilometers westward on the continent. There they were kept alive for forty-six days in tanks of seawater in a dark room. No moon- or sunlight could reach the animals. During all this the time when the oysters opened and closed was registered automatically. It is known that oysters—like mussels, for instance—open more when the tide is high because more food is then available. The activity of the oysters decreases therefore twice a day, in accordance with the tides.

Now it turned out that the oysters in the tanks in Evanston kept that rhythm as if even there tides existed. This is not at all extraordinary in itself. Oysters have a biological clock which can keep up with their familiar rhythm, even if the external synchronizing cause of it disappears. But Brown noticed that the maxima of their activities started to deviate from the moment of high water in their place of origin: The oysters opened some three hours later. According to Brown this shift in time agreed with the difference between high tide in New Haven and the meridian (the moment at which the Moon is at its highest position in the sky) in Evanston. The conclusion was obvious. Now that the tides had disappeared, the oysters had tuned their activity to the position of the Moon at their new home. But in their tank it was impossible to "see" the Moon. Could they then "feel" it directly?

The experiment is still mentioned in several publications about astrology and even in encyclopedias. But some critical remarks should be made. In the first place, the experiment was never repeated, not even by Brown himself. For forty years everybody kept referring to that single test as a proof of cosmic influences. More experiments, preferably with a larger number of oysters and over longer periods of time, would certainly have been desirable for such a remarkable phenomenon.

Paul Quincey, a British physicist who specialized in tides, studied Brown's graph of the "oyster activity" a second time. He found that the shift of the maximum of activity did not follow from a mathematical analysis of the measurements, but from the peaks of a curve which was obviously drawn by hand according to a pattern that Brown himself thought present. This way of presenting the results is rather deceptive: without that imposed curve the maxima in the graph are a lot less clear to identify. Even worse, they become more and more vague as the time passes. There is clearly a shift to be observed, but because of the vagueness it is rather premature to attribute any value to it. According to Brown the shift agreed with the difference in time between high tides in New Haven and the passage of the Moon in Evanston. Curiously he did not mention this difference in time (2.2 hours) himself, while the shifts in his hand-drawn graph varied between 2.2 and 3.3 hours.

Quincey estimates that the shift amounts to 3.5 hours and according to him this is not very convincing. But his strongest objection is that the experiment compared apples to oranges: High tides, as a matter of fact, do not coincide with the passing of the Moon. In New Haven, the tides run on the average one hour and a quarter ahead of the lunar position. Why should the oysters in one place take the tides into account and at another place the location of the Moon in the sky? If they sense the location of the Moon why don't they follow the difference in time (less than one hour) between the passage of the Moon in New Haven and Evanston?

Could the shift be explained in another way? The fact that the biological clock of the oyster slowed down does not have to mean anything mysterious. Maybe the animals were confused by the disappearance of the tidal movement in their environment. Only a more convincing test can settle this question. In that case it would be best to test several groups of oysters in different places, both east and west of their place of origin, with a control group that remains in the same location. Only if the rhythm of the eastern group speeds up, that of the western group slows down, and that of the group in the original location remains the same, then we might ask ourselves if the Moon has something to do with it.

Electromagnetic Radiation

A complete spectrum of electromagnetic radiation continuously reaches Earth from outer space. In spite of the large diversity in which this radiation appears, it is in principle always the same phenomenon: a wave motion of alternating electric and magnetic fields which move with a speed of 300,000 km/s. The difference in the various kinds of radiation is due to their wavelength; the smaller the wavelength, the more energetic the radiation is.

The longest wavelengths are those of *radio waves,* which vary from kilometers to almost a millimeter for microwaves (which have enough energy to heat food). With shorter wavelengths we get into the area of *infrared radiation,* which we can feel as heat radiation. In the narrow zone of wavelengths between 400 and 800 nanometers (a nanometer is a millionth of a millimeter) lies *visible light* (red has the longest and blue/violet the shortest wavelength). At still shorter wavelengths the radiation has so much energy that it can be harmful for humans: *ultraviolet radiation* (which burns our skin when we are exposed to it for some time), *X-rays* (the penetrating action of which is generally known), and the extremely energetic *gamma rays* (which are a result of nuclear explosions, radioactive processes, and extremely violent processes in the universe).

Earth receives most of this radiation from the Sun. Fortunately for us, because high-energy radiation is exceptionally dangerous, a large part of it is stopped by our atmosphere; only visible light, a large part of the radio waves (particularly the short and ultra-short waves) and a little bit of ultraviolet and infrared is transmitted.

In this way the Sun provides us with light and heat, which is essential for our life. Walking around too much in the Sun can cause skin burns and skin cancer. We therefore can certainly not say that the solar radiation has no effect on us. However, this effect is of a much more general nature than the influences astrologers talk about. As far as the Moon and the planets are concerned, the small amount of light we receive from them is just reflected sunlight. With the exception of the Moon, the light of which is strong enough to read a newspaper by, the light of the planets is much too weak to have any influence whatsoever. And this is also valid for other radiation. Only Jupiter produces radio waves by itself, which can disturb certain radio transmissions on Earth, and a little bit of heat radiation, but all of this in much smaller quantities than the Sun. And finally we have to take into account that all radiation received—just like the gravitational force—quickly decreases with the distance from the planet.

Charged and Uncharged Particles

Our Earth also receives a continuous stream of particles from outer space. There are *charged particles* (ions and electrons) originating in the Sun (the solar wind) and coming from outer space outside our solar system (cosmic radiation, possibly coming from exploded stars). Those charged particles do not have much influence on us as they are stopped or deflected by the magnetic field of Earth.

Just to be complete we should also mention *neutrinos*. These are particles without any charge and possibly without any mass, which are produced in nuclear reactions. They are so small (almost equal to "nothing") that they can penetrate practically everything—they even fly straight through Earth—without having any influence. Their influence is so limited that we can only detect them with very special apparatus, although each second several millions of them fly through our bodies.

Solar Activity and the Eleven-Year Cycle

The influence of solar activity on Earth is a controversial issue. A number of phenomena on the Sun show a cyclical character as, for example, the number of sunspots (darker areas on the Sun) which varies over a period of about eleven years. These spots have very strong magnetic fields and produce radio waves. The presence of many sunspots (an "active" Sun) coincides with sporadic eruptions of the solar surface, releasing both X-rays and charged particles. The former cause changes in the higher atmosphere which can disturb radio connections; the latter cause deviations in Earth's magnetic field. For these reasons alone the solar activity is being tracked very carefully.

People have long speculated about possible other influences of solar activity. In particular there appear to be indications of influence on the weather and the climate. Some people believe that they have found an eleven-year cycle in the climatological record, in the thickness of annual rings in trees, and so on. It is also known that there were hardly any sunspots visible during the "Little Ice Age" in the seventeenth century, a period during which it was exceptionally cold (and which, ironically enough, practically coincides with the long reign of France's famous "Sun King," Louis XIV). The influence of the Sun on the weather is controversial, but certainly not impossible; after all, our heat comes directly from the Sun.

Global and Individual Influences

To this list of possible "cosmic influences" we can also add meteorites and comets, which occasionally collide with Earth and cause minor or major catastrophes. The extinction of the dinosaurs at the end of the Cretaceous period, about 65 million years ago, is often attributed to the damage done by such a collision.

Looking at all these factors we can decide that certain extraterrestrial phenomena have an influence on our "sublunar" existence, albeit often very indirectly. In many cases people take this into consideration. All of us take day and night and the change of seasons into account. Sailors and fishermen keep an eye on the tides. Armies want to plan surprise attacks preferably around the New Moon, because they want to profit from the darkness. This is simply a normal taking into account of noticeable natural phenomena. Astrology, however, talks about influences which are unnoticeable.

It is also clear that the well-known influences are much more general, more global than the astrological influences. If X contracts skin cancer by walking in the Sun, then this has nothing to do with the position of the Sun (or of whatever) in the horoscope of X. The known cosmic influences pay no attention whatsoever to such individual questions as love-life, career, or winning the lottery. And it is totally incomprehensible that these influences should have been fixed for once and all at the moment of birth.

Proofs for Astrology?

In spite of these differences the existence of cosmic influences is still used as a justification or even as a proof for astrology. Many astrological books talk in passing about the working of the tides, "radiations," or solar activity, most of the time without going any deeper into the subject. The reasoning suggested is simple: This influence is real, therefore the possibility of other influences should not rejected.

Some researchers are of the opinion that the known influences are much stronger than we would suspect at first. The already mentioned experiment of Brown's oysters is an example. But most of the time these theses do not hold water. For instance there is the theory launched by the British scientists John Gribbin and Stephen Plagemann in 1974 in their book *The Jupiter Effect*. They started out with the assumption that solar activity is regulated by the location of the planets. When this activity is at its peak the rotation of Earth is supposed to be slowed by the solar wind, which would lead to the occurrence of earthquakes. In this way Gribbin and Plagemann predicted a strong earthquake in the area of Los Angles at the end of the 1970s or the beginning of the 1980s. This would coincide with a maximum number of sunspots and a "great conjunction" of the planets in 1982. The theory did not have a leg to stand on: A correlation between planetary positions and solar activity has never been shown; to the best of our scientific knowledge the solar wind does not slow the rotation of Earth and a slowing of the rotation of Earth does not cause earthquakes. And of course . . . the predicted earthquakes did not take place.

Once in a while assertions that the position of the planets has an influence on solar activity are published. Some people believe this can be derived from statistics, but this turns out not to be correct. At first sight it may appear quite likely that planets could have an influence on the sunspots through tidal forces. But the mass of the Sun is 745 times larger than that of all the planets together, and after the calculations have been done it becomes clear that this influence is totally negligible.

But, after all, these digressions have nothing to do with astrology. In astrology no account is taken of the eleven-year sunspot cycle. And the planetary positions that are considered here—just like the mentioned observations of Nelson—are purely heliocentric (calculated with respect to the Sun) while astrology works with geocentric positions (calculated with respect to Earth).

Not a single one of these theories provides a proof for astrology, in the sense that concrete astrological theses or the cosmic nature of the characteristics in which astrologers believe are demonstrated by them. It is indeed questionable if it would *ever* be possible to prove astrology true on the basis of known physical influences. Distances, which are enormously important for physical influences, do not play any role in astrology (neither the difference in distance between the planets, nor the varying distance of each planet separately). Nowhere is there even a beginning of an answer to the question as to why in astrology only planetary positions that are projected onto the plane of the ecliptic are important. And we haven't even mentioned the many inconsistencies and disagreements discussed in this book.

On February 22, 1979, an article appeared in the British scientific periodical *Nature* with the title "Correlation between Heart Attacks and Magnetic Activity." In this article the authors claimed that their investigation had shown that there exists a connection between the total magnetic activity at Earth's surface—which is partly determined by the solar wind—and the number of patients admitted to the hospital with heart trouble. On the days with high solar activity there were clearly more admittances.

In January 1980 a well-known science journalist mentioned in the Belgian weekly *Knack* (which in that country has about the same standing as *Time* magazine) that this investigation triumphantly proved the astrological opinion that the Sun rules the heart. Unfortunately, on October 18, 1979, another article had appeared in *Nature*, in which the investigators described the results of a similar test. However, they could not confirm the results of the earlier article. And in the *Nature* issue of January 3, 1980 (just before the publication of the commentary in *Knack*), the authors of the first article admitted that their investigation could not stand, as the medical information it was based on turned out to be inaccurate! The data in the original hospital records had been checked and turned out to be different from the data they had used for their investigation.

As far as we know now, the supposed relation between the Sun and heart complaints does not exist. But that conclusion was never published in *Knack*.

The Theory of Percy Seymour

In this connection the theory of British astronomer Percy Seymour should be mentioned. Percy Seymour taught astronomy at a polytechnical institute in Plymouth and was head of the planetarium in that city; in his book *Astrology: The Evidence of Science*,* he proposed a physical mechanism which according to him could explain astrological claims. The fact that an astronomer expressed himself in such a positive way about astrology caused elation in some astrological circles in the 1980s.

However, the contents of the book do not fulfill the expectations aroused by the title. Elsewhere Seymour himself admitted that his theory "cannot serve as a foundation for the everyday astrology as usually performed."[1] He carefully avoids the previously mentioned problems which any physical theory that tries to "explain" astrology has to solve, and no new facts are presented. But he does appeal to the results of Michel Gauquelin. As we saw in chapter 6, Gauquelin's claims are now no longer supportable. But what is worse, Seymour suppresses the fact that Gauquelin rejected astrology as such and that he demonstrated the incorrectness of a number of astrological assumptions.

Seymour is an expert on magnetic fields and he looks to them for a possible explanation of astrological influences (without providing any proof whatsoever for even one single astrological proposition). He rejects every "occult" explanation but meanwhile looks for connections with pseudoscientific methods like dowsing and chiromancy.†

His theory is based on the effect of the tides of the Moon on the magnetic field of Earth. That field deflects charged particles from the solar wind and catches them in an invisible, doughnut-shaped structure around Earth, the *magnetosphere*. The Moon exerts a similar tidal influence on these particles as

---

*(London: Lennard Publishing, 1988)

†*Dowsing* is the term for divining, as for water or mineral deposits, by passing a forked stick or rod over the surface of the ground under which the substance is hoped to be found, so that the rod might dip suddenly when brought over the right spot. *Chiromancy* is divination by inspection of the hand, palmistry.

on the oceans and this causes an extremely minor change in the magnetic field. Seymour assumes that this change, which, like the tide, occurs twice a day, exerts an influence on a human being at birth. At the same time he assumes that *all* planets influence us through a similar tidal effect.

The first objection to this theory is that the deviation in the magnetic field caused by the Moon is so weak that it can only be measured by extremely sensitive instruments (on a normal compass nothing can be noticed). Even then the effect is drowned out by other fluctuations, so that often it cannot be perceived at all. The tidal effect of the planets—as we noted already—is immeasurably weaker than that of the Moon; it is so insignificant, in fact, that it does not cause a perceptible variation in the magnetic field.

Seymour's answer to this objection is that the tidal difference in the water level in some bays, estuaries, and river mouths is much larger than the average. He suggests that analogously to this, "magnetic bays" can occur in the magnetosphere in which the effect is amplified. His magic word here is "resonance." This well known natural phenomenon means that a vibration—even a very weak one—can have a much stronger influence on an object if its frequency is equal to the "natural" vibration of the object. In this way a bridge can collapse when a platoon of soldiers marches over it at the right pace. A glass can shatter because of a sound of a certain pitch. Or the rhythmic movement of ebb and flood can cause large tidal differences in a bay of the right dimensions.

An important application of this is the radio; the very weak electromagnetic vibrations of a radio signal are amplified in a receiver, because an electronic circuit (a resonator) in this receiver vibrates with the same frequency as the signal to which it is tuned. In an analogous way—according to Seymour—the human nervous system could be "tuned" to the cyclical changes that the planets cause in the magnetic field of Earth. Each planet has its own frequency, and people with a pronounced personality will be "fine-tuned" to a certain planet. That influence is noticeable to the fetus in the uterus and at birth that condition is "labeled," at least according to the British astronomer.

This theory poses more questions than it even starts to answer. What in the world are these "magnetic bays"? How can they arise and why can they be felt by fetuses and not by sensitive magnetometers? How does the "reception" of the signal work? How can the fetus tell the difference between all these planetary variations, if we know that the tidal effect of Jupiter (assuming that it is noticeable) reappears twice in 23 hours 56 minutes and 24 seconds, while the period for Saturn is barely twelve seconds shorter? And these are only the *average* periods; because of the complicated movements of the planets in the sky these daily cycles can become some tens of seconds shorter or longer. How then can our nervous system recognize the planet due to its "rhythm"? And finally; where is the exact connection with the moment of birth?

Seymour may be an astronomer, but all of this has little to do with scientific theory. He collects all kinds of suggestions and speculations and puts them together in a extremely improbable construction. The use of metaphors such as "magnetic melodies," "heavenly music," and "cosmic programming" are used to hide a lack of facts. In this way he avoids a clear demonstration of proof. Criticisms of his theory are answered with insinuations about the prejudice and intolerance of the opponents, but the content of the criticism is hardly entered into.

In another part of his book Seymour fished Gribbin and Plagemann's previously discussed theory of the Jupiter Effect out of the waste basket. The solar activity, which was assumed (falsely, as we saw) to be dependent on the planetary positions, causes changes in the magnetic field of Earth and, according to Seymour, this in turn influences our nervous system. But here too, we look in vain for proof.

Unknown Influences

Although many astrologers invoke well-known physical influences as an argument for astrology, there are also some (and sometimes the same ones) who look for an explanation to other, still unknown influences.

Some of them search for it in an as yet *unknown radiation*. After all, X-rays have been known for only a century and in the eighteenth century nobody knew anything of radio waves. Who knows what the future may teach us? Or perhaps the unknown factor is hidden in one of the many exotic subatomic particles about which modern theoretical physics talks so much? Of course, we cannot know that now. But we can ask ourselves how it would be possible for the unknown "radiation" to possess exactly those weird specific characteristics which all known rays, particles, and fields are lacking. After all, we may well presume that all physical interactions have certain characteristics in common, as for instance their rapid decrease with distance.

Other proponents of astrology are of the opinion that the influence cannot be of a physical nature. They look for it in the idea of *synchronicity*, a notion mainly known through the work of Swiss psychoanalyst Carl Gustav Jung. Synchronicity is understood to be a simultaneous coherence between phenomena which have no causal connection. A classic example is the story of someone who has a bad dream about an acquaintance he hasn't met in a long time and soon after he learns that this acquaintance died the same night. Or someone who thinks about a certain subject, turns on the radio, and hears to his astonishment a discussion about that same subject. Or someone who won the lottery with a very "personal" number. Quite a few people are unwilling to accept that this sort of coincidence can be explained by chance.

According to the followers of the synchronicity hypothesis, the events in our lives and the positions of the heavenly bodies are attuned to each other by some sort of cosmic order. There is no physical interaction, it is more like two clocks running alike. That idea is quite old and it includes a certain determinism: Are all the events in our life determined beforehand, like the movements of the hands of a clock?

The theory of synchronicity is not far removed from the idea that astrology has something to do with the paranormal. A phenomenon is usually called "paranormal" if it is (apparently) impossible to explain with our scientific knowledge. A whole field of knowledge has been developed for the study of these phenomena: parapsychology. But after more than a century of research parapsychology is still unable to produce any indisputable results and the existence of the paranormal is still being questioned. As a matter of fact, some parapsychologists are of the opinion that correct predictions by astrologers should be considered a form of clairvoyance and not information derived from the horoscope.

However it may be, all these speculations about unknown influences do not answer the question we asked: Can *existing* cosmic influences provide an explanation for the relations with which astrology is occupied? If that were the case—but that has not been shown here—then this would be an argument in favor of the validity of astrology. But to speculate about influences that have *as yet to be demonstrated* can only have meaning if the validity of astrology itself has been proven.

Note

1. Cited in G. Rouckaerts, "Het lied van de Zon," *Knack* (November 5, 1986): 215–17.

Intermezzo X

The Moon and Life on Earth

In discussions about possible influences of the heavenly bodies on humankind it often happens that the "obvious" effects that the Moon is supposed to have on some aspects of human life are quoted. Usually the presumed connection between the phases of the Moon and births is pointed out, as well as the "experience" that psychiatric patients become more restless around the Full Moon. As an additional argument the origin of terms like "lunatic" are often mentioned. Because such an influence is something completely different from the tidal activity and can therefore a priori be considered improbable, it is interesting to check whether such ideas are more than popular beliefs.

Where we have to look in order to find the origin of these ideas is not very clear. The first conception could have arisen from the idea that there was an analogy between the phases of the moon and human fertility: the Moon becoming "full" (the interval between the New Moon and the Full Moon) would then be connected with an increase in fertility; the completion of the lunar evolution, Full Moon, would then correspond to the completion of gestation: birth. By the way, fertility is traditionally one of the characteristics attributed to the Moon in astrology. In all probability the biological fact that the menstrual cycle in human beings lasts roughly a month has promoted this belief in the connection between Moon and births, if it was not the source of it.

Another, now far less known popular belief, is the opinion that hair should preferably be cut during a waning Moon. Cutting hair during a waxing Moon would destroy the forces that allow the hair to grow and which are strongest at that time, with a bigger chance of baldness as a result. Here too, the "growing" Moon is clearly connected with another kind of growth.

But, to confuse the matter, it should be mentioned that in some parts of the world the opposite tradition was held.

The origin of the relation between the phases of the Moon and psychological problems is rather obscure. Two possibilities, which are not mutually exclusive, can here be considered. On the one hand there is the well-known fact (myth?) that some animals are restless when there is a clear Moon above the horizon during nighttime (dogs that bark at the Moon, for instance). From that people could have deduced that our natural satellite also has a psychic influence on man. On the other hand in classical astrology the Moon was associated with water (the tides), which in turn was connected with emotions. The Full Moon would than act on these emotions, resulting in psychic problems.

Finally there is the possibility that these popular beliefs are based on observations: More children were born at the Full Moon, and psychiatrists could have extremely busy days around that time.

The Moon and the Maternity Ward

Let's have a look at the idea that more children are born around the Full Moon. This opinion is very widespread not only among the general public but also among midwives—and they ought to know about it. If they work in maternity wards, they may tell tales about nights with a Full Moon during which one could not keep track of the number of women coming in to give birth. Statements of that kind cannot be rejected out of hand.

In order to check the amount of truth in such "old wives' tales" there is in fact only one good method: counting. If indeed more children are born around the Full Moon than in the period between two Full Moons, then this ought to show up clearly in the birth statistics.

In the course of the years several studies have been performed in order to prove or disprove the existence of such an effect. If we look at all these studies together, then something curious comes to the surface.

For instance in 1959 Menaker and Menaker published an often cited study in which more than half a million births in New York City over a period of ten years were looked at. The results were remarkable: During the *two weeks after a Full Moon* there were about 1 percent more births than in the two weeks before a Full Moon. Now one percent is not all that much, but because of the large numbers involved this 1 percent caused a (statistical) effect that was far from negligible. Clearly, a definite correlation was found between births and phases of the Moon. But a few awkward problems turned up. The maximum correlation occurred not at the Full Moon, as popular belief holds, but in the two weeks around Last Quarter. Moreover how could an excess of only 1 percent ever have penetrated into popular beliefs? The "effect" is all but striking

Miniature representing the Moon with the corresponding sign of Cancer. Illustration from the Italian Renaissance manuscript *De Sphaera* (fifteenth century). Biblioteca Etense in Modena.

and certainly not enough to explain all the stories about overworked midwives.

However, things become more curious yet. One of the authors of this study repeated it eight years later. Half a million births in New York City were studied over a period of thirty-seven months, between 1961 and 1963. This time also an excess of 1 percent was found, but now in the week *before* and the week *after* the Full Moon! A shift of a week had occurred with respect to the previous study, and this time the results were more in accordance with popular belief.

Later yet, in 1973, a study appeared by Osley, Summerville, and Borst, who also studied half a million births in New York City. This time also an excess of 1 percent was established, but now in the two weeks *before* the Full Moon, therefore around the First Quarter!

And in 1980 Criss and Marcum announced the results of their analysis of the 140,000 births that had taken place in New York City in 1968. They too found a small effect, this time around the Last Quarter.

Whether there is really a moon phase-periodicity present in the course of the number of births in New York City is all but clear, but if it exists, it is in any case very weak and certainly not stable in time. Therefore one may well doubt whether this should be attributed to the Moon.

Not all studies obtain this type of result. Rippmann, for instance, performed a study as early as 1957 on slightly fewer than ten thousand births and did not find any effect. The same is true for Abell and Greenspan in a study from 1979 which referred to 11,000 births. Also, studies on a more limited scale by Witter (1983), by Hausser, Bornais, and Bornais (1985) and Desrosiers (1985) turned out to be negative.

A limited, unpublished study by one of the authors of this book (Martens) performed on 2,111 births gave remarkable results somewhat along the line of the studies of Menaker. The births were spread over 120 lunations (periods from one Full Moon to the next Full Moon). The distribution of all births showed a weak wave pattern with a maximum close to the Full Moon. Dividing these 120 lunations into 4 periods of 30 lunations each showed, however, that this particular effect was caused by one single group of 30 lunations with a pronounced peak around Full Moon. The other 90 lunations did not show this pattern.

It appears therefore that in studies of this kind one has to guard against strong variations during a short period, variations which in itself are not due to lunar phases but which in the total of the observations can create that impression. The fact that the place of the maximum changes from study to study and from period to period makes a real "Moon effect" very improbable. Whatever may be the case, it always concerns small variations which could not possibly be noticed in daily life.

Thus the influence of the Moon on births is not shown at all, in spite of the "experience" of midwives and of popular belief.

The Moon and Abnormal Behavior

For obscure reasons the Moon throughout time has also been related to phenomena like werewolves, vampires, and, more popularly, madness. The Full Moon was supposed to cause psychiatric patients to become more restless, more crimes were supposed to be committed, and the number of suicides was said to increase. Some books were published in which this opinion was defended. Astrologers also want to make us believe that this is the truth. For instance the astrological duo West and Toonder in *The Case for Astrology* mention the results of someone by the name of Ravitz, who "ratified the ancient belief that there was more unrest among the insane when the moon was full."[1]

Our remarks about births and the Moon have already made clear that traditional "wisdom" does not necessarily have to be true. For that reason alone the reputed relation between psychiatric unrest and the phases of the Moon is worthy of a thorough inquiry.

Much more has been written about this subject than about the Moon and births. A summing up of all studies would be rather boring to the reader. Fortunately for us, in 1985 Rotton and Kelly performed a meta-analysis on this subject in which they examined 118 sets of data from thirty-seven different studies. These data were divided up into different groups according to the nature of the abnormal behavior: homicide, criminality, suicide and self-mutilation, unrest of psychiatric patients, admittance to psychiatric institutions, calls at crisis centers, and finally the unavoidable "miscellaneous" section. Wherever possible the data were reanalyzed and brought under the same heading, after which the results were combined and evaluated.

For the conclusions we let the authors speak for themselves:

> Although this meta-analysis uncovered a few statistically significant relations between phases of the moon and behavior, it cannot be concluded that people behave any more (or less) strangely during one phase of the moon than another. This is not the same as saying that there is no relation between phases of the moon and behavior. Just as we cannot prove that werewolves, unicorns and other interesting creatures do not exist, we cannot prove that the moon does not influence behavior. However, the burden of proof lies with those who favor the lunar hypothesis. They will have to collect a great deal more—and better—data before they can reject the null hypothesis of no relation between phases of the moon and behavior.[2]

Rotton and Kelly also point to the tendency to consider *every* deviation from chance that was found, even if it does not occur at Full Moon, as a lunar effect, and they remark:

Adopting a more limited but common view of lunar influences, one must conclude that evidence for the lunar hypothesis fails to pass three crucial tests. The first and most important is *replicability*. For every study that has recorded more lunacy when the moon is full, another has recorded less. A second test, which could be regarded as a substitute for replicability, is *statistical significance*. Even when a large number of results are combined, one cannot reject the null hypothesis of no relation between phases of the moon and behavior at conventional levels of significance. A third and closely related test is *predictability*. Given the task of predicting people's behavior, knowing the moon's phase reduces our uncertainty *by less than 1%*. [Emphasis added.][3]

Conclusion

The results of research into the truth of popular beliefs about the relation between humanity and the phases of the Moon have a number of analogous characteristics. In both cases studies have been published that confirm the theses as well as reject them. In both cases the positive results of the research turnout to be variable; in some studies an effect is found around the Full Moon (in accordance with popular belief), in other studies it is found elsewhere. The effect, moreover, is always very small, so that the practical usefulness is negligible.

On this basis we can therefore decide that the existence of an influence of the lunar phases on births and on human behavior has not been convincingly shown. The fact that people nevertheless keep believing in them is probably due to an unending series of anecdotes. A midwife has had a busy night, goes home after work during the early hours and notices a beautiful Full Moon in the clear sky. Such an occurrence is very noticeable and it reminds the midwife of the existing rumors about an increase in births around the Full Moon, rumors that at that moment are confirmed by the facts. After another, equally busy night, the same midwife also goes home, but this time there is no Full Moon in the sky. The absence of it is not noticeable, so no associations are called up this time. If, after a quiet night, she sees no Moon, she will not take anything into consideration. And, supported by popular belief, a calm night with a visible Full Moon will be interpreted as an exception to the rule. It is a fact that the Full Moon is much more striking than the other phases of the Moon; the Moon is then by far at its brightest and only around this time remains visible all night. If one takes all these factors into account, one should not be surprised that these ideas defied time, even among those who should know better. The next time you see a Full Moon either at a late or early hour, admire it quietly, but do not assume the the world population is making a jump.

The presumed influence of the Moon on the growth of plants has also never been proven. The origin of the ideas about this can also be found in the association of the Moon with fertility, so it is no surprise that it was believed, for instance, that it was better to sow by a waxing Moon. Moreover the Moon formerly played an important role—and certainly in the countryside—in determining the time; the beginning of sowing and harvesting was often indicated by lunar phases. Popular almanacs were a combination of practical time divisions and superstition. For the assumption that moonlight in early spring is damaging for the crops there exists a simple explanation. A visible Moon means few or no clouds. Without clouds Earth cools faster than when cloud cover traps the heat. Because of that young shoots can be damaged by frost during a cloudless night, even if no moonlight shines on them.

Notes

1. A. West and J. G. Toonder, *The Case for Astrology* (Harmondsworth, England: Penguin Books, 1973), p. 186.
2. J. Rotton and I. W. Kelly, "Much Ado about the Full Moon: A Meta-Analysis of Lunar-Lunacy Research," *Psychological Bulletin* 97, no. 2 (1985): 300.
3. Ibid., p. 301.

9

ASTROLOGY: PAST AND FUTURE

In contrast to most books about astrology this work did not start with the history of the subject. There are two good reasons for this. In the first place a good understanding of the origin and the evolution of astrology requires at least some understanding of astrological terminology and a knowledge of the fundamental assumptions. And that is only possible, of course, if an explanation of the astrological elements precedes the historical overview. The second reason is the purpose of this work: It is a critical study of astrology, which supplies information and arguments that ought to enable the reader to form a well-founded judgment about the amount of truth of the astrological system. Therefore, it is preferable to judge the system independently of its historical background. In that way confusion of antiquity with truth is avoided. The often heard argument that because something is very old it ought to have at least a kernel of truth is worthless from a logical point of view. For millennia people were convinced that the Sun turned around Earth, but the respectable age of this conviction has not prevented that it has meanwhile been relegated to the museum of scientific theories.

Astrology has to be judged in the same way: It is not because astrology has a history of about 2,500 years behind it that therefore it cannot be in error. Many astrologers use this argument wrongfully ("Can you accept that great scholars have erred for centuries?" Of course we can, why not?). If you want to know the validity of astrology, then you have to forego the past and aim a critical eye at the arguments for and against it.

Yet it is very interesting to have a look at the past of astrology. A little bit of knowledge about the origin and the early evolution of it will throw some more light on some scientific pretensions of the system.

The Origin of Astrology

The cradle of astrology can be found in ancient Mesopotamia, which roughly corresponds to present-day Iraq. From the earliest times people in that area were obsessed with all kinds of predictive techniques. In almost any kind of more or less curious event they saw an omen or the expression of the will of some deity. And since they seem to have had an inclination toward systematics, they started to make extensive lists in which different remarkable phenomena were noted, together with important events that took place around that time. The noticeable event was seen as a sign. These lists are usually called *omina,* the Latin word for signs. Archaeological research has brought many of these texts to light.

As an illustration, here are some examples from the omen series "*Shumma alu*" ("If a city . . ."):

- "If a city is built on a hill, then this is not good for the inhabitants of that city."
- "If the doors of a house face the east, then the owner of that house will become old."
- "If the doors of a house face the west, then the owner of that house will not become old."
- "If a scorpion stings the little finger of the right hand of a man, then that man will be locked up for two years."
- "If in the month of Nisan, between the first and the thirtieth day, a snake falls between husband and wife, then their sons will not live, their house will be destroyed."

Just about any anomalous event or remarkable phenomenon could be considered an omen, including unusual heavenly events. Moreover, meteorological observations, such as remarkable sunsets, were also classified as "heavenly events." Only a very small percentage of the lists found refer to them, however.

For centuries people collected and made notes and no progress was made beyond this stage. This rage for collecting and classifying finally led to the redaction of an extensive series of texts, of which the "heavenly" one is known under the name "*Enuma Anu Enlil*" (according to good assyriological custom referred to by the first words of the text). Here too an example is suitable:

> If at sunrise on 1 Nisan (the Babylonian New Year) the Sun is as red as a torch, a white mist rises from it and the wind blows from the east, then on the 28th or the 29th day of the month a solar eclipse will take place, the king will die in this month and his son will mount the throne.

Very likely this succession of events did indeed happen once. After the death of the king, that sunrise, together with the ensuing solar eclipse, was considered an omen. This event was included in the collection, in the conviction that in the future a similar phenomenon would be followed by similar events. In this sense we can rightly claim that these texts are based on observation—but on a single observation. These texts, however, are still very far removed from the present astrology.

The height of the rage for collecting can be placed at about the seventh century B.C.E. The famous library of Assurbanipal, which provided hundreds of clay tablets with such omina, dates from that time. Besides the older astral texts, like the example cited from the "*Enuma Anu Enlil,*" "ominal" correspondence was also found. It concerns letters of priests who had specialized in the interpretation of astronomical phenomena. The contents of these letters is concerned especially with the meaning that should to be attached to the observed heavenly events. So, for instance, this letter: "I wrote to the king, my lord: 'There will be a (lunar) eclipse. There was indeed an eclipse, it is a sign of peace.' "

It appears as if the fact that the prediction came true was considered a favorable sign. The future was then obviously dependent on the ability of the priests and the state of astronomy: Whatever was "understood" and predictable lost its alarming and therefore unfavorable character. But these texts show as yet very little resemblance to what later would be called astrology.

What happened in the field of astrology after the seventh century B.C.E. is difficult to determine—the available material is too rare. But clay tablets from the sixth century B.C.E. do indicate a rapid development of a *mathematical astronomy* in Babylonia.

As became obvious in the previous chapters, a frame of reference is needed in order to be able to describe the observed phenomena in the sky successfully. Between the seventh and the fifth centuries B.C.E. the Babylonian astronomers brought about such a framework in order to determine the positions of (especially) the Moon and the planets. The exact course of that development is of lesser importance, but from the fifth century B.C.E. on we find the final product of it: the zodiac.

Remarkably, the fifth century B.C.E. is also the period in which the first real "horoscope" is situated. We do not want to keep this historical document from our reader. It is a small clay tablet, on which in cuneiform script the following—poorly preserved—text is written:

Obverse:
Month Nisan, night of the 14th ... (?) ... /
son of Shuma-usur, son of Shuma-iddina, descendant of Deke, was born /
At that time the moon was below the "horn" of the Scorpion /
Jupiter in Pisces, Venus /

in Taurus, Saturn in Cancer,
Mars in Gemini. Mercury, which had set (for the last time), was (still) in(visible) /
(Month) Nisan, the first (day of which followed the 30th day of the preceding month), (the new crescent having been visible for) 28 (USH), (the duration of visibility of the Moon after Sunrise on) the 14th (?) was 4.40 (?) (USH) /
the 27th was the day-when-the-Moon-appeared-for-the-last-time /

Reverse:
(Things will?) be good before you /
Month Du'uz, year 12 /
(year[?])8 ... (rest destroyed)

By assuming that the given positions of the planets refer to the signs of the zodiac which, as was explained in chapter 3, at that time coincided more or less with the constellations of the same name, the dates can be calculated at which these planetary positions occurred. The most probable date for this text turns then out to be April 29, 410 B.C.E.

Of course, this is not the very first horoscope ever "cast." It would be an extreme coincidence if that document were ever found. And even if it were discovered, nothing like "first effort at casting a horoscope" would be written on it. If we take this into account and if some period has to be assigned for the origin of astrology, then the fifth century B.C.E. ought to be considered as the most likely.

Even a superficial study of these texts shows that there are fundamental differences between the new horoscopy and the earlier omina. The *personal* character of the astrology is particularly striking. While astral omina were concerned exclusively with the country ("If Mercury is visible in the month Kislimu, then there are thieves in the country") or with the king as personification of the state, but certainly not with the common man, in the new version all attention is now aimed at the individual. Originally this was limited to the higher classes, but in principle it was applicable to everybody.

Another important element by which the new astrology differed from the omina was the importance of planetary constellations: the position of all the planets in the zodiac and the geometrical relations between them. This novelty, of course, could only appear after the development of the mathematical astronomy, by means of which it had become possible to determine the place of those planets which were not visible at that moment. With the omina, on the contrary, the concern was with the interpretation of an isolated phenomenon and not of a complex whole.

Finally, for the horoscope a well determined point of time, the moment of birth, was taken as the point of departure to make predictions, while with the older techniques phenomena had to be waited for patiently. The new system was more precise, more ordered, more exact, but no more correct.

What could possibly have happened during the "missing centuries" that are so important for the origin of the real astrology? It is a pity that these centuries are so poorly documented in this area. A plausible hypothesis follows.

During the seventh century B.C.E. the astral omina were studied intensely. New observations were performed, new omina were composed and the collection grew and grew. But then doubt arose, and slowly the conviction spread that the traditional texts actually provided very little certainty as far as predicting future events was concerned. Some omina based on the same phenomenon contradicted each other and many omina never came true.

All of this could have led to a distrust of the ancient texts, a crisis of confidence, so that the decision was made to repeat the "research" from the beginning: pin down observations of simultaneous heavenly and earthly phenomena of which one could be sure. For that purpose it was necessary, however, to have access to a good system of reference for the determination of the position of the celestial bodies. Moreover techniques were necessary to determine the exact place of these bodies in the sky at a given moment. In other words, a solid mathematical astronomy was a necessary condition for the rise of astrology. Driven by that impulse, the development of the already existing astronomy was accelerated. The last step of dividing the ecliptic into twelve equal signs was made, which produced a very useful system of reference. Mathematical models (the so-called zig-zag functions) were developed to calculate the positions of the Moon and the other celestial bodies. Astronomical observations were systematically noted in diaries. Because of this from about the fifth century B.C.E. on, all mathematical methods and astronomical data that were needed for the development of a personal astrology were available. Add to that the conviction that personal predictions were possible—as evidenced by the above cited "*Shumma alu*"—and the horoscope could be born.

Whatever the precise development might have been, astrology is about 2,500 years old. Of course, that is a very respectable age, but in astrological circles much greater, sometimes fantastic ages are mentioned. The oldest horoscope dates from a time when the Babylonian and the Assyrian empires already belonged to the past and Mesopotamia was ruled by the Persians.

In contrast to what some people claim, astrology was not born in Egypt, India, or China. We want to warn the reader of a number of books which insist on taking the origin of astrology back to the Egypt of the pharaohs (a myth which, as we shall see, already existed in antiquity; the Egyptian civilization has always fascinated other nations). A general characteristic of these papers is that they systematically neglect the existing evidence, which clearly situates the development in Mesopotamia. Because not a single document from the classical Egyptian period that refers to astrology is known, the authors of these papers are compelled by necessity to find their inspiration in alternative interpretations of nonastrological remnants. For instance West and Toonder try to give an astrological interpretation to the building plans of a number of Egyptian temples.

The famous zodiac of Dendera, a sculptured zodiac in Egyptian style, is presumed by some authors to picture the firmament as it looked 10,000 years ago. In reality this zodiac dates from around the beginning of the common era and is a typical product of Hellenism. Among the innumerable inscriptions and papyruses from the time of the pharaohs there is not a single one that contains astronomical data. When astrology proper arose, Egypt was a Persian province and the creative period of the Egyptian civilization was long past. The horoscope is about as old as the Parthenon in Athens. The Great Pyramid is some twenty centuries older.

The Earliest Astrology

As far as we can judge, Babylonian astrology always remained primitive. The zodiac and a division of it were known and the classical planets (Sun, Moon, Mercury, Venus, Mars, Jupiter, and Saturn) were used. Also, a text has been found that allows us to presume that something like an extremely primitive house system existed. This can be derived from the following phrases: "If a child is born when Mars is standing in the *tallu* . . . / . . . Venus is standing to the *MI-SHIR* . . . / . . . Jupiter is standing to the *dur.* . . ." It is not clear what these terms exactly mean, but it is very well possible that here a reference is made to an angular division with respect to the horizon. The precursors of the Ascendant, Descendant, Midheaven, or Imum Caeli? Maybe a simple rule for the aspects was also applied, at least if sentences like "If a child is born while Jupiter comes forth and Venus (had) set, then . . ." may be interpreted in that way. In this case only a form of opposition—the rising of one planet while the other was setting—was used.

The "new" astrological system did as yet keep some clear connections with the older astronomical tradition: The importance attached to the first sighting of a planet after a conjunction with the Sun is an indication of this ("If a child is born and that day Jupiter was visible for the first time after conjunction with the Sun, then . . ."). At that time the astrologers did indeed "watch the stars."

For a clear insight in the relation between this "first" astrology and the later developments, a survey of the interpretations that were associated with the different planetary positions would be welcome. However, extensive texts about this subject have not been found. Yet groping in complete darkness is not necessary: Some Babylonian texts include short sentences which suggest what the complete "art" might have been. Consider, for instance, the following horoscope from 235 B.C.E.:

> Year 77 (of the Seleucid era, month) Siman, from the fourth (day until some time) in the last part of the night of the fifth (day),
> Aristokrates was born.
> That day: Moon in Leo. Sun in 12.30° in Gemini.
> The Moon sets its face from the middle toward the top; (the relevant omen reads:) "If, from the middle toward the top, it (the Moon) sets its face, (there will ensue) destruction." Jupiter ... in 18° Sagittarius.
> The place of Jupiter (means): (His life will be) regular, well; he will become rich, he will grow old,
> his days will be long (numerous). Venus in 4° Taurus.
> The place of Venus (means): Wherever he may go, it will be favorable (for him);
> he will have sons and daughters. Mercury in Gemini,
> with the Sun. The place of Mercury (means): The brave one
> will be first in rank,
> he will be more important than his brothers, ...
> Saturn: 6° Cancer. Mars: 24° Cancer ...
> the 22nd and 27th of each month. ...

This horoscope shows some remarkable features. There is the general tendency of the pronouncements that are connected with the planets: Those for Jupiter and Venus are favorable, in accordance with the characteristics which these planets also have in modern astrology. In addition the name of the subject of the horoscope is striking: Aristokrates. Not a Babylonian, but a Greek. Probably a descendant of a soldier or an officer of the army of Alexander the Great. They belonged to the social upper crust in Hellenistic Babylon.

Besides the few horoscopes a "textbook" is also known, which provides a survey of a number of astrological methods and rules. Here too, the pronouncements for Jupiter and Venus are favorable. What is remarkable is that the interpretations for these two planets, which occur in the abovementioned horoscope, are found almost literally in this textbook! Maybe the astrologer who drew that horoscope of Aristokrates used a copy of this same manual?

Development

The "honor" of working out this simple astrology into the complicated system we now know belongs to the Greeks. In the fourth century B.C.E. the Babylonian sounds were heard in Greece (certain cryptic statements in the work of Plato point in this direction), but only in the third century, when—among others—the Babylonian priest Berossos opened an astrological school on the Greek island of Kos, did the march of astrology begin in earnest.

A very important factor in the spread of astrology were the conquests of Alexander the Great. By the end of the fourth century B.C.E. this Macedonian king conquered from Greece the whole Middle East, from Egypt and Asia Minor to the Indus Valley. He wanted to have the whole of the known world fused into one large world empire with a common—mostly Greek—culture. Although after his death in 323 B.C.E. his empire was divided among his generals, the cultural fusion, known as Hellenism, did take place.

In the conquered areas the popularization of the Greek language and culture was strongly promoted. In return the Greeks came into contact with strange oriental religions, ideas, and customs. Among these ideas was astrology. In this way it became possible that in Egypt bas-relief sculptures were made with astrological symbolism in old-Egyptian style at the behest of rulers who spoke Greek, and temples were built in Syria in the Greek style for Persian or Egyptian gods.

The early history of astrology in the Hellenistic world is obscure, but there are some indications here and there that throw some light on it. For instance in a number of astrological/magical texts there are references to a book which is called *Salmeschiniaka*. Although this (lost) work was written in Greek, the name makes one suspect that the source was in all probability Babylonian: The word *salmi* is Babylonian and means "image." From a number of surviving fragments we can conclude that the book covered the subdivision of the Egyptian months—which consisted of thirty days each—in periods of five days—the length of the Babylonian week—in which the characteristics of the astrological "rulers" of each division were discussed. A Greek text that divides the Egyptian months into Babylonian weeks—talk about cultural fusion! The book dates from about the third century B.C.E., possibly the period in which astrology was brought from Babylonia to Egypt.

The further development of astrology took place mainly in Alexandria, the world center of Hellenism. There *hermeticism*, a philosophic-religious system which according to its adherents represented the "ancient higher wisdom," also developed. That knowledge was supposed to have been revealed by the god Hermes Trismegistos, the Greek name for the Egyptian god Toth, traditionally the god of wisdom. However, in reality this ancient knowledge dates from the second and third centuries before our era and it shows a predominantly Greek philosophical point of view, bedded in an—exotic—Egyptian magic context.

Hermeticism was a worldview, an attempt to obtain a total insight in the fundamental structure and the workings of the cosmos, the ordering of the universe, the place of man in it and the meaning of existence. The answers to the important philosophical and religious questions could be found in the *Hermetica* or hermetic scriptures. These consisted of texts about philosophy, astrology, magic, alchemy, and similar subjects. Magic was an important part of it, and it is in this environment that astrology was developed further.

In Greek and Roman astrological documents one finds references to a number of hermetic astrological works which were known as *Hermaikai*

Diataxeis or "Teachings of Hermes." Some classified the *Salmeschiniaka* among them, but that happened to just about everything which was considered to contain ancient wisdom. The most important astrological work in that series of "Teachings of Hermes" was attributed to the duo Nechepso and Petosiris and is probably the first real astrological textbook. Judging from the fragments which have been preserved and the references made to it by some ancient authors, most elements of Hellenistic astrology were represented in it.

A striking characteristic of the work by Nechepso and Petosiris is the justification of astrology. Here there are no references to centuries of observation and systematizing; here is no place for such down-to-earth arguments in the "higher hermetic wisdom." Astrology is here a *revelation* of the gods themselves: King Nechepso had a vision during which he beheld the order of the cosmos, while the priest Petosiris summoned the goddess Ananke (Greek for Necessity) with magic formulae in order to obtain knowledge. In a later hermetic iatromathematical text (*iatromathematica* means medical astrology) the physician Thessalos narrates how he also had a vision in which Asklepios, the god of medicine, reveals to him the astrological relations between planets and medicinal herbs.

That the book was attributed to a king and a priest of ancient Egypt is typical for these documents. In fact a late-Egyptian pharaoh Necho or Nechepso is known, but he lived some four centuries before the book was written and more than a century before the rise of astrology. The second name associated with these texts is Petosiris. In Egypt a tomb was found of a priest of Toth (Hermes) of that name; from the graffiti in his tomb it is clear that this man was honored as a wonder-worker long after his death. The times in which he lived, the fourth century B.C.E., leaves us to suspect that he too was not directly implicated in the redaction of the books which were ascribed to him. It is clear that these respected names of Necho/Nechepso and Petosiris were only used to suggest that the work was ancient and to attribute more authority to it. This false authorship is not at all exceptional for Hellenistic documents; many religious and magical works were presented as revealed by a god—in the first place Hermes Trismegistos himself—or from a king, priest, sage, or prophet. For that matter, many apocryphal Bible books originated at the same time. That the real author of the books of Nechepso and Petosiris deemed it necessary to attribute his texts to such authorities can point as much to giving in to the taste and the demands of the time as to the confidence he had in his own piece of work.

Parallel with this hermetic-religious development in Egypt there was a philosophical-scientific development in Greece. The astrological teachings were adopted and spread by the philosophical school of the *Stoa*. The stoics, as they were called, accepted a rather fatalistic philosophy: Earthly life was a vale of tears against which the true philosopher could arm himself by detachment from all earthly pleasures. The stoic principle was "He who has nothing can lose nothing."

The philosophical school of stoicism was established in Athens around 300 B.C.E. by Zeno of Cition (a city in Cyprus). It is said that Zeno was from semitic stock, so that from the very beginning stoicism was not a purely Greek movement. It spread rapidly in the Hellenistic and later also in the Roman worlds. Strikingly enough Zeno's successor as leader of the Stoa was also a barbarian (a non-Greek in the language of those times); a native of Mesopotamia, he is known as Diogenes of Babylon. A later prominent stoic, Archidemos, even established a section of the school in Babylon itself. It is therefore not surprising that stoicism was influenced by Oriental ideas, such as the immutability of Fate (everything is fixed beforehand and no escape is possible). For the stoics the cosmos was a living being within which everything, even human life, is connected causally. Typical of those teachings was the *cyclic* character of history: Everything has happened before and will, after the destruction of the world by fire and the following rebirth, occur again in an infinite succession of cosmic cycles.

This deterministic idea found a natural ally in astrology. It brought, after all, the possibility of foreseeing the future and preparing with a certain peace of mind for what was unavoidable (escape was not possible anyway). For many this was one of the attractive aspects of this philosophy: The relation between humanity and the cosmos was explained in a rational way and the possibility was offered to make the best of it in this life. The planets completely determined development in the sublunar sphere and everything was subordinate to them. Because of its association with stoic teachings (which were extremely popular in later antiquity), astrology became philosophically respectable. Rival schools, such as skepticism and epicurism, radically rejected astrology, but they were far less successful.

Stoics, however, were very rationally inclined. A scientific explanation was sought for astrology in order to make it philosophically acceptable. The only valid reason they could think of was experience. That in turn led to the claim that astrology was based on centuries of observation and systematizing. In this context "centuries" is much too mild an expression: The observations could never be old enough for the authors of antiquity. Berossos, for instance, according to some sources, attributed to astrology the venerable age of 432,000 years, according to others it was 468,000 years. Epigenes of Byzantium alleged that the Babylonians had observations dating back to 730,000 years ago. His contemporary Critodemos, on the other hand, was more modest and stuck to 490,000 years. Simplicius, one of the last philosophers of antiquity, thought in turn that 1,440,000 years was a nice number.

Together with this "historical" justification, efforts were made to bring astrological principles into accordance with Greek science. The characteristics of the signs and the planets which, as we already noticed, are reflections of the images of the constellations and gods of the same names, were "derived" from the Greek physical elements (fire, earth, air, and water) with their corresponding attributes (hot, cold, dry, moist) and in this way were fitted into the Greek concepts about the cosmos. The worldview of Aristotle also contributed to this.

The acme of this integration is to be found in the work of the Alexandrian astronomer and astrologer Ptolemy (Claudius Ptolemaeus, ca. 150 C.E.). Among other things he wrote two books that would be considered standard texts centuries after his death: The *Mathematikè Syntaxis* (later known as the *Almagest*) for astronomy and the *Tetrabiblios* ("Four Books") for astrology. In Ptolemy's astrological work mysticism is practically absent. Wherever possible Greek scientific principles are invoked. The *Tetrabiblios* is above all things a theoretical tract. Nowhere is it explained how in actual practice a horoscope is to be cast and interpreted. Nowhere is there any example. In spite of its age (or because of it?) it is still considered a reference work by modern astrologers, but it can be doubted how many among them have ever read the book.

Summing up, we can conclude that the combined influences of the Babylonian inheritance, Greek philosophical and scientific opinions, as well as Egyptian mystical considerations gave astrology its final shape.

Around the beginning of our era we can as a result discern three kinds of astrology in the Greco-Roman world:

- *scientific astrology*, explained by the theses of the Greek natural philosophers;
- *philosophical astrology*, which was mainly adhered to by the stoics;
- *mystical astrology*, which was considered to be a revelation of a god.

Adherents of the last branch studied the hermetic documents, which were supposed to contain ancient secret knowledge. That knowledge could then be applied in all kinds of magical practices, such as the consecration of amulets, the determination of the suitable time to pick magic herbs, and so on. Even in later times this connection of astrology with magic has never disappeared completely.

Two important parts of the astrological practice, which also flowered during the first centuries of our era, were the *melothesia* and the *iatromathematica*. The melothesia was an astrological doctrine which connected certain parts of the body with signs and planets. In this system the head was ruled by Aries, the neck by Taurus, arms and lungs by Gemini, and so on. From later times many pictures have been preserved which depict these ideas in the shape of the "astrological man": a small figure of a man with the signs of the zodiac distributed over his body. Up until the eighteenth century such a figure was a fixed part of an astrological almanac; it was, among other things, used to point to the right organs and times for bloodletting.

Iatromathematica or medical astrology (the Greek *iatros* means physician) was supported partly by this melothesia. With the aid of the horoscope the astrologer indicated the parts of the body which were most susceptible to illnesses, for instance because of unfavorable aspects with the corresponding planet or the presence of ill-aspected planets in a sign. An unfavorably placed Sun, which rules the heart, for instance, or Saturn (unfavorable) in Leo, the sign of the heart, could point to susceptibility for heart disease. Magical correspondences between the body and the signs or the planets on the one hand and between the signs or planets and certain plants or minerals on the other hand could advise the physician-astrologer about the cosmic cause of an illness, the expected development of it, and the magical plants or minerals which could be used as a medicine.

So much for the astrological theory as it is known from textbooks and traditional tracts. The day-to-day practice was almost completely limited to two applications: the *genethlialogy* or personal astrology, which predicted someone's fate from the birth data, and the *katarchai* or horary astrology in which the astrologer was consulted in connection with the omens for success or failure of a project.

In antiquity a certain tension between the two forms was always present: Were the adherents of the fatalistic natal astrology, who claimed that Fate was unchangeable, that everything in the natal horoscope was fixed, and that horary astrology was superfluous, right, or were the defenders of katarchai, who assumed that "foreseeing" was also "preventing" correct?

It is striking how little has changed in this area throughout the centuries: Personal astrology and horary astrology are still the two branches of the art which are practiced the most.

Many astrological methods and ideas that are mentioned in ancient textbooks remained purely theoretical and have never found general application. As examples of this we cite the following:

- The *Partes*, points in a horoscope which are found by some juggling with the longitude of other points. The best known among them is the *Pars Fortunae* or the Part of Fortune. In antiquity about ten of these partes are mentioned, all of them formed by all kinds of arithmetical combinations of horoscope elements. During the flowering of Arab astrology these points had a revival; an author like Abraham Ibn Ezra mentioned no fewer than ninety-seven of them!
- An *eight-fold* house system, although all horoscopes found or mentioned use twelve houses.
- The division of the horoscope in twelve parts according to the *athla*, a kind of house system which starts at the Pars Fortunae instead of the Ascendant.

Propagation

From the Hellenized eastern part of the Mediterranean, astrology started its triumph. At the beginning of the common era the center of activities was located in the cosmopolitan city of Alexandria, where all kinds of philosophies and religions ran into each other. The intensive commercial contacts aided the spread of astrology. Yet the great break-through of astrological practice must have occurred rather late. The oldest known horoscope from Egypt dates from 38 B.C.E. The earliest known Greek horoscopes date only from the first century of our era. Only in the next century did horoscopes start to occur frequently.

One of the areas in which an invasion of astrology would not quite be expected is Palestine. It would seem that Judaism would offer resistance to practices surrounding heathen planetary gods, but in reality it is found that the exclusion of non-Jewish ideas and practices was not all that strict. The Essenes, for instance, a strictly ascetic group within Judaism, were known for the practice of medicine and magic. In the well-known Dead-Sea Scrolls, documents found near one of their centers, three horoscopes occur, including one for the expected messiah!

From the second century of our era Rome started to annex large areas of the Hellenized world. One result of this was that Hellenistic culture spread over the Roman Empire. In this way astrology became known in Rome, the more so since the stoic philosophy also exerted a strong influence there. This "invasion," however, did not run its course without opposition; repeatedly the "*Chaldaei*" (Chaldeans or Babylonians, as the astrologers were called) and other foreign prognosticators were chased out of Rome, among other things because they formed a dangerous competition for the traditional Roman predictive arts. But time and again these measures became dead letters. Also, in more intellectual circles a strong dose of skepticism was present; arguments against astrology of the Greek skeptic Carneades (second century B.C.E.) were taken over in the next century by the orator-statesman-philosopher Cicero as well as by the epicurean poet Lucretius. In the long run, however, the battle was lost; slowly but surely the often praised Roman common sense collapsed and from the imperial time on it was completely seduced by the astrological pretensions. Already during the reign of the emperor Augustus the Roman poet Marcus Manilius wrote an astrological ode, the *Astronomica*.

A clear illustration of the success of astrology is the influence which astrologers exerted at the imperial court in Rome. Thrasyllos, an Alexandrian philologist and astrologer who became a friend of the later emperor Tiberius during the stay of the latter at Rhodes, was an advisor one had to reckon with during the reign of Tiberius (14–37 C.E.). For that matter it was told of

Tiberius that he applied himself to astrology under the guidance of Thrasyllos. Thrasyllos' son, Balbillos, served as an astrologer to the emperors Claudius and Nero.

With few exceptions Roman emperors before the breakthrough of Christianity believed strongly in astrology. Edicts equated the investigation of the horoscope of the emperor with *lèse-majesté*, a capital offense. This was not without reason of course; he who studied the horoscope of the emperor usually did so with the aim of determining his day of death, whether or not in the hope of succeeding him. And, in a reverse way, some emperors, at the advice of their astrologers, were on their guard for those whose horoscope predicted an imperial future. Subjects of such an "imperial horoscope" were sometimes done away with as a precautionary measure. And yet, as was remarked cynically, not a single emperor has ever succeeded in slaying his own successor.

In the second century there appeared a short-lived revival of the criticism of astrology, particularly in the work of Sextus Empiricus, the last great skeptic of antiquity. But meanwhile the influence of astrology increased even further with the rise of the Oriental mystery religions. Especially in the very popular cult of the Persian god Mithra (at one time probably the most important competitor of Christianity) quite a bit of astrological symbolism can be traced. The same was true for the Syrian sun-god Baal or Ela-Gabal who for a time was the official imperial god, after a priest of that cult (who was mockingly called Heliogabalus after his god) was proclaimed emperor in 218 C.E. He built a temple to his god as *Sol Invictus Elagabalus*, the Invincible Sun, on the Palatine and attempted to make his worship the principal religion at Rome. Half a century later the emperor Aurelian re-established the cult of Sol Invictus as special protector of the emperors and of the empire. Here too, astrological symbolism played a role. Until the emperor Constantine the Great made Christianity the official imperial religion, the Sun was *the* preeminent symbol of the unity of the Roman Empire. It was in 312 C.E. that Constantine proclaimed the day devoted to the Sun, Sunday, as the Day of the Lord and the Christian day of rest. The celebration of the birth of the Sun on December 25 was so popular that Christianity adopted that day for the celebration of Christmas. The sun god himself was depicted as a Greek Apollo with a halo of sun-rays around his head, and Roman emperors with divine pretensions often had themselves depicted on their coins with such a halo. This was so generally accepted as an expression of divinity that in later Christian iconography it was adopted as the aureole of the saints.

It is most likely that from Alexandria astrology spread into the Indian subcontinent around the year 150 C.E. Some remnants in Indian astrological systems, such as the names of the signs, the use of certain geographical parameters in old textbooks, and the application of methods that became obsolete in the West still point to that transfer.

From India astrology became known in China around the twelfth century. The origin of the so-called *Chinese astrology*, however, has to be found elsewhere. This "astrology" is a system in which time is divided in periods of twelve years. Each year bears the name of an animal: Rat, Ox, Tiger, Hare, Dragon, Serpent, Horse, Goat, Monkey, Cock, Dog, and Boar. By combining this twelve-year cycle with the five traditional Chinese elements—fire, earth, water, wood, and metal—a longer cycle of sixty years is created. After each period of sixty years the same combinations of animal and element reappear. Whoever is born in a certain year is presumed to show the characteristics that are particular for that year. Because there is no question of planets or of factors which, such as in the horoscope, make the interpretation unique, the use of the term "astrology" is out of place. All who are born in the same year would have the same characteristics.

Where does this system come from? It is striking that the basic cycle contains *twelve* units and that the *names* are derived from animals. Of course, this reminds one of the zodiac. The zodiac, however, is a division of the celestial dome, while the cycle of twelve animals is a division of time. For the determination of the place in the sky Chinese astronomy used twenty-eight lunar mansions, a more primitive system than that used by the Babylonians. This points to a later adoption of the series of twelve, probably sometime during the first century of the common era.

This cycle of twelve animals is also found in a large part of Asia, from the central Asiatic plains to Japan. It turns out that in antiquity a similar division was known in the west: the *dodekaoros* (Greek for "twelve hours"), a division of the day in twelve hours, each of which had the name of an animal and was brought into connection with a sign of the zodiac. The animals which were associated with it show some differences with those from the Far East: Cat, Dog, Snake, Beetle, Ass, Lion, Goat, Bull, Hawk, Monkey, Ibis, and Crocodile. The presence of the Cat, Beetle, Monkey, and Ibis betrays an Egyptian origin of this sequence, but it is very much a question if the origin is to be sought there. The division into twelve parts can refer to Babylonia, but also to the movement of Jupiter in the sky; after all this planet circles the ecliptic once roughly every twelve years. The exact origin of this cycle, as far as the time (some centuries before our era?) or the region (Middle East?) are concerned, remains obscure.

As soon as Christianity gained the day in the Roman Empire, the climate for astrology became less favorable. Church father Augustine particularly attacked astrology, although before his conversion to Christianity he had been an enthusiastic adherent of it himself. Astrology, with its associations between planets and gods, was a "pagan" phenomenon and the Jews had already equated fortune-telling with idolatry. To make predictions based on a kind of celestial mechanism appeared to be a mockery of the divine omnipotence. The accompanying fatalism and determinism meant a limitation of free will. Finally the idea of consecutive cosmic cycles was incompatible with the Christian vision of time: for the Christians the creation of the world; the birth, death, and resurrection of Christ; and the Last Judgment are unique, singular events.

But even then the astrologers were extremely inventive defending their doctrine. According to them Christianity and astrology could be reconciled. The accusation of fatalism was refuted with the saying "*Astra non necessitant sed inclinant*" (The stars do not compel, but only incline). In order to take astrology away from the religious domain, mystical and philosophical astrology were relinquished, so that these two fell into decay. On the other hand the "scientific" astrology could easily be adapted to the requirements of the new time, although the relation with the Church remained unclear. It was therefore possible that Firmicus Maternus, the author of a late Roman astrological manual, also wrote an attack on pagan religions in which not a single word was uttered about astrology.

In the Byzantine Empire very little changed in this field. Astrology was busily practiced at the court in a "Christianized" form. By way of contacts between the Byzantine Empire and the increasing influence of Islam, astrology was also imported in the Arabic world, where it knew great success. Arabian astrology (which was also influenced by Indian astrology) reached its zenith around the year 1000 C.E. Muslim astrologers added very few new elements to astrology, but their tables and calculations reached a precision that was unheard of in the Christian world. Islamic theologians, jurists, and philosophers condemned astrology almost unanimously, but this had very little effect. Astrology triumphed at the courts of the caliphs and sultans as well as among the common people. In some regions cadis (Islamic judges) were officially also astrologers, even to the present century.

Renaissance and Decay

After the fall of the Roman Empire astrology became dormant in Western Europe, but from the eleventh century on there was a clear revival. Contacts with the Islamic world, particularly via Spain, led to the translation of Arabic astrological texts. At the same time the West became enamored with Aristotle's worldview. Due to the authority of the religious teachings of Albertus Magnus and Thomas Aquinas astrology became totally acceptable for the Roman Catholic Church. Aquinas emphasized that the celestial bodies could not influence the human soul directly, but only through the body. By resisting these influences—just as other bodily passions can be resisted—they can be limited and therefore there is no determinism.

With the rise of the Renaissance and humanism from the fifteenth century on, the interest in astrology increased further. Among the Greek texts which were studied anew in their original form (previously most were known through Latin or Arab translations) there were also astrological and occult texts. It can be said with certainty that, parallel to the Renaissance in the arts and sciences, there was an occult Renaissance. Books appeared to both defend and attack astrology. At the courts of princes and kings the astrologer was a welcome figure and some towns even had an official town astrologer. Even popes asked the advice of their court astrologer for the determination for important and less important ceremonies. Some universities established a chair of astrology and innumerable astrological almanacs were printed for the public at large.

This success did not last. In the sixteenth century because of the Reformation and Counter Reformation a sphere of religious strictness arose in which ever more distance was taken from any unchristian world of thought. Around that time also, the foundations of modern science were laid down, the results of which created more and more doubt about the physical basis of the astrological worldview. In the seventeenth century astrology indeed experienced another period of decay. In intellectual circles the subject was ignored and from the pulpit it was opposed as a remnant of old superstitions. It is striking that only a few anti-astrological writings from that time were authored by scientific researchers. Almost all of them were from the pens of clerics and satirists (such as Jonathan Swift, who was both). In scientific institutions astrology soon became taboo and even governments took measures against it. For instance in 1682 the French king Louis XIV outlawed all astrological almanacs.

During the eighteenth century the climate was possibly even more hostile. For the philosophers and the Encyclopedists of the Enlightenment astrology was no more than a memory of an era of backwardness that was definitely over and done with. The final result was that the astrological practice all but disappeared from the European continent, while a certain interest in the astrological symbols remained alive in only a few limited occult circles. In England astrology remained in existence in the form of popular almanacs and here and there it found a sporadic practitioner.

Renewed Popularity

This situation remained thus until the second half of the nineteenth century. At that time theosophy came into existence in the Anglo-Saxon world. This movement was established by the Russian adventuress Helena Petrovna Blavatsky, who brought all kinds of occult ideas together. This in turn created more attention for astrology. From about 1880 there was indeed a revival in England with practitioners who bore such colorful names as Alan Leo, Sepharial, and Zadkiel. The use of these pseudonyms indicates that astrology

Astrology: Past and Future

was not very respectable yet. By the end of the century the spark jumped to Europe and since that time the interest in astrology generally has grown strongly in the Western world.

From time to time there were a few delaying factors. For one thing astrology was taboo under the communist regimes, even if it was only because it appeared to be contrary to the scientific-materialistic worldview of Marxism. After the fall of communism in Eastern Europe in the 1990s, astrology and other occult ideas had a spectacular revival. In Nazi Germany astrology was also suppressed, albeit more because of mistrust than out of disbelief.

Both world wars were followed by a revival of astrology, but the real breakthrough took place at the end of the 1960s when so many established values were criticized and people sought salvation in all kinds of alternative ways of thinking. During the 1980s things quieted down a bit, but since that time astrology has gained a firm place in the world of the New Age, next to natural ways of living, alternative medicine, crystal healing, Oriental and other meditation groups, and more or less fanatical movements. The increased interest for these currents seems partly to be blamed to the spiritual emptiness caused by the decrease in church membership.

At the end of the millennium (which for some astrologers is associated with the Age of Aquarius) a revival can be expected of all kinds of chiliastic ideas* and astrology will almost certainly play a role in that. Whether the popularity of astrology will be maintained in the next century cannot be predicted, but in the short run we certainly don't expect that it will disappear.

The Present Situation

In the modern Western world, astrology has for a long time not had any official recognition. Science, particularly psychology and the natural sciences, totally writes it off. If some academic shows any interest in it, then this is purely a personal matter (usually accompanied by quite a bit of naivete and ignorance). For the media—particularly the more popular or sensationalistic facets—astrology is a welcome pagefiller. And this refers not only to newspaper horoscopes; astrologers are regularly given an audience to make their predictions for the new year. Articles about occult and "alternative" subjects obviously have a large readership.

The astrological world shows characteristics of what sociologists call a subculture: a group that holds certain ideas that are not shared by the rest of the population. But this is true only for the group of the professional and of the more "serious" amateur-astrologers. Some superficial familiarity with astrology

---

*Such ideas pertain to or hold the doctrine of the millennium (the belief that Christ will reign in bodily presence on Earth for a thousand years).

by the man in the street—most people know their "sign"—or the presence of a horoscope section in a newspaper or a weekly magazine are not sufficient to promote the casting of horoscopes as a generally accepted social phenomenon. Among the more serious practitioners of the "ancient knowledge" we can generally find two large trends. On the one hand are the *esoterics*, who emphasize the subjective interpretation of the horoscope (the so-called humanistic astrology in the United States is an example of this) and the relation with other occult ideas, and, on the other hand are the more *scientifically oriented astrologers*, who would love to see clear proofs for the correctness of astrology. The personal experience—whether or not reliable—of the authors of this book is that discussion with the latter group is very well possible, although we never will agree with each other, of course, while the terminology and the way of thinking of the former is, in our modest opinion, totally opaque, mixed up, and unintelligible. As is so often the case, it shows that in this case also the tendency for "deeper knowledge" is not conducive to clearness of thought.

Since the end of the Middle Ages, when a number of "fine-tunings" were added to the system, the number of changes in the astrological practice has been minimal. The rules for the interpretation of the horoscope are for the most part still the same as they were at the end of the Roman Empire. The terminology has become more "scientific," nowadays more psychological terms are used, but it is essentially still the same.

Astrology is a historic fossil. That verdict can hit hard for the adepts of astrology, but it is therefore no less true. Astrology arose as a prejudiced search for a connection between celestial happenings and life on Earth, and there does not exist even the least indication that reliable observation ever played a role in it. Religious ideas and outdated conceptions were much more important in ordering and drafting astrological rules than experience. The increase in scientific knowledge during the last centuries has never been able to influence these rules to any important extent.

Astrology implies a world vision: a vision on nature, man, and the cosmos. As such it is one of the many efforts undertaken to determine the role and the place of man in nature. The "scientific" astrology was one of the first attempts to work out a world vision in which the idea of a *natural law* was formulated. No fickleness of invisible gods any longer, but the inexorable rules of law of cosmic phenomena. It would therefore be a sign of narrow-mindedness to deny the historic role of astrology in the development of certain ideas. But human knowledge goes on, and ideas which once were considered valid have been replaced by better models of reality. In this view astrology today can only be valued in its historic context, just like the old worldview of Aristotle. No matter how much respect we can have for the role these ideas have played, this should not prevent us from acquainting ourselves with more recent and better based conceptions. Fossils can teach us a lot, but their meaning for the present is limited.

10

CRITICISM IN A NUTSHELL

A number of arguments that are often cited in discussions about the subject of astrology have not been covered yet. Because we do not want to withhold these from our readers, a short survey will follow here.

Birth Horoscope or Conception Horoscope?

From an astrological point of view life starts at birth, which is most of the time determined by the moment of the first cry of the newborn. This is a strange idea: A human being does not come into existence at birth but roughly nine months earlier. Would it therefore not be more correct if astrology started from the moment of conception for casting a natal horoscope? But that implies insurmountable problems. It is, after all, not possible to estimate the moment of conception with the precision of a few minutes, as astrology would want it (except maybe in the case of in vitro fertilization!). That is why the astrologers resort to the much more accurately described moment of birth. Their justifications for this can go into two directions:

1. They use the moment of birth "for lack of something better," but admit that a "conception horoscope" would be preferred.

Fine, but in that case they have the obligation to explain how a *birth* horoscope can indicate the characteristics that ought to belong to the conception horoscope. As seen from Earth the planetary movements are after all so complicated that no simple connection exists between the planetary positions at a certain moment and the positions of these same planets nine months earlier or later. Some astrologers believe they are able to solve this problem by the application of the ancient traditional rule, the so-called *Trutina Hermetis*. According to that rule the Moon in the conception horoscope has to be found in the same place as the Ascendant in the birth horoscope and vice versa. Absolutely no rational basis exists for that rule; the only function it has appears to be helping astrologers in distress.

> 2. That first cry is the first contact with the outside world and at that very moment the cosmic effects of that same moment are grafted upon the baby.

Okay, but in that case it has to be called very remarkable to hear that the abdominal wall of the mother can obviously foil the astrological influences, but the walls of the maternity ward cannot. Can one conclude from this that a person can protect herself from astrological fate by hiding behind a few centimeters of meat?

Astrological Twins and Other Multiple Births

Contrary to what astrologers would like to make us believe, the personal horoscope is not all that unique. For the casting of a horoscope one starts from a certain place and an exactly determined time. The requirement for these exact data may give the impression that a horoscope can only be connected to one person, but that is not the case.

Changes in the sky go very slowly. Even the apparent rotation of the celestial dome—and therefore the change in Ascendant and houses—has a speed of only one degree per four (time) minutes. For children born in the same place within a time interval of a few minutes (which can happen in any large maternity ward) the horoscopes do not differ in any essential way.

Also, the place does not have to be the same in order to obtain an identical horoscope. Horoscopes are particularly sensitive to differences in geographical longitude. In order to find a difference in longitude of one degree it is necessary to travel some 70 kilometers east- or westward at a latitude of 50 degrees (at lower latitudes this distance is even larger, becoming 111 kilometers at the equator). Babies who come into the world at the same time in a large city therefore have the same birth horoscope.

Finally the natal chart "moves" over the surface of Earth. All places at the same latitude have the same house configuration for a certain sidereal time, as was explained in chapter 6. The whole Ascendant turns, as it were, in one day around Earth, a displacement of about one degree longitude in four minutes. Because of this movement the house configuration at a certain moment in Brussels is the same as one hour before that in Prague. Meanwhile, of course, the position of the planets in the horoscope also changes, but this change proceeds much more slowly. The Moon moves by far the fastest in the sky, but not faster than one degree in two hours.

This means that the same birth horoscopes can be found in places that are a few thousand kilometers apart from each other (and then we are using the rather high precision of one degree, otherwise the distances may become a lot larger). The same horoscope "shifts" in two hours over the surface of Earth and is valid for everyone born "under" it.

Some defenders of astrology point out that, according to the birth register, Johann Wolfgang Goethe was the only person born in Frankfurt am Main on August 28, 1749. The horoscope of the brilliant German poet is therefore unique, they say. They obviously forget to check the birth registers of the villages and towns in a zone of some tens of kilometers around Frankfurt and in a band of at least a thousand kilometers east and west of this zone.

Do people with the same horoscope show the same course of life? It appears that this is not the case. It is estimated that the number of persons with the same horoscope as Albert Einstein is about 260. As far as is known no 260 people with the qualities of Einstein were born in 1879. But there are indeed quite a few astrologers who have shown that Einstein's genius is clearly present in his "unique" horoscope.

Some astrologers assert having found examples of identical courses of life. For instance the astrologer Goodavage composed a list of time-twins. He asserted that their lives showed striking similarities. A check by Eriksen brought so many errors to light, however, that the study can be considered completely worthless. So-called simultaneous events in reality turned out to be not simultaneous at all. And, after checking, certain "astrological twins" turned out not even to have the same horoscope!

An often cited case is the time-twin of King George III of Britain. The story goes that when the future king was born on June 4, 1738, at about the same time a certain Samuel Hemming also saw the light of day. The lives of the two showed clear similarities. On the day George was crowned, Hemming took over the hardware store of his father. Both were supposed to have married on the same day and to have had the same number of children. Both were also supposed to have been hit by illness and accident at the same moments. And both supposedly died on January 29, 1820, of similar causes.

A good story, but is it true? We are only aware that this could possibly be based on the death announcement on a certain Richard Spear, but official documents and reliable witnesses appear to be absent. And the astrologers, who forever copy from each other, do not provide more clarity.

As an aside we can also take the opportunity to cite the astrological research on "real" twins. Between the birth of twins there are intervals ranging from a few minutes to more than one hour, often sufficient to cause major differences in the house divisions. Twin brothers or sisters who are genetically identical and grow up in the same environment can have clear differences in their horoscopes (for instance, the Ascendant can be a different sign). Does that supply the twins with an equivalent difference in character? Of course, astrologers think that this is the case, and some of them tried to investigate this. The best known study of this kind was performed by French scientific researcher Suzel Fuzeau-Braesch, who investigated the horoscopes of 238 young twins. The twins' parents matched brief astrological descriptions with their personalities: They had to decide which one of the two children was more sociable (or sensitive, or affectionate . . .) and which one was less. In 68.5 percent of the cases the description was assigned to the corresponding child. By chance, one should expect a hit rate of 50 percent. Fuzeau-Braesch's very significant results were considered by many people—including herself—as new and decisive evidence for astrology. But her work was afterward criticized by Suitbert Ertel and Geoffrey Dean, two researchers we have met previously. They objected, among other things, that her results were incompatible with previous findings and could not be replicated, and that the interval between births did not increase with increasing personality difference (as required by her hypothesis). They found evidence of bias due to the response sets Fuzeau-Braesch used and stereotypes about twins (she knew the twins' sex and birth order). After reanalyzing the original data, they arrived at a hit rate of only 53.6 percent. Moreover, French skeptic Henri Broch remarked that some of the data Fuzeau-Braesch used were quite unreliable. Although Fuzeau-Braesch claimed she worked with much precision, Broch, in verifying only a limited number of data, discovered that she gave erroneous information about the birth place of four sets of twins. In one case of twins no birth record of them was found in the given birth place.

Public Predictions

As promised, in this book we concentrated on natal astrology and not so much on predictive astrology. The major part of the criticism of natal astrology is, of course, also valid for making astrological predictions of the future. In the case of predictions a number of additional problems crop up. For instance there is the question if it is at all possible to predict the future to begin with and how "the stars" can determine our future. Maybe it is possible to imagine that our character is cosmically influenced at birth, but that from the sky at birth it can also be derived that we will win the Irish Sweepstakes or that we run the risk of a traffic accident appears to us real magic, to say the least. And then there is the fundamental question, of course, as to whether the predictions really come true. Here we will only pay some attention to the type of astrological predictions with which the public at large is familiar.

Criticism in a Nutshell 249

It is the tradition for some publications to have a few astrologers make predictions at the beginning of the new year about what humanity by and large can expect in the coming year. Specialized periodicals even publish monthly predictions. Although many astrologers turn up their noses at this kind of predictive astrology, others appear to consider themselves competent in this field.

It is always interesting to save these predictions and to check them afterward. Time and again the same characteristics are found when reviewed a year later: Specific predictions did not come true, striking events were not predicted, and what was predicted and came true was usually vague or predictable.

Regularly claims are made that some astrologer successfully predicted a striking event (an earthquake, an airplane crash, the death of a celebrity). A further look into the original pronouncement almost always shows that the prediction was actually very vague. An earthquake was predicted but the place ("somewhere in the northern hemisphere") and the time ("in the month of February") was mentioned only in vague terms. Since these kinds of events happen at least once a year somewhere on Earth (and earthquakes at least once a month), it is up to the astrologers to improve their predictions.

Equally unimpressive are predictions which anybody knows have to come true sooner or later. A war, for instance, ends sooner or later. The French astrologer André Barbault, whom we mentioned earlier, predicted year after year the end of the Algerian war of independence until the prediction finally came true.

The few correct predictions which are slightly impressive usually concern events that are not all that improbable. Hits purely by chance cannot be excluded. As Voltaire once remarked, the astrologer does not have the privilege of erring all the time. If in the United States one astrologer predicts an electoral victory for the Republican presidential candidate and the other predicts the same for the Democratic candidate, the chances are extremely good that one of these predictions will come true!

Unexpected events are seldom found in predictions. Who predicted the nuclear disaster of Chernobyl in 1986? Among the predictions for 1989 one searches in vain for the fall of the Berlin Wall or the bloody revolution in Rumania (perhaps because they occurred very late in the year?).

It is a miracle that, in spite of the blunders, so many astrologers take the risk of making predictions and so many people swallow this hook, line, and sinker. About ten years ago the authors of this book met on television with the well-known commercial Belgian astrologer Daniël Van Ooteghem, who publishes predictions about the development of the stock market in *Para-Astro*, his own monthly review. The general tendency of these predictions is usually very vague: rates will fluctuate, some stocks will gain, and others will fall. In October 1987 he predicted that "Generally speaking October will be a decent month for the market. Many favorable and new trends are present. Still the

250 Making Sense of Astrology

big hurrah is past and it is necessary to act thoughtfully. By the end of October there will be some restraint. There is distrust then, and there is a minor slowdown."

He gave not the slightest indication for Black Monday on October 19, 1987, the largest stock market crash on Wall Street since 1929.

If you think that after a blunder of this caliber Dr. Van Ooteghem (he has a Ph.D. in chemistry) would sing a different tune, you have it all wrong. During that time he also took care of an astrological section in the Belgian weekly *Knack*. On February 17, 1988, he wrote "That astrology can also play a role in the financial world was shown here by predicting more than a year ago the crash of end '87, beginning '88. It happened even earlier than expected."

Nowhere does Van Ooteghem tell us that his "art" abandoned him when the crash was really about to occur. Predicting that a collapse was about to come was not sensational. You did not have to be an astrologer and even not a great expert on the stock exchange to understand that the rising trend of 1987 could not last forever.

Aside from that, if astrology can predict the trends of the stock market (or the lottery results or horse races) why aren't the astrologers swimming in money? That would be really convincing. Some of them claim that they do not want to misuse their "foreknowledge" but that is not very believable, since a lot of astrologers have no problem earning big money with their predictions.

Apocalyptic Predictions

The astrological predictions with the largest response are in all probability the announcements of major catastrophes. Exceptional planetary positions are after all supposed to announce uncommon occurrences. In the past some dire predictions led to international panic. For instance the gathering of all planets in Libra in 1186 would, according to the astrologers, cause all kinds of catastrophes, such as hurricanes and earthquakes. Everywhere precautions were taken, but in the end nothing exceptional happened. With hindsight this conjunction was associated with the beginning of the terrifying conquests of Ghengis Khan, but he had been enthroned five years earlier and his major campaigns did not start until ten years later. Predictions for 1236 and 1524 caused similar panic waves. Again the expected disasters stayed away. In the Middle Ages at least ten such predictions of calamities met with a similar wide response. Sometimes the calculations were not even correct.

Nowadays astrologers have become somewhat more cautious, but that does not prevent their dire predictions from reaching the news from time to time. These usually come from pseudoscientific authors who do not consider themselves astrologers. In Intermezzo IX we discussed the "Jupiter Effect" contrived by Gribbin and Plagemann that would cause earthquakes around 1982. A new disaster is already predicted for May 2000 (note the "chiliastic" year!): Jupiter and Saturn will be located together behind the Sun (which happened before in 1881 and in 1921).

What about Mass Accidents?

The Romans already asked themselves whether all victims of a maritime disaster or all those killed in the same battle had indications in their horoscopes for a common violent death. This comprises a predictive problem that astrologers have not yet solved.

Their most often cited argument is that in such a case the horoscopes of nations, countries (in the case of natural disasters or wars), ships, airplanes, and so on are decisive. Your personal horoscope may be as favorable as you can imagine, if the horoscope of the plane you take predicts a crash, you're gone! It is, of course, a marvelous alibi that makes astrological predictions extremely complex. If strictly applied, a personal horoscope could only be interpreted after consulting the horoscope of the country, the town, the car used, other means of transportation, and who knows what else.

The Great Predecessors

If the facts cannot be used to justify astrology, then authority and tradition can be called in. How often do astrologers refer to illustrious historical figures who practiced astrology or who at least believed strongly in it? Since these Great Men (nobody mentions Great Women) certainly were not stupid, astrology has to be true, according to this argument.

Calling in the help of authorities—whether for or against astrology—is, of course, no proof, and it is even not an honest argument; it can at the most impress the layman. If a few scientists, like Seymour or Fuzeau-Braesch, express themselves in a positive way about astrology, then astrologers do not hesitate to sum up the academic titles and functions of these "eminent scientists." But if hundreds of other eminent scientists—including Nobel laureates—sign a declaration against astrology, then they see in it only the prejudices of "official science."

But even then the Illustrious Names can hardly serve the case for astrology. The belief in astrology (and in other outdated subjects like witches and warlocks) of these people ought to be judged in its historic context. They too were children of their time and shared the convictions and worldview of their contemporaries. Without that realization even the greatest mind from the past can now seem ridiculous. Important scholars from the Middle Ages like Albertus Magnus and Thomas Aquinas not only believed in the value of astrology, but also in the existence of unicorns and other fabulous animals. Moreover, in the past, scientific research methods to investigate certain claims simply did not exist.

That astronomer Johannes Kepler (1571–1630), who for the first time gave a correct description of the movements of the planets, was also a critical astrologer is in no sense detrimental to his historical importance for astronomy. Kepler, who for that matter had to earn his living as an astrologer (officially called "Imperial Mathematician"), wanted to reform astrology drastically because, in his opinion, there was too much chaff among the wheat. His astronomical discoveries are not worthless because he was inspired by mystical conceptions; the mystical conceptions themselves proved to be untenable.

The same is true of Sir Isaac Newton (1643–1725), the founder of classical physics. Besides his work in mathematics and physics he spent an enormous amount of energy on alchemy and biblical chronology. These latter aspects of his work are now almost totally forgotten because they produced hardly anything of worth, while the former work is by some considered to be the greatest intellectual achievement ever produced by man.

Newton in his turn is sometimes represented as a defender of astrology. There circulates a classical anecdote which goes roughly like this: When Edmund Halley (an astronomer, known especially because of his comet) expressed his disbelief in astrology in the presence of Newton or, according to another version, blamed Newton for occupying himself with astrology, the latter answered with, "Sir, I have studied these things, you have not." This pronouncement is supposed to prove that the most important founder of modern science also had a warm heart for astrology. However, the anecdote is apocryphal. The cited pronouncement is found in a completely different context in the biography of Newton by Sir David Brewster (1831): "Every time... Dr. Halley tried to say something about *religion* he (Newton) corrected him and said: 'I have studied these things, you have not.'" Newton's interest in religion was indeed enormous, while in his (very extensive) writings no direct reference to astrology can be found. We do not know whether the story told by Brewster is authentic, but in any case it has nothing to do with astrology. Let us not forget that it was precisely in Newton's time, and not the least because of Newton's work, that astrology quickly lost its support in scientific circles (and in England Newton was the uncrowned king of these circles).

This example gives an idea of the reliability with which astrologers call in the authority of Illustrious Minds. We will not even answer the stories which profess to show Einstein's interest in astrology. These interests can only be found in astrological books.

Nostradamus

French physician and astrologer Nostradamus (Michel de Notredame, 1503–1566) was famous during his lifetime for his predictions. He was employed by the (very superstitious) queen Catherine de Medici and is still famous for his *Centuries*, a collection of 940 quatrains in which interesting events through the end of the world were supposed to be predicted. In themselves the poems of Nostradamus are so opaque, so vague, and so confused (there is no discernable order in the quatrains) that without additional interpretation not a single historical fact can be traced from them. But his commentators have done their very best, with an enormous imagination and sometimes with a straight distortion of the text, to trace the most exciting facts in them. Because of the large number of commentaries (in the French language alone more than four hundred books about Nostradamus are written) there is no lack of interpretations. Apart from that these very free interpretations sometimes contradict each other. However famous—and however nonsensical—these predictions are, they have very little to do with astrology. Nostradamus was indeed an astrologer. He cast horoscopes and composed astrological almanacs, and some passages in his *Centuries* refer to planetary positions, but it is obvious that the prophecies cannot be derived from horoscopes. Even commentators who are not at all critical point out that in the *Centuries* Nostradamus, as a "seer," a "prophet," or a "psychic," directly wrote down "revelations," without astrology. As a matter of fact some anecdotes are known about Nostradamus's clairvoyance, and horoscopes do not appear in them.

11

CONCLUSION

Astrology: sense or nonsense? Is astrology true? These were the questions we asked at the beginning of this book. From the first chapter the intelligent reader understood that the answer would not be an overwhelming "yes." The reader was warned: This book was not intended to be an apology for astrology but—we hoped—an understandable explanation of the reasons why certain persons look rather skeptically at the subject.

If one wants to make a reasoned judgment about the validity of astrology, it is of course preferable to listen to a voice other than that of the astrological textbooks. Only by weighing the arguments pro and con against each other can one hope to get to a defensible conclusion.

It is a pity that all too often arguments against astrology are raised which are based on the critic's tacit assumptions about astrology—and which immediately lose their value if it becomes apparent that the attacked astrologer does not agree with these assumptions. And likewise we occasionally find criticism of statements which astrologers never uttered.

An example of the first kind is the argument that according to science there exist no forces or cosmic influences that could exert an astrological effect on man. This is right, but it also assumes that science knows *all* the influences that reach us from the cosmos, something with which not everybody agrees. However, as soon as the astrologer raises the possibility that as yet undiscovered forces or influences could possibly exist (which then strangely would have exactly those characteristics that the astrologer needs), the argument loses its value. It is not an easy task for the critic to answer this rationally. Discussing forces which are not yet discovered and which may never be discovered because they do not exist is after all very difficult.

An additional weakness of this argument is that the critic obviously assumes

Conclusion 255

Miniature representing the planets and the zodiac, from the French Medieval manuscript *Très riches heures du duc de Berry* (fourteenth century). Museum in Chantilly.

that astrologers are looking for a physical explanation of astrology. Nothing could be farther from the truth. Most astrologers are at peace with the idea that these hypothetical astrological influences exist, but that they cannot be discovered by any scientific research. "Experience" is the foundation of their belief in astrology, not a possible mechanism or a scientific explanation.

An example of the second kind of unsound reasoning is the argument of "free will." Astrologers are sometimes accused of an exaggerated determinism. If everything is determined by "the stars," man has no free will and he is not responsible for his actions. According to some people this opens the road to all kinds of debauchery and irresponsible behavior. For them this is sufficient reason to damn the inducement to it, astrology.

The number of astrologers who hold such a strongly deterministic idea is small. Usually they take on a more shaded attitude: Humanity does not have to be at the mercy of the horoscope. On the contrary, knowledge of the horoscope can lead to more self-knowledge and self-control, so that negative tendencies in the horoscope will be softened and one can make good use of the positive characteristics. The astrologer then *controls* fate according to the principle "a warned man counts for two." Astrologers can refute the—very old—argument of "free will" without much trouble.

The same is true of the claim that astrologers are swindlers who ruthlessly exploit the credulity of their customers in order to make a fortune. Without any doubt there exist some astrologers who are true to this picture. Some astrological practices are purely commercial businesses (we have heard stories of an astrologer who sends a judicial warrant to clients who do not pay his—obviously high—fee quickly enough). But that does not say anything about the value of astrology as a system. The "argument" is simply invalid.

Because of the weakness of such, sadly enough too often heard, arguments, it pays to look deeper into the better criticisms. But that is not as easy as it appears to be. The literature is spread all over and therefore difficult to trace. Most of the few critical books (which unfortunately do not always give the best arguments) have been sold out for a long time. On the other hand, whole stocks of astrological books can be found without any trouble in most bookstores. And, understandably, in most of those books the critical remarks are totally ignored.

The most difficult part of criticizing the subject is the fact that good arguments ask for extensive knowledge of astrological methods as well as of one or more branches of science. The collapse of the house system above the Arctic Circle is a prime example of this. The argument requires some insight into astronomy as well as geometry. For the origin of astrology the best material is often found in older, specialized historical works, which can only be found in large university libraries. And to provide well-founded answers to the argument of astrological "experience," psychology has to be consulted. And we have not even mentioned statistics. Astronomy, geometry, statistics, psychology, history . . . all of these have to be used and that makes the critique rather difficult to access.

We have tried to present some of the better arguments. Some readers may have found it unusual that so much explanation was given of astrological methods, but in order to evaluate something critically one has to know and understand it, otherwise the impression remains that something profound must be hidden behind the juggling of angular displacements and planets. And the argument of "experience" of course should not be pushed aside without much ado.

What we call the "better criticism" is summarized in the answers which can be given to three questions, answers which throw their own light on the true nature of astrology:

- *How did astrology arise?* What are its foundations? Were those foundations reliable observations, as astrologers would like to make us believe, or were they religious and mythical considerations? History makes clear that the historical basis is not supported by any factual data. The origin of the characteristics of the signs and the planets (Uranus, Neptune, and Pluto) are good examples of this.
- *How consistent is the astrological system internally?* The single fact that astrologers contradict each other at about every point and the firm convictions of their own correctness—supported by their "experience"—must call up doubts about the reliability of the applied methods.
- And finally there is the question about *the results of scientific research.* Here too, there is very little to offer any comfort to the astrologers. Not a single classical astrological element is shown to be able to resist statistical research. And whatever astrologers may claim about that, this kind of research is eminently suitable to give a verdict on this subject.

Scientifically speaking astrology is as dead as a doornail.

Still, casting horoscopes has a lot of success, a success that is exclusively fed by the argument of positive experiences with the system: "Astrology works." But even that argument could not hold against a critical approach. Every available evidence indicates that the psychological processes which play a role in accepting astrology are so important that the question of objective validity becomes unimportant for those concerned. *Psychology alone* was shown to be more than sufficient to explain belief in astrology and related techniques of soothsaying. The "stars" do not even have to be mentioned.

How subjective and worthless that much-praised "experience" is became clear when the claims of the astrologers about their successes in practice were checked. The research of Dean showed that astrologers, in spite of their strong belief in their methods, were not able to obtain the favorable results which they had predicted for themselves. The much-praised astrological "experience" is just plain worthless.

Making Sense of Astrology

The astrological influences of signs and planets do not exist. That does not mean that no relations between the cosmos and certain human characteristics *could* exist. But even if these influences exist (which, as things stand now, appears to be extremely unlikely, but we could be mistaken), they could hardly mean a support for the astrological practice. Their effect, by their very nature, must after all be very weak—otherwise their existence would have been proven a long time ago—so that they can only be traced by large-scale statistics. Their *practical* importance is therefore a priori excluded. This means that undiscovered cosmic influences cannot come to the rescue of astrology.

The final judgment of astrology then is without any doubt negative. But does it have to be condemned? There never was a lack of anathemas, certainly not from the religious side. Fortune-telling was condemned as a form of idolatry in the Old Testament (Deuteronomy 17:10). Astrology and other predictive techniques are at present also disapproved by most Christian churches: Whoever consults the horoscope appeals to Satan and demonic forces. This does not have to mean that the adequacy of astrology is therefore acknowledged; it is the intention which is condemnable. The most recent universal catechism of the Roman Catholic Church condemns astrology explicitly and denies its validity. In practice most Christians appear not to care a bit about that, with the exception of the more or less fundamentalist assemblies. In the Muslim world the situation is about the same. Astrology is popular in most of the Islamic countries—just like a thousand years ago—but it is damned by the fundamentalists and in a country like Iran it is taboo.

The ecclesiastical authorities nowadays warn mostly against the New Age movement, which partly profits from the decreasing influence of the traditional religions. A publication of Belgian Roman Catholic Cardinal Godfried Danneels about this had the significant title "Christ or Aquarius?" Not only the irreconcilability with the faith as such is pointed out, but also the disadvantage in the area of morality. Some people appear to flee into occult ideas in order to escape their own responsibility and their own moral engagement.

This last form of criticism also appears among groups who take a critical stance toward religion. In liberal-humanist circles astrology is a kind of obscurantism and superstition. That attitude is an inheritance of the Enlightenment, when astrology—after the words of the French astronomer and revolutionary Jean-Sylvain Bailly—was designated as "the most long-lasting illness which has ever affected reason," or even of the old Greek skepticism. In practice this attitude does not differ much of that of the scientific world, as evidenced by a declaration against astronomy signed by 186 prominent scientists and published in 1975 by *The Humanist*.

In modern psychology, on which astrology likes to lean, astrology does not play any role. Astrology enjoys no recognition in science. But astronomers especially do not hide their distaste of astrology. Whoever has read this book knows why. Astrology is as absurd for the modern astronomer as the ancient *auspicia* (predicting the future from the flight of birds) is for a modern ornithologist. Moreover, it is no fun for an astronomer to have to listen constantly to weird talk about planets and "signs" by people who in all likelihood never looked at a planet and who could not recognize any constellation in the sky. That explains the sometimes vehement reactions from that side. French astronomer Paul Couderc, with the assistance of UNESCO, preached a straight crusade against commercial astrologers.

Condemnation from science does not make that much of an impression. For most of the people the opinion of scientists is only one of the possible truths. However, it should be clear for everybody now that *astrology is not a science*, whatever the astrologer asserts. The theories and the calculations may give astrology a more objective and scientific appearance than for instance palm or card reading, but fundamentally there is no difference among all of these practices. Astrology is not based on scientific principles but on the prejudices of the astrologers. The horoscope does not say anything about objective reality.

Since the seventeenth century governments have outlawed astrological practices and other forms of fortune-telling, possibly under clerical pressure, possibly to prevent flagrant abuses. Today commercial forms of fortune-telling are still prohibited in some developed countries, but those prohibitions are no longer enforced and are nearly forgotten.

All those condemnations and prohibitions have not been able to stop the success of astrology. Maybe the effect has been the opposite: The astrologers certainly like to present themselves as the underdogs. According to them they are constantly persecuted by a modern inquisition (for them criticism is the same as persecution). Forbidding something puts it in the area of a taboo and that makes it especially attractive (think of the anathemas against drugs and even against racism).

Is astrology really harmful or dangerous? In order to answer that question definitively more research would have to be done on the impact of astrology on society. Quantitatively this influence is not negligible. For the Brussels urban area the telephone directory mentions about sixty astrologers (many of whom are also a "medium" [psychic] or a "clairvoyant")—more than one for every 17,000 inhabitants. In France there are supposed to be more astrologers (known by the tax inspectors) than Roman Catholic priests. How much money is spent on astrological consultations, books, periodicals, courses, pay-telephone lines, and computer programs is hard to estimate, but it has to be an enormous amount.

Most of the astrologers are of good faith and believe that they do useful work. Without any doubt there are quite a few people with problems who obtain good advice from an astrologer, or who are just pleased that someone is paying attention to their problems. The question remains whether they would have been better off consulting a physician, psychologist, priest, or some other kind of counselor or adviser. In addition, there is no guarantee that the astrologer one consults is capable (but remember that capable astrologers appear to produce no better results than less capable ones!), or even "serious." How can the customer know that this astrologer is not a swindler, a leader of some sect, or a fanatic with dangerous ideas?

The "serious" astrologers try to protect their profession by organizing in their own societies, which draw up norms for recognition and rules of conduct. But because of the hopeless differences of opinion and the lack of any objective criteria, this does not succeed very well. Abusive language, name-calling, envy, schisms, and lock-outs are the rule rather than the exception.

Besides the professional astrologers there are quite a few people who are interested in and attracted to astrology. They look at it for consolation, as a source of insight, a recreation, or even as an alternative for religion. This seems to be rather innocent as long as their dependence does not become too great.

It certainly becomes serious if astrology gets hold of people who do not (want to) have anything to do with it. Is it acceptable to investigate the horoscope of someone who applies for a job? Is it thinkable that the moment of a surgical intervention depends on an astrologically "favorable" moment? Is it acceptable that a president of the most powerful nation in the world seeks the advice of an astrologer?

Finally, astrology belongs to the sometimes very dangerous world of the irrational. We do not mean by this the world of imagination, romanticism, or even mysticism. We do mean the world in which "believing" and "knowing" are wrongly mixed up and in which prejudices and ill-founded ideas are of more importance than facts and common sense. In that atmosphere racial theories and other delusions flourish. We do not mean that astrologers would be racists, but in some circles there are connections between the two.

The ideas of the superiority of the white race originated in theosophy (which played an important role in the revival of astrology). By the end of the nineteenth century occult societies arose in Germany and Austria which worked out and propagated these racial ideas further. On the basis of calculations of cosmic cycles the revival of the pure Aryan race and the rise of the Great German Empire were predicted. The most notorious figure was Jörg Lanz von Liebenfels, a former monk, a madman who founded a "New Temple Order." His repugnant racist pulp sheet, the *Ostara*, which appeared in Vienna at the beginning of the twentieth century, formed the main source of inspiration of Adolf Hitler. Later Lanz von Liebenfels started to practice mundane ("political") astrology. He predicted that 1920 was the end of the Moon Period or the era of the vulgar masses, a period characterized by the influence of Turks and Jews, capitalism, democracy, and the rise of the proletariat. Following this was the Jupiter Period during which power would not be exerted by parliament, but by "brilliant, ariosophic-mystically educated patricians and leaders (Führer)." The rise of fascist dictatorships was greeted by him as a sign of the new time. Again, we do not want to insinuate anything with respect to astrologers in general. Hitler did not have any special interest in astrology and outlawed occult societies (although the SS had some kind of institute for occult studies). But it is no coincidence that astrology as well as racist ideas could flourish in the same environment, and sometimes still flourish today. In this book we have given examples of absurd reasonings that are used to confirm astrological prejudices. Similar reasoning can be used for other, more dangerous prejudices.

As such astrology is not totally without any danger. But rather than damn and condemn it we want to inform the public about what astrology is (not) able to do. The potential customer has, after all, a right to proper information. Only then can he pass judgment and, if necessary, take steps if he feels cheated. Present-day laws protecting consumers, which are becoming more strict, can help with this. Astrology is a commercial business; the reaction to it should preferably be businesslike too.

In this book astrology was viewed critically. What the reader does with the cited arguments is her own business. We can only hope that she, by acquainting herself with the contents, has obtained a more balanced view of the relation between humanity and the cosmos. Humanity is part of nature and therefore also of the cosmos, that much is certain. But according to us it is evidence of a certain lack of courage to project personal problems on the cosmos and to expect a "hint from above" as a solution for them. Two thousand years ago such a thing was understandable and the founders of astrology cannot be reproached for that. But nowadays, in a time of interplanetary space flights, the vision of man and his place in the universe ought to have been adjusted to the new insights. Old ideas have to be seen in the right perspective, as phases in the development of human knowledge, which after a while were replaced by new and better knowledge.

Astrology was such a phase, one of the efforts people undertook to find their place in the cosmos and through that to control the fear of the uncertain future. It was, certainly in antiquity, a great vision, which was attractive because of its universal character. But that worldview did not survive the tests of science. The planetary gods were chased out and infinite time and space have taken their places. Or should have taken them . . .

Astrology was not born yesterday and will not have disappeared by tomorrow. Astrologers are still hawking it in the marketplace of ideas, but *caveat emptor*, as the Romans said, Let the buyer beware!

POSTSCRIPT

As was mentioned previously, we tried for some completeness for this book. It may sound arrogant, but for us the file appears to be definitively closed. Lots of interesting studies of astrology can be performed, for instance on its captivating history, but it does not look as if in the short, or even the long run, new facts will appear that would change the final judgment about the value of astrology.

Discussions about astrology are fruitless. There have always been objections against astrology and most of them remain valid up until today. But it is particularly the results of experimental research that appear to be irrefutable. The research of Dean (see chapter 8) was so destructive that we may speak of the Waterloo of astrology. If a similar investigation in the future were to give positive results, then that would be nothing less than a miracle. As a matter of fact it would remain incomprehensible that astrologers in one experiment failed massively, collectively, and over the whole field, if astrology appeared not to be worthless after all.

Still the possibility has to remain for astrologers to test their reputed talents objectively, if only because of the principle that nothing can be excluded a priori. Well, that is possible. Several persons and institutions offer prizes to those who—under controlled conditions—can show a talent which scientifically speaking is impossible or highly improbable. Making astrological predictions or descriptions of character will certainly be considered, but, naturally, only after binding agreements about it have been reached. For more information about objective, controlled testing, contact the Committee for the Scientific Investigation of Claims of the Paranormal (CSICOP), Box 703, Buffalo, New York 14226–0703.

BIBLIOGRAPHY

General Literature about Astrology

Couderc, P. *L'Astrologie,* 5th ed. Paris: Presses Universitaires de France, 1974. Written by a well-known French astronomer, this was one of the rare critical books of high scientific level about astrology before the rise of the skeptical publications in the 1970s. It was published in the popular French scientific series *Que sais-je?* It is significant that after Couderc's death no new edition was printed, but a new book appeared—as no. 2483 of the same series—with the same title, but with a totally different attitude, written by the uncritical astrology researcher Suzel Fuzeau-Braesch (see chapter 10).

Dean, G., and A. Mather. *Recent Advances in Natal Astrology.* Cowes, England: Recent Advances, 1977. An extensive literature research of the studies undertaken to assess the value of the astrological elements. Not very easy to understand and very technical.

Eysenck, H., and D. K. B. Nias. *Astrology, Science or Superstition?* Harmondsworth, England: Penguin Books, 1982. An excellent critical overview of scientific studies about astrology and cosmic influences.

West, A., and J. G. Toonder. *The Case for Astrology.* Harmondsworth, England: Penguin Books, 1973. A good example of the way in which astrologers try to accuse their critics of ignorance. The authors took pains to prove that astrology had its origins in Pharaonic Egypt, against all known evidence about those origins (see chapter 9). In an updated edition, they no longer hold this thesis.

264   Making Sense of Astrology

Historical Works about Astronomy and Astrology

Boll, F., and C. Bezold. *Sternglaube und Sterndeutung: die Geschichte und das Wesen der Astrologie.* Leipzig: B. G. Teubner, 1931.

Bouché-Leclercq, A. *L'Astrologie Grècque.* Brussels: Culture et Civilisation, 1899/1963. Still the standard work about Greco-Roman astrology. The first chapters on the origin and early history of astrology in Babylonia, however, are out of date.

Dreyer, J. L. E. *A History of Astronomy from Thales to Kepler.* New York: Dover Books, 1953 (first published in 1906 as *History of the Planetary Systems from Thales to Kepler*). Excellent history of astronomy to the Renaissance. It treats the reaction of astronomers to the discovery of precession.

Festugière, A.-J. *La Révélation d'Hermès Trismégiste: I. L'Astrologie et les Sciences Occultes.* Paris: Gabalda & Cie, 1944. Still a standard work about hermeticism and the role of astrology in it. Gives an excellent description of the classical worldview.

Gundel, W. *Sternglaube, Sternreligion und Sternorakel.* Heidelberg: Quelle & Meyer, 1959.

Neugebauer, O. *The Exact Sciences in Antiquity.* New York: Dover Books, 1969.

———. *A History of Ancient Mathematical Astronomy* (3 vols.). Berlin: Springer Verlag, 1975. The absolute standard work about mathematical astronomy of the ancient Babylonians, Greeks, and Romans.

Tester, J. *A History of Western Astrology.* Wolfeboro, N.H.: The Boydell Press, 1987.

Van der Waerden, B. L. *Erwachende Wissenschaft II: Die Anfänge der Astronomie.* Basel/Stuttgart: Birkhäuser Verlag, 1968.

Chapter 1. Introduction

"Good Heavens! Washington Learns an Astrologer Dictates the President's Schedule." *Time,* May 16, 1988.

Chapter 2. The Starry Sky

Allen, R. H. *Star Names, Their Lore and Meaning.* New York: Dover Books, 1963 (first published in 1899 as *Star-Names and Their Meanings*). An excellent overview of the origin of names of stars and constellations in different cultures.

Chapter 3. The Zodiac

Barbault, A. *Petit Manuel d'Astrologie.* Paris: Editions du Seuil, 1972. A brief introduction about horoscopes with attacks of the skeptics. The author defends the very contestable thesis that the zodiac was tropical from the beginning.

Böker, R. and H. Gundel. *Zodiakos*. Munich: Alfred Druckenmöller Verlag, 1972. Extensive paper about the zodiac in antiquity.
Boll, F. *Sphaera*. Leipzig: B. G. Teubner, 1903. The standard work about the dodekaoros.
Gauquelin, M. "Zodiac and Personality: An Empirical Study." *Skeptical Inquirer* 6, no. 3 (1982).
Hutin, S. *Histoire de l'Astrologie*. Verviers, Belgium: Marabout, 1970. The author, an expert in occultism, is sometimes very ignorant in astrology. That astrology has an age of 26,000 years is for him "the most certain hypothesis."
Martens, R. "De geschiedenis van het lentepunt." *Heelal* 287 (1981). A concise history of the vernal equinox.
McGervey, J. D. "A Statistical Test for Sun-Sign Astrology." *The Zetetic* 1, no. 2 (1977).
McIntosh, C. *The Astrologers and Their Creed, an Historical Outline*. London: Arrow Books, 1981. One of those "historical" books which link the origins of Aries' attributes with a flock of sheep (symbolic or not).
Ungnad, A. "Besprechungskunst und Astrologie in Babylonien." *Archiv für Orientforschung* (1944): 251–84. Contains a suggestion about the origin of Aries (p. 256).
Van der Waerden, B. L. "History of the Zodiac." *Archiv für Orientforschung* (1954): 216–30.

Intermezzo I. The Age of Aquarius

De Vos, H. *Astrologische Uitdaging*. Antwerp/Amsterdam: De Nederlandsche Boekhandel, 1975. The author, founder of an astrological society and well-known astrologer in Belgium, writes that the Age of Aquarius is only a "hippie tale" and that constellations do not have any significance in astrology.

Intermezzo II. The Eysenck Case

Eysenck, H. "The Importance of Methodology in Astrological Research." *Correlation* 1, no. 1 (1981): 11–14.
Gazet van Antwerpen, "Innovative Research into Cosmic Factors and Personality," November 27, 1978.
Kelly, I. W., and D. H. Saklofske. "Alternative Explanations in Science: The Extroversion-Introversion Astrological Effect." *Skeptical Inquirer* 5, no. 4 (1981): 33–47.
Mayo, J., O. White, and H. Eysenck. "An Empirical Study of the Relation between Astrological Factors and Personality." *Journal of Social Psychology* 105 (1987): 229–36.
Pawlik, K., and L. Buse. "Selbst-attribuierung als differentielle psychologische Moderatorvariabele: Nachprüfung und Erklärung von Eysencks Astrologie-Personlichkeit Korrelationen." *Zeitschrift für Sozialpsychologie* 10 (1979): 54–69.
Saklofske, D. H., I. W. Kelly, and D. W. McKerracher. "An Empirical Study of Personality and Astrological Factors." *Journal of Psychology* 110 (1982): 275–80.

Chapter 4. The Astronomical Planets

Beatty, J. K., and A. Chaikin. *The New Solar System.* Cambridge: Cambridge University Press; Cambridge, Mass.: Sky Publishing Corporation, 1990.
Grant, E. *Physical Science in the Middle Ages.* Cambridge: Cambridge University Press, 1977.
Hall, A. R. *The Scientific Revolution 1500–1800.* Boston: Beacon Press, 1966.
Koestler, A. *The Sleepwalkers.* Harmondsworth, England: Penguin Books, 1977.

Chapter 5. The Astrological Planets

Cumont, F. "Les noms de planètes en l'astrolâtrie." *L'Antiquité Classique* (1935): 5–43.

Chapter 6. The Houses

Benski, C., D. Caudron, Y. Galifret, J.-P. Krivine, J.-C. Pecker, M. Rouzé, E. Schatzman, and J. W. Nienhuys. *The "Mars Effect": A French Test of Over 1000 Sports Champions.* Amherst, N.Y.: Prometheus Books, 1996. The final report on the CFEPP test.
Comité Para. "Considérations critiques sur une recherche faite pas M. M. Gauquelin dans le domaine des influences planétaires." *Nouvelles Brèves* 43 (1976).
Gauquelin, M. "Bibliographic Chronology of Michel Gauquelin's Planetary Heredity Research." *Correlation,* 6, no. 1 (1986): 16–17.
———. *Birth and Planetary Data Gathered since 1949.* Series C, vol. 1: Profession-Heredity. 1972. Paris: LERRCP.
———. *Cosmic Influences on Human Behaviour.* London: Futura, 1976.
———. *The Mars Effect and the Sports Champions. A New Replication.* Paris: LERCCP, 1979.
Nienhuys, J. W. "Astrologie voor skeptici." *Skepter* 7, no. 3 (1994): 5.

Intermezzo VII. The Skeptics and the Mars Effect

Comité Français pour l'Etude de Phénomènes Paranormaux (CFEPP). "L'effet Mars est-il réel?" *Science & Vie* (October 1982): 44.
Comité Para. "On the Mars Effect: A Last Answer to M. Gauquelin." *Zetetic Scholar,* no. 10 (1982): 66.
Ertel, S. *An Assessment of the Mars Effect.* Invited paper presented at the sixth annual meeting of the SSE, Austin, Texas, 1987.
———. "Raising the Hurdle for the Athletes' Mars Effect: Association Covaries with Eminence." *Journal of Scientific Exploration* 2 (1988): 53–82.
Gauquelin, M., and F. Gauquelin. "Star U.S. Sportsmen Display the Mars Effect." *Skeptical Inquirer* 4, no. 2 (1979): 31–43.

Kamman, R. "The True Disbelievers: Mars Effect Drives Skeptics to Irrationality."*Zetetic Scholar,* no. 10 (1982): 50–65.

Kurtz, P., M. Zelen, and G. Abell. "Response to the Gauquelins." *Skeptical Inquirer* 4, no. 2 (1979): 44–63.

———. "Results of the US Test on the 'Mars Effect' Are Negative." *Skeptical Inquirer* 4, no. 2 (1979): 19–25.

Nienhuys, J. W., ed. *Science or Pseudo? The Mars Effect and Other Claims. Proceedings of the Third EuroSkeptics Congress. October 4–5, 1991, Amsterdam.* Utrecht: Stichting Skepsis, 1992. Contains De Jager, Jager, and Koppeschaar's remarks, with replies by Ertel and Françoise Gauquelin and a commentary by Nienhuys.

Rawlins, D. "Report on the U.S. Test of the Gauquelins' 'Mars Effect.'" *Skeptical Inquirer* 4, no. 2 (1979): 26–31.

Rawlins, D. "STARBABY." *Fate* (October 1981): 68–98.

Truzzi, M. "Personal Reflections on the Mars Effect Controversy." *Zetetic Scholar,* no. 10 (1982): 74–81.

Chapter 7. The Aspects

Brazu, J.-L. *Dictionnaire de l'Astrologie.* Paris: Librairie Larousse, 1983.

Ianna, P. A., and C. J. Margolin. "Planetary Positions, Radio Propagation and the Work of J. H. Nelson." *Skeptical Inquirer* 6, no. 1 (1981): 32–29.

Meeus, J. "On the 'Correlation' between Radio Disturbances and Planetary Positions." *Skeptical Inquirer* 6, no. 4 (1982): 30–33.

Chapter 8. Astrology and Psychology

Carlson, S. "A Double-Blind Test of Astrology." *Nature* 318 (December 5, 1985): 419–25.

Dean, G. "Can Astrology Predict E and N? 1. Individual Factors." *Correlation* 5, no. 1 (1985): 3–17.

———. "Can Astrology Predict E and N? 2. The Whole Chart." *Correlation* 5, no. 2 (1985): 2–24.

———. "Can Astrology Predict E and N? 3. Discussion and Further Research." *Correlation* 6, no. 2 (1985): 7–52.

———. "Does Astrology Need to Be True? Part 1: A Look at the Real Thing." *Skeptical Inquirer* 11, no. 2 (1986): 166–82.

———. "Does Astrology Need to Be True? Part 2: The Answer Is No." *Skeptical Inquirer* 11, no. 3 (1987): 257–73.

Dickson, D. H. and I. W. Kelly. "The 'Barnum Effect' in Personality Assessment: A Review of the Literature." *Psychological Reports* 57 (1985): 367–82.

Hyman, R. "'Cold Reading': How to Convince Strangers That You Know All about Them." *The Zetetic* 1, no. 2 (1977): 18–37.

Milani, M. *Girolamo Cardano, mistero e scienza nel Cinquecento.* Milan: Camunia Ed., 1990.

Nanninga, R. "The Astrotest: A Tough Match for Astrologers." *Seventh European Skeptics Conference, Proceedings* (A. Sarma, ed., 1995).
Zusne, L., and W. H. Jones. *Anomalistic Psychology.* Hillsdale, N.J.: Lawrence Erlbaum Associates, 1982.

Intermezzo IX. Cosmic Influences

Bernard, E. A. "Réflexions sur les cause de l'activité solaire et l'organisation en battement de ses pseudopériodicités." *Ciel et Terre* 94, no. 6 (1978): 385–403.
Brown, F. A. "Persistent Activity Rhythm in the Oyster." *American Journal of Physiology* 1978 (1954): 510–14.
Gribbin, J., and S. Plagemann. *The Jupiter Effect.* London: Macmillan, 1974.
Henbest, J. N. "The Pull of the Planets on the Lives of Men." *New Scientist* (May 12, 1988). Criticizing Seymour's work.
Meeus, J. "Activité solaire et séismes." *Ciel et Terre* 92, no. 4 (1976). No correlation is found between solar activity and earthquakes.
———. "Planètes et activité solaire." *Ciel et Terre* 94, no. 1 (1978): 19–27. No correlation is found between the position of planets and solar activity.
Quincey, P. "The Strange Case of the New Haven Oysters." *Skeptical Inquirer* 17, no. 2 (1993): 188–93.
———. "Why We Are Unmoved as Oceans Ebb and Flow." *Skeptical Inquirer* 18, no. 5 (1994): 509–15.
Rouckaerts, G. "Het lied van de Zon." *Knack* (November 5, 1986): 215–17. In this—very uncritical—article in a Belgian magazine, Seymour admits that his theory cannot serve as a foundation for everyday astrology.
Seymour, P. *Astrology, the Evidence of Science.* London: Lennard Publishing, 1988. In his preface to an updated edition (1989), Seymour replies to Henbest's criticism and gives a more obvious exposition of his theory.

Intermezzo X. The Moon and Life on Earth

Abell, G. O., and B. Greenspan. "The Moon and the Maternity Ward." *Skeptical Inquirer* (Summer 1979): 17–25.
Criss, T. B., and J. Marcum. "A Lunar Effect on Fertility." *Social Biology* 28 (1981): 75–80.
Desrosiers, J. "La pleine lune, panacée cosmique ou prostaglandine pré-historique." *L'Union Médicale du Canada* 114, no. 7 (1985): 555–62.
Hausser, C., R. Bornais, and S. Bornais. "L'influence du cycle lunaire sur les accouchements." *L'Union Médicale du Canada* 114, no. 7 (1985): 548–50.
Martens, R., I. W. Kelly, and D. H. Saklofske. "Lunar Phase and Birthrate: A 50-Year Critical Review." *Psychological Reports* 63 (1988): 923–34.
Menaker, W. D. "Lunar Periodicity with Reference to Births." *American Journal of Obstetrics and Gynecology* 98 (1967): 1002–1004.

Menaker, W. D., and A. Menaker. "Lunar Periodicity in Human Reproduction." *American Journal of Obstetrics and Gynecology* 77 (1959): 905–14.
Osley, M., D. Summerville, and L. B. Borst. "Natality and the Moon." *American Journal of Obstetrics and Gynecology* 117 (1973): 413–15.
Rippmann, E. T. "The Moon and the Birth Rate." *American Journal of Obstetrics and Gynecology* 74 (1957): 148–50.
Rotton, J., and I. W. Kelly. "Much Ado about the Full Moon: A Meta-Analysis of Lunar-Lunacy Research." *Psychological Bulletin* 97, no. 2 (1985): 286–306.
Witter, F. R. "The Influence of the Moon on Deliveries." *American Journal of Obstetrics and Gynecology* 145 (1983): 637–39.

Chapter 9. Astrology: Past and Future

Burchkardt, J. *The Civilization of the Renaissance in Italy.* New York: Harper & Row, 1975. With some considerations about astrology in Renaissance Italy in the last chapters.
Carus, P. *Chinese Astrology.* La Salle, Ill.: Open Court, 1907/1974. "Chinese Occultism" should have been a better title, since it doesn't tell much about astrology after all. The author was a strong supporter of *panbabylonism*, a tendency, very popular before World War I, which tried to reduce the origins of all cultures to influences from Babylonia.
Cramer, F. H. *Astrology in Roman Law and Politics.* Philadelphia: The American Philosophical Society, 1954. A standard work about the role of astrology in the Roman world. A follow-up about astrology in the Byzantine Empire was never published due to the author's premature death.
Cumont, F. *Astrology and Religion among the Greeks and Romans.* New York: Dover Books, 1912/1960.
———. "Ecrits hermétiques." *Revue de Philologie* 42 (1918): 63–79, 85–108.
———. *Oriental Religions in Roman Paganism.* New York: Dover Books, 1956.
Dupont-Sommer, A. "La secte des Esséniens et les horoscopes de Qumran." *Archaeologia* 15 (1967): 24–31.
Encyclopedia of Islam. S.v. "Astrology." Leiden, 1937.
Ezra, Abraham Ibn: *Le Livre des Fondements Astrologiques.* Paris: Ed. Retz (*Bibliotheca Hermetica*), 1977. French translation of two astrological works by a twelfth-century Jewish astrologer. The 97 partes are mentioned (for the partes see also Bouché-Leclercq, *L'Astrologie Grecque.*)
Ferguson, J. *The Religions of the Roman Empire.* London: Thames and Hudson, 1982.
Festugière, A. *Hermétisme et Mystique Païenne.* Paris: Aubier-Montaigne, 1967.
Frigara, X. and H. Li. *Tradition Astrologique Chinoise.* St-Jean-de-Braye: Editions Dangles, 1978.
Gundel, W., and G. H. Gundel. *Astrologumena.* Wiesbaden: Franz Steiner Verlag, 1966.
Halsberghe, G. H. *Het Rijk van de Zonnegod: de eredienst van Sol Invictus.* Antwerp: Scriptoria, 1982.
Hamel, J. *Astrologie-Tochter der Astronomie?* Leipzig: Urania Verlag, 1987.
Howe, E. *Astrology and the Third Reich.* Wellingborough: The Aquarian Press, 1984. An

excellent book about astrology since the eighteenth century. The first part treats the revival of astrology, especially in the Anglo-Saxon world. The second part contains the biography of astrologer Karl Ernst Krafft, who was said to be Hitler's personal astrologer (which was not the case). "Capain" Louis de Wohl's allegation that he served the Allies during World War II as an astrologer is retraced to a practical joke.

Kroll, W. "Nechepso," *Pauly-Wissowa* RE, 1935.

———. "Salmeschiniaka," *Pauly-Wissowa* RE. Supplementband V. 1935.

Lindsay, J. *Origins of Astrology.* London: Frederick Muller, 1972. A historical study about the role of astrology in the Greek and Roman worlds.

Nasr, S. H. *An Introduction to Islamic Cosmological Doctrines.* London: Thames & Hudson, 1978. Interesting, but the author does not always seem to understand his sources. Represents an Islamic fundamentalist point of view: Science is subordinate to revealed religion. Some passages may seem rather strange to a Western reader.

Neugebauer, O. "Demotic Horoscopes." *JAOS* 63 (1943): 115–26.

Neugebauer, O., and H. B. Van Hoesen. *Greek Horoscopes.* Philadelphia: The American Philosophical Society, 1959.

Nougayrol, J., and J.-M. Aynard. *La Mésopotamie.* Paris: Bloud et Gay (*Religions du Monde*), 1965.

Oppenheim, A. L. *Ancient Mesopotamia.* Chicago: University of Chicago Press, 1977. "The arts of the diviner" are discussed in chapter 4.

Sachs, A. "Babylonian Horoscopes." *Journal of Cuneiform Studies* 6 (1952): 49–75.

———. "Naissance de l'astrologie horoscopique en Babylonie." *Archaeologia* 15 (1967): 13–19.

Slosman, A. *De astrologie van het oude Egypte.* The Hague: Miranda, 1985. An extreme case of a publication which wants to reduce the origins of astrology to Pharaonic Egypt. It contains unintelligible astronomy, mythic history, and an alternative interpretation of hieroglyphs.

Stierlin, H. *L'Astrologie et le Pouvoir.* Paris: Payot, 1985. The author gives an overview of astrological symbolism used by rulers since Hellenistic times. He defends the thesis that the Roman emperor Hadrian's "Naval Theater" in Tivoli was an astronomical/astrological planetarium.

Thomas, K. *Religion and the Decline of Magic.* Harmondsworth, England: Penguin Books, 1978. Contains a very interesting study of the astrological practice in Britain in the sixteenth and seventeenth centuries. It shows that the decline of astrology was essentially due to the clergy's opposition: "The clergy and the satirists chased it into its grave, but the scientists were unrepresented at the funeral" (p. 418).

Vermes, G. *The Dead Sea Scrolls in English.* Harmondsworth, England: Penguin Books, 1976. The three horoscopes in the Dead Sea Scrolls are on p. 418.

Weidner, E. "Die Astrologische Serie Enuma Anu Enlil." *Archiv für Orientforschung* 17 (1954–1956): 71–89.

Chapter 10. Criticism in a Nutshell

Broch, H. Personal communication on Internet.
Cowling, T. G. *Isaac Newton and Astrology*. Leeds, England: University Press, 1977. A refutation of the anecdote about Newton. The same anecdote is adopted uncritically by Hutin, *Histoire de l'Astrologie*, and—with reservations—by West and Toonder, *The Case for Astrology*.
Fuzeau-Braesch, S. *L'Astrologie, la Preuve par Deux*. Paris: Robert Laffont (*Dossiers Sciences Frontières*), 1992.
Ertel, S., and G. Dean. "Are Personality Differences between Twins Predicted by Astrology?" *Personality and Individual Differences* 21 (1996): 449.
Meeus, J. "Doomsday: The May 2000 Prediction." *Skeptical Inquirer* 12, no. 3 (1988): 290–92.
Trachet, T. "Astrologie bij Newton." *Heelal* 360 (September 1987): 205–206.

Chapter 11. Conclusion

Catechism of the Catholic Church. Vatican City: Libreria Editrice Vaticana; Chicago: (dist. by) Loyola University Press, 1994. The "consultation of horoscopes, astrology" are mentioned with "to call the help of Satan and the demons." Those practices are condemned by the Church as contrary to the Third Commandment. The same text considers it erroneous that they should "unveil" (quotation marks in the text) the future.
Feyerabend, P. *Against Method*. London: New Left Books, 1975.
———. *Science in a Free Society*. London: New Left Books, 1978.
Goodrick-Clarke, N. *The Occult Roots of Nazism. Secret Aryan Cults and Their Influence on Nazi Ideology. The Ariosophists of Austria and Germany, 1890–1935*. London/New York: I. B. Tauris, 1992. With much attention to Lanz von Liebenfels.
"Objections to Astrology: A Statement by 186 Leading Scientists," *The Humanist* (September/October 1975).

INDEX

Abell, George, 160, 161
Age of Aquarius, 74–77, 243
Albertus Magnus, 241, 252
Alcibitius (al-Kabisi; *see* division of the houses)
Anaxagoras, 88
anthroposophy, 205
Aquinas (*see* Thomas Aquinas)
Arabian astrology, 237, 241
Aries, the origin of, 56–57, 60, 65, 66–67
Aristotle, 87
Ascendant, 48, 109, 113, 125, 127, 138, 139, 145, 149, 152, 156, 166, 167, 170
aspects, 43, 166–85
asteroids, 102–103
astrological twins, 246–48
astrology
   history, 231–44
   origin, 17–18, 227–33
   types, 15–17
Augustine (Aurelius Augustinus), 240–41
autumnal equinox, 31
ayamansha, 76

Babylonians, 51–54, 227–31
Bailly, Jean-Sylvain, 258
Balbillos, 239
Barbault, André, 56, 64, 203

Barnum Effect, 200
Berlin Wall, 249
Berossos, 235
Black Monday, 250
Black Moon, 180
Blavatsky, Helena Petrovna, 206, 242
Broch, Henri, 248
Brown, Frank, 209

Campanus (*see* division of the houses)
Cardano, Girolamo, 202
Carlson, Shawn, 192
Carneades, 238
Catherine de Medici, 253
CFEPP, 134, 164, 165
chance, aversion to, 205
Chernobyl, 249
Chinese astrology, 240
Christianity, 20, 240–41
Cicero, Marcus Tullius, 238
Clark, Vernon, 190
cognitive dissonance, 202
cold reading, 200
comets, 36
Comité Para, 133, 158, 159, 160
communism, 243
constellations, 36–40, 44–46, 59, 63
Copernicus, Nicolaus, 87–88

274 Making Sense of Astrology

cosmic influences, 207–18
cosmobiology, 118
Couderc, Paul, 158, 259
CSICOP, 133, 160, 162

dangers of astrology, 259–60
Dath, Jean, 159
Dead Sea Scrolls, 238
Dean, Geoffrey, 72, 73(n), 105, 129, 137(n), 141, 192, 193–97, 248, 257, 262
De Marré, Luc, 159
Dendera, zodiac of, 12, 231
Descendant, 113, 125, 127, 139, 145, 149
determinism (*see* free will)
division of the houses, 112, 113–16, 138–43
  Alcibitius, 119, 141
  Campanus, 119, 122, 139
  equal house system, 118
  Koch, 119, 122, 141
  Morin de Villefranche, 119, 141
  Placidus, 118–19, 122, 141
  Porphyry, 119
  Regiomontanus, 119, 122, 139, 141
  topocentric system, 119, 141
  Zariel, 119, 139
Dodekaoros, 240
Dommanget, Jean, 159
double-blind test, 191, 192

Ebertin, Elsbeth and Reinhold, 118
eclipse (*see* lunar eclipse, solar eclipse)
ecliptics, 29, 109, 113, 127, 138, 149, 152, 154, 166, 172
Einstein, Albert, 252
electromagnetic radiation, 211, 217
Eminence Effect, 162–63
Enlightment, 20, 242, 258
Enuma Anu Enlil, 227–28
equal house system (*see* division of the houses)
equinox (*see* autumnal equinox, vernal equinox)
Ertel, Suitbert, 162, 163, 165, 248
experience, reliability of (*see* fallacy of personal validation)
Eysenck, Hans, 78–81, 176, 191

fallacy of personal validation, 187–89, 198, 201, 206
fate, 204–205
free will, 240–41
Fuzeau-Braesch, Suzel, 248, 251

Gauquelin, Michel, 72–73, 129, 130–36, 157–65, 174, 203, 215
George III, 247–48
gravitation, 207–11
Gribbin, John, 213, 251
Halley, Edmund, 252
hermeticism, 233
Hipparchos, 53
Hitler, Adolf, 118(n), 260
horary astrology, 16, 237
houses, 43, 112–37, 138–43, 144–47, 148–56, 256–57 (*see also* division of the houses)
Humanist, The, 160, 258
hypothetical planets, 104–105

iatromathematica (*see* medical astrology)
Imum Caeli (IC), 113, 139
Indian astrology, 239, 241
interpretation-after-the-fact, 201

Jerome, Lawrence E., 160
Jung, Carl Gustav, 217–18
Jupiter Effect, 213, 217, 250–51

Kepler, Johannes, 88, 118, 252
Koch (*see* division of the houses)
Koppeschaar, Carl, 163
Kurtz, Paul, 160, 161
KZA test, 161, 162

Lanz von Liebenfelz, Jörg, 260
Louis XIV, 242
Lucretius Carus, Titus, 238
lunar eclipse, 34

magnetosphere, 215–17
Manilius, Marcus, 56–57, 238

Index   275

Mars Effect, 133, 134, 135, 136, 157–65
Mather, Arthur, 72, 73(n), 105, 129, 137(n), 141
Mayo, Jeff, 176
medical astrology, 16, 22, 234, 236–37
Medium Caeli (MC; *see* Midheaven)
melothesia (*see* medical astrology)
meteors, 36–37
Midheaven, 113, 122, 125, 127, 138, 139, 149, 152, 166, 167, 170
Mithra, 239
Morin de Villefranche, Jean-Baptiste (*see* division of the houses)
Moon, 31–33, 89, 219–25
  influence on abnormal behavior, 223–24
  influence on births, 220–22
mundane astrology, 16

Nanninga, Rob, 196
natal astrology, 16, 17
Nazi Germany, 243
Nelson, John, 176–79
New Age, 243, 258
Newton, Sir Isaac, 88, 252
Nienhuys, Jan Willem, 163, 164, 165
Noblitt, James Randall, 174
nodes, 33, 34, 180
Nostradamus (Michel de Notredame), 253

orb, 167, 169, 172, 183
oyster test, 209–11

panics, 250–51
paranatellonta, 60–61
paranormal, 218
Pars Fortunae, 180, 237
particles, 212
Petiot, Marcel, 203
Placidus de Titus (*see* division of the houses)
Plagemann, Stephen, 213, 251
planets, 34–37, 43, 82–111, 118
polar problem, 148–56
popular astrology, 15–16

Porphyry (*see* division of the houses)
Porte, Jean, 158
precession, 44, 51–56, 62, 75
predictive astrology, 16–17
psychology and astrology, 186–206, 257, 258–59
Ptolemy (Klaudios Ptolemaios), 53, 87, 171, 236

Quincey, Paul, 210

radiation (*see* electromagnetic radiation, solar radiation)
Ram, Theo, 104, 105
Rawlins, Dennis, 161, 162
Reformation, 242
Regiomontanus (*see* division of the houses)
Renaissance, 241–42
resonance, 216
Rumania, revolution, 249

Saturn Effect, 135, 136
selective memory, 202
self-fullfilling prophecy, 202
semiarcs, 141
Sextus Empiricus, 239
Seymour, Percy, 215–17, 251
Shenkel, R. J., 197
signs, 11, 42, 44–46, 96, 97, 113, 118, 127, 172 (*see also* Ascendant, Descendant, Midheaven, and *Imum Caeli*)
  origin of characteristics of, 55–61
  difference from constellations, 44, 46
Snyder, C. R., 197
solar eclipse, 33–35
solar radiation, 211
Sol Invictus, 239
stars, 27, 28, 38, 40–41 (*see also* constellations)
Steiner, Rudolf, 76, 205(n)
stoicism and stoics, 234–35
sunspot cycles, 212, 214
synchronicity, 217–18

Teissier, Elizabeth, 179

theosophy, 205–206, 242
Thomas Aquinas, 241, 252
Thrasyllos, 238, 239
tides, 18, 85, 208–209
time twins, 247
Toonder, Jan Gerard, 223, 231
topocentric system (*see* division of the houses)
Trutina Hermetis, 246

Uranian astrology (*see* Witte school of astrology)

Van Ooteghem, Daniel, 249–50

vernal equinox, 31, 44, 52, 115
Vernon Clark test, 190

West, Anthony, 223, 231
Witte school of astrology, 104–105

Zariel (*see* division of the houses)
Zelen, Marvin, 160, 161
Zelen test, 161–62, 163
zodiac, 43–73
　divisions of, 50–51
　sidereal, 52–56, 61–65
　tropical, 44, 52–56, 61–65